Palgrave Studies in Governance, Leadership and Responsibility

The fall-out from many high profile crises in governance and leadership in recent decades, from banking to healthcare, continues to be felt around the world. Major reports have questioned the values and behaviour, not just of individual organizations but of professionals, industries and political leadership. These reports raise questions about business corporations and also public service institutions. In response this new series aims to explore the broad principles of governance and leadership and how these are embodied in different contexts, opening up the possibility of developing new theories and approaches that are fuelled by interdisciplinary approaches. The purpose of the series is to highlight critical reflection and empirical research which can enable dialogue across sectors, focusing on theory, value and the practice of governance, leadership and responsibility.

Written from a global context, the series is unique in bringing leadership and governance together. The King III report connects these two fields by identifying leadership as one of the three principles of effective governance however most courses in business schools have traditionally treated these as separate subjects. Increasingly, and in particular with the case of executive education, business schools are recognizing the need to develop and produce responsible leaders. The series will therefore encourage critical exploration between these two areas and as such explore sociological and philosophical perspectives.

More information about this series at
http://www.palgrave.com/gp/series/15192

Anna Sörensson
Besrat Tesfaye
Anders Lundström
Georgiana Grigore • Alin Stancu
Editors

Corporate Responsibility and Sustainability during the Coronavirus Crisis

International Case Studies

palgrave
macmillan

Editors
Anna Sörensson
Mid Sweden University
Östersund, Sweden

Besrat Tesfaye
Södertörn University
Huddinge, Sweden

Anders Lundström
Mid Sweden University
Östersund, Sweden

Georgiana Grigore
University of Leicester
Leicester, UK

Alin Stancu
Bucharest University of Economic Studies
Bucharest, Romania

ISSN 2662-1304 ISSN 2662-1312 (electronic)
Palgrave Studies in Governance, Leadership and Responsibility
ISBN 978-3-030-73846-4 ISBN 978-3-030-73847-1 (eBook)
https://doi.org/10.1007/978-3-030-73847-1

This Palgrave Macmillan imprint is published by the registered company Springer Nature Switzerland AG.
The registered company address is: Gewerbestrasse 11, 6330 Cham, Switzerland

Contents

Notes on Contributors

Fajer Al-Husaini is a PhD researcher at Henley Business School. She has graduated from the Gulf University for Science and Technology, Kuwait, with a bachelor's degree in Marketing and an MBA in Marketing Concentration (class valedictorian). Her research interests include branding of science and technology, applications of branding to secure research funds and understanding the impact of branding variables on the perceived quality of research produced by national labs. She is also working at the Kuwait Oil Company in the field of communications where she is responsible for maintaining the Company's brand image through communication initiatives, initiating CSR projects and conducting reputation studies.

Lizbeth Arroyo is a PhD candidate in the Department of Business at the University of Barcelona (UB). Her doctoral research is focused on the interplay between legitimacy, identity and context of digital entrepreneurship. In 2020 her paper *Understanding the Moral Space of Digital Entrepreneurship: The Where, The Who and The How of Digital Legitimation* was nominated for the Best PhD paper prize of the *Strategy Management Society (SMS)* conference. Secondary lines of research include innovation communities, collective entrepreneurship, circular economy, and diversity and inclusion. She participates in projects for regional development and entrepreneurship, such as GUESSS project.

Maria Bogren is PhD in Business Administration within entrepreneurship by Mid Sweden University, Östersund, Sweden. She is an assistant professor and researcher at the Department of Economics, Geography, Law and Tourism at Mid Sweden University, Sweden. She has worked at this university since 2002, in different positions. Besides her PhD, she holds a Licentiate degree in Business Administration within organizational theory, a master's degree in Business Administration, a bachelor degree in Sociology and a Bachelor of Science in Human Resource Development and Labor Relations. All degrees are from Mid Sweden University. She has published articles and book chapters mainly within the field of entrepreneurship. Her research interest is broad, including, for example, women's entrepreneurship, growth, social capital, networking and SMEs within nature-based businesses.

Håkan Boter is Professor Emeritus at Umeå School of Business and Economics, Umeå University. Earlier he was also a professor at Mid Sweden University. He was an initiator for Centre for Inter-Organizational Innovation Research (CiiR), with close collaboration with University of Technology (LTU) and financial support from VINNOVA, 2010–2018. He had long experience from research and PhD training in developing countries. He was an initiator and participant in a long-standing exchange program with University of Dar es Salaam, where 20 PhDs graduated. He was a partner in Global Business School Network (GBSN), whose purpose was to strengthen entrepreneurial skills at universities in the third world. He had long-standing activities with tailor-made competence program in networks of SMEs, internationalization processes in SME and eight research groups over ten years.

René Díaz-Pichardo holds a PhD in Management from Tecnológico de Monterrey, Mexico. He works as a professor and researcher at South Champagne Business School, France, and participates as an associate researcher at Université de Technologie de Troyes, ICD-CREIDD, France. His research interests include sustainability and environmental management in subsistence businesses and fragmented industries. He is a member of the National System of Researchers in Mexico, Level I, and has acted as thesis director of students at the doctoral and master levels in Mexico and France.

Rita Goyal is Lecturer in International Business and Strategic Leadership and an *ASPiRE* fellow at Centre for Business in Society at Coventry Business School, Coventry University, UK. She has published a few journal articles and book chapters on a range of topics including corporate board effectiveness, board diversity, women on boards (WoB), value-creating boards, gender discrimination on boards and enlightened board Chairs. She has interviewed 50+ Chairs, CEOs and board directors and Company Secretaries of top listed and closely held companies in the UK. She regularly writes and presents articles in international academic and practitioners' conferences. Earlier she has worked for two decades in various middle and senior management roles.

Georgiana Grigore is Associate Professor of Marketing at University of Leicester, School of Business. She is also chair of an annual international conference in "Social Responsibility, Ethics and Sustainable Business", which she co-founded in 2012. Her major area of research is in marketing and corporate responsibility concepts and practices, including changes that result from digital media. In the last years, she has published several books, including *Corporate Responsibility and Digital Communities* and *Corporate Social Responsibility in the Digital Age* (2018) that explore a contemporary intersection of two fields: corporate responsibility and digital technology. Her publications also include applications of post-psychoanalytic theories to consumer-brand relationships and shopping in marketing theory. Her research received external funding, including from Arthur W. Page Center (2014/2015 and 2015/2016) and British Academy/Leverhulme (2017/2019). She completed an EU-funded doctorate in Marketing at the Bucharest University of Economic Studies using relationship-marketing theory to examine the impact of corporate responsibility on stakeholders. Prior to her doctorate, she received a master's degree in Strategic Marketing and a bachelor's degree in Marketing from the same university. Before her PhD, Georgiana was a marketing specialist and consultant in the retail industry and a trainer for a series of practitioner workshops and marketing and corporate responsibility courses.

Esther Hormiga is an associate professor in the Business department at Universitat de Barcelona (UB). She is the director of the UB Business PhD program and the coordinator of the UB Organizational Development

Research Group. Her research interests focus mainly on the analysis of entrepreneurial behavior and intangible assets of new ventures.

Andrew Kakabadse is Professor of Governance and Leadership at Henley Business School and Professor Emeritus at Cranfield School of Management. He was a Board Member on boards of ABIS and Windsor Leadership Trust. He was visiting professor at the University of Ulster, Macquarie University, Australia. His research covers boards, top teams and the governance of governments. He has published over 45 books, 88 book chapters, over 235 articles and 18 monographs. He is advisor to the UK Parliament and numerous corporations, NGOs and other governments.

Nada Kakabadse is Professor of Policy, Governance and Ethics at Henley Business School. She was visiting professor at American, Australian, Israeli, French, Kazakhstani and Chinese universities. She is an elected and active member of the European Academy of Science and Arts (EASA) and is the head of its EU Representation Office in Brussels. She has co-authored 20 books and has published over 200 scholarly articles. Her interests are leadership, boardroom effectiveness, governance, CSR and ethics, diversity and the policy design of the state.

Anders Lundström Professor Emeritus at Mid Sweden University, was one of the creators and managing director of the Swedish Foundation for Small Business Research (FSF) and invented the Global Award for Entrepreneurship Research in 1996. He has been chairing three world conferences in the area of entrepreneurship, small business and innovations. He has created the Innovative Policy Research in Entrepreneurship and Small Business (IPREG), an international network consisting of research organizations in 14 European countries. He has been president of International Council of Small Business (ICSB), a worldwide network organization. He has been working as full professor and project manager at Mid Sweden University for a multidisciplinary EU-funded project, SESPA, of social/societal entrepreneurship with 25 researchers from 6 different disciplines. He has also been visiting professor in China. He has worked at the Business School at Gothenburg University in earlier years,

EIASM in Brussels and SIND/NUTEK. He is now managing director of the Foundation of Innovative Policy Research—PREG.

Giulio Nardella is Assistant Professor of Strategy and Responsible Business at Loughborough School of Business and Economics, Loughborough University, UK. His research mainly explores issues concerning corporate social irresponsibility, the international strategic management of corporate reputation and behavioral theory. To date, his research has been published in leading journals such as the *British Journal of Management* and *Journal of World Business*. His research has also won multiple awards at International Business and Management conferences such as AOM and BAM.

Ijeoma Nwagwu holds a doctorate and master's in Law from Harvard Law School. She is on the faculty of Lagos Business School where she played a key role in developing research projects funded by the Gates Foundation and Ford Foundation, and in advancing the role of business in sustainable development through the Lagos Business School Sustainability Center. She is qualified as a barrister and solicitor of Nigeria. After attending the Nigerian Law School, she worked as an attorney for the Civil Liberties Organisation and produced documentaries on law, human rights and development with Channels Television and the Institute for Democracy in South Africa. Nwagwu taught at St. Mary's University College, London, and worked on World Bank education sector projects. She has presented papers in international conferences and published in the areas of corporate social responsibility, sustainability leadership, social impact, law and development as well as nonprofit leadership and management. She serves on numerous boards including the board of BudgIT, a civic tech organization. She also serves on the international advisory board of the Sustainability Centers Community of the Network for Business Sustainability, a collaborative of academic experts and business leaders focused on advancing corporate sustainability.

Adaeze Okoye is a senior lecturer at the University of Brighton. She holds a PhD from the University of Hull and a master's degree in Environmental Law and Policy from the University of Dundee. Okoye.

She is also a barrister and solicitor of the Supreme Court of Nigeria and an associate academic fellow of the Honourable Society of the Inner Temple. She was a visiting fellow at the Institute of Advanced Legal Studies, University of London in 2015–2016. She is a 2010 alumni of the Institute for Global Law and Policy (IGLP) workshop, Harvard Law School. Her book, *Legal Approaches and Corporate Social Responsibility* (Dec. 2016), explores legal approaches to law and the corporate social responsibility relationship. She has also written about law and development, corporate governance, joint development agreements and environmental management systems in the oil industry.

J. Javier Sanchez-Asín holds a PhD in Economic and Entrepreneurial Sciences and a University Degree in Chemistry. He is CEO at the *Entreprise – University of Zaragoza Foundation*, and has been the Managing Director of a Business Innovation Centre (EU-Commission BIC) for 11 years. He is part-time Associate Professor of Economics of Strategy, Innovation and Technological Change and Essentials of Management at the University of Zaragoza. His main research interests are in the field of economics of entrepreneurship and labor economics. He is member of the *Organizational Value Creation* research group (CREVALOR).

Patricia S. Sánchez-Medina holds a PhD in Conservation and Exploitation of Natural Resources and works as a professor and researcher at the Instituto Politécnico Nacional (CIIDIR Unidad Oaxaca), Mexico. Her research interests include environmental management in subsistence contexts and family businesses. She is a member of the National System of Researchers in Mexico, Level II, and has acted as thesis director of students at the doctoral, master and bachelor levels.

Ulrich Schmudde is PhD candidate in Business Administration at Mid Sweden University, Östersund (Sweden). Schmudde has a master's degree in Business Administration from Mid Sweden University and completed bachelor studies in Foreign Trade as well as in Tourism and Travel Management from University of Applied Sciences, Worms, Germany. Schmudde has published articles about sustainability, tourism and city development.

Anna Sörensson holds PhD in Business Administration within international marketing from Åbo Akademi (Finland). She is an assistant professor and researcher at the Department of Economics, Geography, Law and Tourism at Mid Sweden University, Sweden. She has worked at this university since 2001, in different positions. Besides her PhD, she holds a master's degree in Business Administration, a master's degree in Economics and a master's degree in Education from Mid Sweden University, Sweden. She also has a master's degree in Law from Stockholm University. She has published articles and book chapters mainly within the field of marketing, tourism and sustainability. Her research interest is broad and includes, for example, nature-based businesses, sustainable development and education.

Alin Stancu is Professor of Corporate Social Responsibility and Public Relations in the Department of Marketing from The Bucharest University of Economic Studies, Romania. His main areas of research include customer care, consumer experience, corporate responsibility and public relations. He is the co-founder of The International Conference on Social Responsibility, Ethics and Sustainable Business (www.csrconferences.org) and co-editor of the book series: Palgrave Studies in Governance, Leadership and Responsibility.

Irina Surdu is Associate Professor of International Business Strategy at Warwick Business School, University of Warwick, UK. Her research agenda focuses on the international growth and subsequent investment strategies of multinational enterprises, organizational learning and corporate irresponsible behavior across different country markets. Her research has appeared in journals such as *Journal of International Business Studies*, *Journal of World Business*, *International Business Review*, *Journal of International Management* and *British Journal of Management*. Her recent book titled *The Oxford Handbook of International Business Strategy* has been published with Oxford University Press. Her research has won multiple awards at International Business and Management conferences such as AIB UK-I, AOM, BAM and EIBA. She is an associate editor of *Multinational Business Review* and part of the editorial board of *Journal of International Business Studies*.

Besrat Tesfaye is Associate Professor of Business Studies at the Department of Social Sciences, at Södertörn University. She teaches courses in innovation, entrepreneurship, human resource management, organization, marketing and consumer behavior. Her research focuses primarily on entrepreneurship and small business. She has studied entrepreneurship from different perspectives, including gender and ethnicity, and in contexts such as academic institutions, marginalized communities and low-income economies. She is researching the impact of the patent system on innovation in smaller enterprises, with emphasis on how the SMEs use and benefit from the patent system. In another multidisciplinary project, "Re-inventing the Suburbs", Tesfaye is studying the emergence (or lack of) high-technology clusters in knowledge-intensive environments in the southern suburbs of Stockholm City.

Jaume Valls-Pasola is Professor of Management and Business Administration at the University of Barcelona (UB) where he has been the director of the Barcelona Entrepreneurship Institute (2015–2018). He is a member of the Business Department and the Business and Management Research Group of UB. His research interests are in the fields of innovation management, innovation communities and entrepreneurship. He is co-editor of the open access *Journal of Evolutionary Studies in Business* that was promoted by UB in 2016.

List of Figures

List of Tables

1

What Happens to Corporate Responsibility in a Worldwide Health Emergency?

Anna Sörensson, Georgiana Grigore, Anders Lundström, Alin Stancu, and Besrat Tesfaye

1.1 Introduction

Since the COVID-19 pandemic swept across the globe, corporate conditions have changed radically. The pandemic has caused a societal and economic crisis around the globe. Due to the uncertain but rapid course of the spread of infection, great efforts have been required from all

A. Sörensson (✉) • A. Lundström
Mid Sweden University, Östersund, Sweden
e-mail: anna.sorensson@miun.se; anders.lundstrom@miun.se

G. Grigore
University of Leicester, Leicester, UK
e-mail: gg186@leicester.ac.uk

A. Stancu
Bucharest University of Economic Studies, Bucharest, Romania
e-mail: alinstancu@mk.ase.ro

A. Sörensson et al. (eds.), *Corporate Responsibility and Sustainability during the Coronavirus Crisis*, Palgrave Studies in Governance, Leadership and Responsibility,
https://doi.org/10.1007/978-3-030-73847-1_1

countries in the management of this worldwide health emergency (Gehrke 2020). Efforts range from the medical management of the virus in the form of adequate access to healthcare, protective equipment and necessary treatment of patients, to the issue of financial sustainability of various organisation (Gehrke 2020), or the societal risks that businesses should undertake in times of uncertainty (Crane and Matten 2020). All these issues then raise questions about insecurity in society, the role that the businesses might play in avoiding or reducing such societal risk and the implications of uncertainty for economies. In addition, measures to limit the spread of infection differ significantly between countries, and the World Health Organization's recommendations adapted to the conditions and political governance of the various countries. For some industries, this has led to a sharp decline in sales, while other industries have seen a boost in their activities due to high demand for certain products and services.

Research on corporate social responsibility (CSR) expanded considerably before the pandemic, and some suggest it is one of the fields in business or management studies that is most read and cited (Crane and Matten 2020). CSR is theorised as dealing with the relationship between business and society, ensuring that businesses maintain their legitimacy, or social licence (Grigore et al. 2020, 2021). The European Commission defines CSR as "the responsibility of enterprises for their impacts on society", and they state that organisations "should have in place a process to integrate social, environmental, ethical human rights and consumer concerns into their business operations and core strategy in close collaboration with their stakeholders". In a broader sense, CSR attempts to bring together the interests of commercial, not-for-profit, and governmental actors to do good in society (Stancu et al. 2011; Campbell 2007), and to build bridges between private and public sectors (i.e., UN Agenda 2030). However, Crane and Matten (2020) note that "the pandemic has clearly

B. Tesfaye
Södertörn University, Huddinge, Sweden
e-mail: besrat.tesfaye@sh.se

challenged a number of existing CSR assumptions, concepts, and practices". Indeed, COVID-19 has caused a sentiment of vulnerability and instability in business and in society, and the crises therefore put corporate responsibility to the test (Kramer 2020). Some of the questions raised are: Do businesses have a responsibility to help save lives? And does society have any responsibility to support businesses?

In a recent *Harvard Business Review* article, Kramer (2020) reminds us how 38 years ago, seven people in Chicago died from taking poisoned Tylenol pills. This was a rare and localised event, and Johnson & Johnson immediately pulled all Tylenol from their stores, taking a loss to avoid even a single additional death. Business should never cause such harm, regardless of the cost. This case study is still taught in business schools as it reminds us about the prioritisation of saving lives. People still talk about that decision, which is well alive in our collective memories. It is likely that the ways in which companies respond to this Coronavirus crisis will also be remembered for many years to come. Will they help to save lives, or insist on being saved? Organisations talk about having a social purpose and set of values driving their strategies, or about how much they care for their employees, customers, suppliers, communities and future generations. Now is the time for them to make good on that commitment. How do they respond to the crises? Who are they responsible to?

In other studies, we hear that businesses have faced major impacts from the pandemic (Manuel and Herron 2020). The pandemic affected societies and economies, and this then shapes the ways in which governments, businesses and people act (Donthu and Gustafsson 2020). Supply chain disruption, working from home, operational implications (for example, total or partial production shutdowns in the context of national state of emergency or high number of infected employees), and new costs related to decontamination are some of the most discussed impacts of this pandemic. Industries such as tourism, hospitality, airlines or travel are impacted due to travel restrictions and lockdowns, and therefore are losing customers and revenues, whilst e-commerce, home entertainment and social media platforms are booming. The customers have changed their purchasing behaviours and there has been a rapid increase in demand for online shopping, which firms had to meet to maintain sales. So how do companies respond to such fluid times?

Some companies have reframed their visions and mission and repurposed their production lines or services to manage the effects of the pandemic. Immediate organisational responses include companies like Nissan, or McLaren Automotive joining the race to produce ventilators that could help patients with breathing problems (BBC 2020a; McLaren 2020), Luis Vuitton saying it wants to use its perfume production lines to start making hand sanitiser (BBC 2020b), whilst electronics giant Foxconn switched some of its production from Apple iPhones to make surgical masks (The Guardian 2020a). Other organisations had to redefine what is essential or non-essential in the workplace, and digital technologies afforded new opportunities for organising work from home. He and Harris (2020: 176) argue that the "Covid-19 pandemic offers a great opportunity for businesses to shift towards more genuine and authentic CSR and contribute to respond to urgent global social and environmental challanges".

Different studies have shown different results regarding CSR during the COVID-19 pandemic. In a recent study, 47 per cent of the companies surveyed also stated that the company's sustainability budget had not changed, and 14 per cent said that it had actually increased during the pandemic (LRF 2021). Another study has shown that the Covid-19 pandemic will have a negative impact on companies' sustainability work. That is the opinion of global sustainability experts. Almost half of the respondents, or 49 per cent, answered that sustainability will be prioritised down as a result of the pandemic, which consumes much of companies' energy and resources (FAR 2020). The fact that CSR and sustainability issues have increased in importance is partly due to the fact that they afford opportunities to contribute to a better society, and also because customers demand sustainability commitments. As such, it has become even more important to primarily take care of their employees during this time (LRF 2021).

However, in the first few weeks of the lockdown we heard how Richard Branson faced backlash over plea for a £500m bailout to help his Virgin Atlantic airline survive the Coronavirus pandemic (The Guardian 2020b). Many pointed out that the entrepreneur has paid no personal income tax since moving to the tax-free British Virgin Islands 14 years ago (The Guardian 2020b). We also heard about furloughed Sports Direct employees claiming they have been asked to work at least once a week (McCulloch 2020). And this controversy came after owner Mike Ashley pressed the government to allow Sports Direct stores to stay open arguing that selling fitness equipment is essential to people stuck at home (although we might suspect the actual motive was profit). These examples have been met with public anger and frustration, which, one might argue, stem from the apparent hypocrisy of organisations that have avoided corporate social responsibility yet expect society to make concession to *them* in a time of crisis. This is a strange reversal towards claims for societal business responsibility in a crisis. As the third lockdown starts to end, we further see all sorts of organisations in the UK, for example, asking for it to do so more quickly. People may be dying still, but businesses want a return to "normal" even if that normal risks lives.

If we think about the aforementioned Tylenol example, the ways in which organisations respond will be remembered and might hinder or enhance the organisational reputation. Now, if we take the question of who organisations should be responsible to, we can draw from previous research. Previous CSR studies suggest several approaches regarding the responsibilities of corporations: business, stakeholder and societal approaches (Grigore et al. 2017). Briefly, the business approach argues that a corporation should maximise profit survival, and its responsibility is, first and foremost, to its shareholders (Friedman 1970). The stakeholder perspective (Freeman 1984) contends that corporations are responsible to groups beyond shareholders who are impacted by and can impact the corporation. The societal approach suggests that corporations have commitments to society at large and that the polyvocal (or multivocal) nature of society, not the corporation, determines what is right and proper (Waddock 2004). So, organisations may want to ask these questions about how they meet their responsibility to various actors during the Coronavirus crises. Do they attempt to ensure profitability for shareholders regardless of societal impact and risk? How about the responsibilities to their employees, do organisations have a workplace health and safety risk assessment, or do they continue to pay salaries? How about suppliers—are companies giving advance payments to small suppliers?

And how about the responsibility to community and vulnerable groups—do they provide food, deliveries to the vulnerable? Such dilemmas will be addressed and dealt with in the chapters of this book.

1.2 Corporate Responsibility and COVID-19: International Perspectives

We seek to understand how society and businesses are affected by and respond to the Coronavirus crisis in various parts of the world. We aim to explore: (1) new CSR perspectives given the pandemic situation, (2) SME perspectives and responsibility during the early stages of the pandemic and (3) how large companies responded to the crisis. Overall, then, the book asks readers to reflect on what the current crisis means for businesses, markets, communities and society more broadly. It has a global reach and includes conceptual or empirical studies from Spain, Mexico, Sweden, Nigeria, Ghana and Kuwait, from various sectors and it also explores both small and large organisations/companies. The common ground is that the pandemic has hit on a global level and all businesses around the globe are affected.

1.2.1 COVID-19 and New CSR Perspectives

In Chap. 2, Arroyo, Sanchez-Asin, Valls-Pasola and Hormiga tackle the role and relevance of the Coronavirus makers network in the context of CSR's situation in Spain during the crisis in the first half of 2020. It analyses how the network emerged, how it was organised, its results and social impact, and the key factors that explain its success and its relations with large companies.

Then, in Chap. 3 Díaz-Pichardo and Sánchez-Medina analyse the evolution of the CSR initiatives of Mexican enterprises during the first six months of the pandemic. Authors demonstrate how enterprises have shown an evolution in the types of initiatives proposed, starting from helping the population in need to satisfy their immediate necessities and to help others retake their economic activity in the "new normal".

However, with hundreds of thousands of businesses closing and millions of people unemployed and in poverty, Mexico is facing its worst economic crisis in history. The authors reflect on the current situation in Mexico.

In Chap. 4, Surdu and Nardella problematise the outcomes of corporate social irresponsibility (CSI). Their work reveals how and why the assumptions that corporate irresponsibility leads to negative organisational outcomes, such as negative impacts on reputation or financial performance, are not always supported. The authors show that there is a disconnect between what the CSI theory assumes and what happens on the ground, or the CSI practice. The chapter is ripe with examples of corporate irresponsibility during the pandemic from various sectors and how these led to mixed outcomes for organisations and society. Finally, the authors end the chapter by presenting managerial implications and they also discuss the role of policy in managing corporate social irresponsibility.

These chapters address CSR during the pandemic from an organisational perspective focused on network as well as how companies are helping people during the pandemic. The chapters could be useful for different organisations and society to show how policies can be useful in CSR implementation.

1.2.2 CSR, SMEs and COVID-19

In Chap. 5, Sörensson, Bogren and Schmudde investigate the case of the Swedish tourism industry during the first six months of the COVID-19 crisis. Using data from 100 SMEs in three sectors of the tourism industry—accommodation and restaurants, culture and entertainment, and travel agencies—they analyse the effect of the pandemic on firms with focus on their sustainability values. They note that the impact of the pandemic on individual segments and firms vary, but overall, the tourism industry is struggling. Consequently, there is a shift from sustainability values of the firms towards economic sustainability values. Authors also note that tourism firms which have managed to create higher sustainability value for their customers have higher prospects for survival.

In Chap. 6, Tesfaye and Lundström gain insight into how SMEs manage the COVID-19 pandemic from both economic and CSR perspectives. The results indicate that the impact of the COVID-19 pandemic is related to the state of the industry in which the case companies are located, and the pre-crisis status of the companies. The perceptions of the entrepreneurs also differ. Some entrepreneurs perceive the crisis as a threat to the business, while others see opportunities for innovation. These perceptions likely guide the strategic choices and managerial practices of the entrepreneurs. Digitalisation is a common denominator with regard to social responsibility. However, the primary focus is on socially responsible practices for health and safety of employees.

In Chap. 7, Boter, Lundström and Sörensson analyse how Swedish small companies have been affected by the pandemic. The data consists of interviews with 1200 small companies from four different industry segments and the results show different outcomes. Some company groups have had, and still have, significant negative effects, while other categories have only been marginally affected. There are a small group of companies that has noticed growing sales and occasionally also signals from the market that new products and services are needed in the near future.

These chapters address mainly small businesses and how they have been affected by the pandemic and their work with CSR. It is clear that companies in some industries have been affected more than others. The clearest impact is the tourism industry, which has been hit hard during the pandemic.

1.2.3 CSR in Large Companies During COVID-19

Chapter 8 by Okoye and Nwagwu explores illustrative cases of large multinational enterprises (MNE) response—Lafarge in Nigeria, and Unilever in Nigeria and Ghana—in terms of their approach to and practice of corporate social responsibility and sustainability during the pandemic, and their response to the COVID-19 crisis in a complex environment marked by deepening poverty and climate change issues. These examples are chosen as indicative of MNEs active in the West African region.

In Chap. 9, Goyal, Kakabadse and Kakabadse argue that when dealing with uncertain or complex situations—such as a global-wide pandemic—board members turn to their backgrounds and experiences when making decisions. Specifically, by drawing on depth interviews with 42 board members, the authors demonstrate the importance of religious beliefs in interpreting available information and the shaping of their values, as well as organisations' strategic aspirations. They conclude by discussing the implications of board members' religious beliefs on decision-making during the COVID-19 crises.

In Chap. 10, Al-Husaini explores how corporate social responsibility has grown in the state of Kuwait. The chapter discusses CSR best practice in a global crisis based on the three pillars seen in the work of Kuwait's Oil Sector during COVID-19. The Kuwait Oil Sector, led by Kuwait Oil Company (KOC), took responsibility for providing Kuwait's Ministry of Health with urgent aid through CSR projects such as building the largest quarantine facilities in the country, constructing the Kuwait Field Hospital and developing several media campaigns to highlight such extensive efforts to the general public and promote individual responsibility during COVID-19.

These chapters address how large companies are reacting to the pandemic and CSR. Different perspectives are discussed as well as different countries with specific contexts. The chapters show how CSR still is useful during the pandemic in these countries.

1.3 Concluding Thoughts

The book invites readers to further reflect on new areas for CSR research, especially in times of crises. Whilst previous research deals with new theories or models post-financial crises (see "Corporate social responsibility in the post-financial crisis era" by Theofilou, Grigore and Stancu, 2016, as one example, Theofilou et al, 2016), little is known about the impact that a worldwide health crisis might have on businesses, organisations, society and CSR research. Crane and Matten (2020) suggest that COVID-19 might help us imagine new ways of theorising private enterprises, for example, or might push our thinking beyond CSR to identify alternative modes of organising or new models of the firm where businesses' purposes are truly aligned with societal goals.

The COVID-19 pandemic has generated a global health, economic and social crisis that requires the collaboration and commitment of all of us (ref), both in the private sector as well as in the public sector. The pandemic has led to more sustainable behaviour like fewer flight trips with less pollution from the airline industry. This book shows different perspectives on CSR during the pandemic. The work with implication of the 2030 Agenda and the Sustainable Development Goals (SDGs) may lead to new CSR strategies post COVID-19. Practical implications from this book are that the COVID-19 pandemic will increase people's awareness and expectations of companies and their behaviour. Today, people have higher expectations and companies must balance profitability with different stakeholders' demand for CSR actions. In sum, now is the time to make investment in CSR, to be able to move to a future post-COVID-19 that will be more sustainable.

References

Aßländer, M. S., & Curbach, J. (2017). Corporate or governmental duties? Corporate citizenship from a governmental perspective. *Business & Society, 56*(4), 617–645.

BBC. (2020a). *Nissan halts carmaking in Sunderland and may make ventilators*. BBC. Retrieved from https://www.bbc.co.uk/news/uk-england-tyne-51972329.

BBC. (2020b). *Coronavirus: Louis Vuitton owner to start making hand sanitiser*. BBC. Retrieved from https://www.bbc.co.uk/news/business-51868756.

Campbell, J. L. (2007). Why would corporations behave in socially responsible ways? An institutional theory of corporate social responsibility. *Academy of Management Review, 32*(3), 946–967.

Crane, A., & Matten, D. (2020). COVID-19 and the future of CSR research. *Journal of Management Studies*.

Donthu, N., & Gustafsson, A. (2020). Effects of COVID-19 on business and research. *Journal of Business Research, 117*, 284.

FAR. (2020). Retrieved from https://www.tidningenbalans.se/nyheter/hallbarhetsarbetet-blir-lidande-i-pandemin/.

Freeman, R. E. (1984). *Strategic management: A stakeholder approach*. Boston: Pitman.

Friedman, M. (1970). A theoretical framework for monetary analysis. *Journal of Political Economy, 78*(2), 193–238.

García-Sánchez, I. M., & García-Sánchez, A. (2020). Corporate social responsibility during COVID-19 pandemic. *Journal of Open Innovation: Technology, Market, and Complexity, 6*(4).

Gehrke, T. (2020). After Covid-19: Economic security in EU-Asia connectivity. *Asia Europe Journal, 18*, 239–243.

Grigore, G., Molesworth, M., & Watkins, R. (2017). New corporate responsibilities in the digital economy. In *Corporate social responsibility in the post-financial crisis era* (pp. 41–62). Cham: Palgrave Macmillan.

Grigore, G., Molesworth, M., Vonţea, A., Basnawi, A. H., Celep, O., & Jesudoss, S. P. (2020). Drama and Discounting in theRelational Dynamics ofCorporate Social Responsibility. *Journal of Business Ethics*, 1–24.

Grigore, G., Molesworth, M., Miles, C., & Glozer, S. (2021). (Un) resolving digital technology paradoxes through the rhetoricof balance. Organization, 28(1), 186–207.

He, H., & Harris, L. (2020). The impact of Covid-19 pandemic on corporate social responsibility and marketing philosophy. *Journal of Business Research, 116*, 176–182.

Kramer, M. R. (2020). Coronavirus is putting corporate social responsibility to the test. *Harvard Business Review*.

LRF. (2021). Retrieved from https://www.pressmachine.se/pressrelease/view/pandemin-paverkar-inte-foretagens-hallbarhetsarbete-sager-hallbarhetsrapporten-fran-lrf-media-25068.

Manuel, T., & Herron, T. L. (2020). An ethical perspective of business CSR and the COVID-19 pandemic. *Society and Business Review*.

McCulloch, A. (2020) Sports Direct 'pressured furloughed staff to work', reports suggest. *Personnel Today*. Retrieved from https://www.personneltoday.com/hr/sports-direct-alleged-to-have-pressured-furloughed-staff-to-work/.

McLaren. (2020). Case study: Ventilator Challenge UK. How McLaren answered the nation's call in the fight against covid-19. Retrieved from https://www.mclaren.com/racing/inside-the-mtc/case-study-ventilator-challenge-uk/.

Stancu, A., Grigore, G. F., & Rosca, M. I. (2011). The impact of corporate social responsibility on employees. In InternationalConference on Information and Finance (Vol. 21, pp. 11–16).

The Guardian. (2020a). Foxconn makes masks for its iPhone workers amid coronavirus crisis. *The Guardian*. Retrieved from https://www.theguardian.com/technology/2020/feb/07/foxconn-makes-masks-for-its-iphone-workers-amid-coronavirus-crisis-apple.

The Guardian. (2020b). Richard Branson faced backlash over plea for a £500m bailout to help his Virgin Atlantic airline survive the coronavirus pandemic. Retrieved from https://www.theguardian.com/business/2020/apr/12/richard-branson-facing-backlash-over-plea-for-uk-bailout-of-virgin.

Theofilou, A., Grigore, G., & Stancu, A. (Eds.). (2016). Corporate social responsibility in the post-financial crisis era: CSRconceptualisations and international practices in times of uncertainty. Springer.

Waddock, S. (2004). Creating corporate accountability: Foundational principles to make corporate citizenship real. *Journal of Business Ethics, 50*(4), 313–327.

Part I

COVID-19 and New CSR Perspectives

2

The Coronavirus Makers Network. Understanding the Success of an Innovation Community Facing COVID-19 in Spain

Lizbeth Arroyo, J. Javier Sanchez-Asin, Jaume Valls-Pasola, and Esther Hormiga

2.1 Introduction

The COVID-19 pandemic is the defining global health crisis of our time and one of the greatest challenges we have faced since World War II. Since its appearance in Asia late last year, the virus has spread to all continents, affecting every aspect of our lives, from the family and social environment to employment, production and the distribution of goods and services. Estimations for the economic prospects of all countries are bleak, and the pandemic is likely to have a lasting impact on the determinants

L. Arroyo • J. Valls-Pasola (✉) • E. Hormiga
Universitat de Barcelona, Barcelona, Spain
e-mail: jaume.valls@ub.edu

J. J. Sanchez-Asin
Universidad de Zaragoza, Zaragoza, Spain

A. Sörensson et al. (eds.), *Corporate Responsibility and Sustainability during the Coronavirus Crisis*, Palgrave Studies in Governance, Leadership and Responsibility,
https://doi.org/10.1007/978-3-030-73847-1_2

of long-term growth prospects, further eroding living standards in the years ahead. Even though the pandemic was predictable and indeed predicted (Gates 2014), it has taken most of the world by surprise. Neither administrations nor companies were prepared for this health crisis, nor its socio-economic repercussions.

The crisis has exposed weaknesses both in terms of pandemic management and in the networks that ensure socio-economic stability and global cooperation. Struggling to cope with its impact, governments and companies are facing challenges concerning labour and for ensuring essential supplies and social stability. Difficult choices had to be made to achieve the necessary trade-off between health security, growing social anxiety and economic consequences. Even when the pandemic is over profound and long-lasting economic, social, political and cultural repercussions are expected.

In this context of crisis, the integration business-society plays a central role to respond to post-pandemic challenges (Porter and Kramer 2006, 2011). The pandemic triggered actions by all kinds of social agents and organisations to address the situation. From the collaboration between the business world and civil society has risen a movement to face this health crisis—as the maker movement. Although the established pieces of literature in corporate social responsibility (CSR) (Porter and Kramer 2011), social innovation (Defining Social Innovation 2020) and maker movement (Unterfrauner et al. 2020) address them as a mechanism for social progress, it is worth asking how the maker movement emerged during the COVID-19 breakout, how the relationship with companies was established, and how its success can be explained?

This chapter aims to analyse how the network emerged, how it was organised, its results and social impact and the key factors that explain its success. The relations with large companies in the framework of their CSR policies are also considered. To this end, a case study has been designed (Eisenhardt 1989; Eisenhardt and Graebner 2007; Yin 2013). To examine this phenomenon in greater depth, a single case has been selected: the Coronavirus Makers community. A unique programme that arose from the maker community in Spain set up to respond to the specific needs of the health system in the context of the COVID-19 health emergency. This research was based on analysing secondary sources of information and two in-depth interviews with two coordinators of the network.

Main findings offer insights framed in a health crisis about the development process of an innovation community, the maker profile and the roles they adopt within the organisation, the factors that made the community success and finally the relationship between the community and company's CSR initiatives.

The chapter is organised into four blocks. The first is a synthesis of the theoretical framework concerning innovation communities. This section is followed by an introduction to the basic concepts of the social impact/CSR binomial. The methodology, results and discussion are then presented, and the analysis closes with some concluding remarks.

2.2 Theoretical Framework

The integration of business-society can be framed in the collaboration between companies and agents that promote social innovation as innovation communities do (Fichter 2009). A good example is the *maker movement* that aims to solve challenges or needs by taking an approach based on sharing the knowledge generated. Makers address social imbalance empowering people to "make" solutions for encountered problems, democratising access to digital technologies and their know-how and their ambitions to change society providing better opportunities for individuals (Unterfrauner et al. 2020).

In this chapter, it takes an innovation community approach to understand the nature of the maker community. It also examines the basic concepts relating to the social impact/CSR binomial, and the context of CSR in Spain during the COVID-19 crisis. These three topics are relevant for the analysis of the Coronavirus Makers network that is presented in Sect. 2.3.

2.2.1 The Maker Movement as an Innovation Community

Over the last 20 years, the development of internet-based communications and the increasing digitalisation of knowledge-intensive tasks have made it feasible to solve problems employing crowd approaches. For some authors, innovation is democratised through the community because the product consumers/users act as innovators (Fauchart and Foray 2016). In Von Hippel's (1994) terminology, this is the *user innovation revolution*, which goes beyond open innovation as it is an open-source approach. In this sense, the *maker movemen*t is associated with the "Do It Yourself" philosophies; even some authors express that it is more a do-it-together culture (Dufva 2017; Giusti et al. 2020) that gave rise to a new entrepreneurial ecosystem (Mortara and Parisot 2016). It is also claimed to be open and provide democratised access to modern fabrication technologies and to equip citizens with digital skills (Unterfrauner et al. 2020).

According to Lakhani (2016), the innovation community emerges from groups of people united through a common technology or used condition. They connect either online or physically to share willingly and freely their problems and solutions to the various use conditions of that technology. When specific results are obtained, the community is committed not only to sharing but also to obtaining a collective outcome that leads to an operational solution. Following this conceptualisation, a *maker community* describes a broad community built on an individual's ability to be a creator of new technologies and practices, "a maker" (Morreale et al. 2017; Papavlasopoulou et al. 2017). They are engaged with new technologies, mostly 3D manufacturing (Papavlasopoulou et al. 2017; Dufva 2017) in a collaborative work that depends on community members (Morreale et al. 2017).

Another relevant aspect that interrelates innovation communities with the maker movement is how market failures can motivate users to become innovators (Fauchart and Foray 2016). That is to say, that makers will take advantage of the collective power and handicraft skills to carry out a better result than that which would be obtained by others means (Dufva

2017). However, contrary to the theoretically established transaction cost advantages of innovation communities (von Hippel and von Krogh 2003), the maker movement is driven by doing something that solves daily life needs (Dougherty 2012). However, recently, authors suggest a bigger socially impact purposes (Unterfrauner et al. 2020).

A core element of the maker movement as an innovation community is its attractiveness. One of the most remarkable attributes is the complete freedom in the selection of the tasks encourages members to perform them accordingly with their priorities and convictions (Baldwin and Clark 2006). No one plays an intermediate role between the task and the problem solver. It is the participants themselves who decide whether they have sufficient relevant skill sets and interests to contribute to a given collective project. The decentralised nature of the project encourages individuals to self-assign specific tasks that they consider appropriate for them without having to go through assignment mechanisms that are decided upon by the community's leadership (Fichter 2009). Although in the literature on the maker movement, it is not clear the existence of a defined leadership.

The benefits to be a part of the maker movement in terms of an innovation community make sense with Dougherty (2012) when describing a maker as an enthusiastic tinkering-skilled individual. Learning, having fun, gaining status or social recognition are seen as rewards for being a member of the community. Some studies on motivations for participating in communities also consider as perceived benefit enjoying the project, the intellectual challenge, the satisfaction that completing the task brings, being in direct contact with a real need of the user, career development or merely improving learn-by-doing skills (Lakhani 2016). From Sect. 2.3 on, we will illustrate the case of the Coronavirus Maker movement as an innovation community.

2.2.2 Social Impact and CSR

The context of crisis urges the symbiosis business-society to search for new and more efficient forms of social impact and to develop the know-how to respond to new needs. By one side, *social innovation* is a key term for understanding how innovation is viewed in our society today. It conceptualised as "the process of developing and deploying effective solutions to challenging and often systemic social and environmental issues in support of social progress" (Defining Social Innovation 2020). It socially impacts changing people's way of life, their environment, health and wellbeing, their personal and property rights, and their aspirations (Vanclay 2002, 2003). From civil society has risen movements to balance the social inequalities—as the maker movement.

By the other one, in the case of company activities, their impacts sometimes are socially and environmentally questionable. Under the argument of "do the right thing" (Porter and Kramer 2006), companies must take the lead in bringing business and society back together (Porter and Kramer 2011). They embrace CSR works as a mechanism to develop actions to reinforce corporate strategy through social progress (Porter and Kramer 2011).

Social impact and CSR share common values, that is, to address the social implications of corporate activities with a concern for human rights, livelihoods, community engagement in decision-making, ethical behaviour and the valuing of local knowledge and the environment [Carroll 2008; Crane et al. 2009]. CSR activities show what areas companies are looking to create a social impact in (Porter and Kramer 2011).

The pandemic has offered great opportunities for companies to engage with their CSR strategies and agendas actively. CSR is at its best where stakeholder views are considered and used to inform corporate policy and practice (Jamali 2007), as evidenced through corporate–community partnerships, long-term community investment and the creation of sustainable communities by concentrating on adding value throughout the supply chain (Blowfield and Frynas 2005; Wood et al. 2006; Porter and Kramer 2006).

In Spain, during the COVID-19 health crisis, its effects have transformed CSR significantly in terms of business ethics and the way sustainable businesses are developed (EY Spain 2020; FORETICA 2020). Business priorities in CSR have changed, focusing on society in general and people's health in particular (SERES 2020a, 2020b). For example, donations in kind (medical supplies, food and electronic devices, among others) and monetary donations stand out, which combined account for more than 19% of total actions (CANVAS and Monge 2020).

Among the corporate actions, it includes activity reductions or services redefinition. For example, manufacturing companies have adapted their activity to the context of the crisis, even modifying their production chains to manufacture essential products: ventilators, personal protection equipment, hand sanitisers and so on. Many products have been donated where they were needed. There are examples of large retailers making masks in their workshops or protective gowns for health staff, and hotels converted into hospitals, banks deferring mortgage loan payments, power companies giving moratoriums on electricity or gas bills, private centres offering free online courses, gyms providing free workouts on the internet, supermarkets scheduling special opening hours for the elderly and making donations to food banks and charities and so on.

As for those involving employees, notable cases are those maintaining activity and employment and reinforcing health, safety and welfare measures. Also prominent are programmes carried out by companies to adapt their activities to the new needs arising from the crisis. It is also remarkable to find 26 actions regarding the establishment of alliances and signing up for initiatives or social platforms, something which denotes a high level of commitment to society, with the intention of permanence, and a strong component of cooperation.

The resources most offered by organisations are (i) in the area of social welfare: basic needs, medical supplies, medical care services and online caregiving; and (ii) in the economic area: deferred payments of bills, improved financial conditions for services, training platforms and programmes, and other engaging digital contents. The primary beneficiaries of the cases analysed have been health agents, with 27% of the total contributions. Forty-one per cent of organisations have focused some of their actions on this group. Other relevant beneficiaries are a society in general (22%); people at risk of social exclusion (15%); vulnerable groups (13%); companies, self-employed and customers (13%); educational agents (6%) and others (3%).

2.3 Methodology

This chapter aims to analyse the maker movement as an innovation community in times of crisis. Specifically, it seeks to explore their nature, their composition and their relations and dynamics with institutional agents and companies. To this end, a case study has been designed (Eisenhardt 1989; Eisenhardt and Graebner 2007; Yin 2013). To examine this phenomenon in greater depth, a single case has been selected: the Coronavirus Makers community.

The Coronavirus Makers collaborative network was selected because it groups more than 20,000 researchers, developers and engineers. They altruistically put their knowledge and resources at the service of the community in order to provide solutions for one of the main problems the healthcare system was facing at that time—the shortage of medical supplies to cope with the increasing number of COVID-19 cases. The idea was to design and manufacture a specific type of personal protection equipment (PPE) that was feasible for the maker network: mainly visors, masks and ear guards. Nevertheless, there were other remarkable products, especially a ventilator designed in a record time of 15 days.

The main source of data for this chapter was the open-ended interview. The people interviewed were one of the Coronavirus Makers movement's leading promoters, Esther Borao, and one of its coordinators in Catalonia, A lvaro Jansa. The first interview was held on July 24, 2020, at the site of ITAINNOVA, Aragon's Technological Institute belonging to the Government of Aragon (during this interview, all safety measure derived from pandemic were followed), and lasted 105 minutes. The second was held online on August 7, 2020, and lasted 64 minutes. The interviews were structured around four theoretical categories, emphasising the emergence of innovation communities, their social impact, the factors behind their success and their relationship with companies. Secondary sources (news in national newspapers, podcasts, web pages, etc.) were also used to contextualise the case.

Data analysis included narrative analysis and first-order and second-order constructs (Gioia et al. 2013). The first step was narrative analysis to identify the main elements of the interviewees' narratives related to the emergence of the innovation communities, success factors, social impact and the relationship between innovation communities and companies through CSR initiatives.

It is worth noting the particular context in which the Coronavirus Makers network was created. On March 12, Spain was only two days away from the declaration of a state of alarm by the Spanish government. Lockdown was decreed that would last until April 26, when a process of returning to the so-called new normal began in various phases. The epidemic threshold (a cumulative incidence of people affected by the virus exceeding 5 cases per 100,000 inhabitants) was reached in Spain on March 8, with the Community of Madrid being the first region in which this happened (February 24). After the first week of March 2020, the Spanish media began to talk about a possible collapse of the healthcare system due to COVID-19 and the imminent lack of resources caused by a rapid increase in admissions to hospital Intensive Care Units (ICUs). The media also showed scenes of the poorly equipped medical staff using self-made personal protective equipment (PPE), including garbage bags.

2.4 Results

The emergence of Coronavirus Makers confirms Lakhani's (2016) definition of innovation communities as described in Sect. 2.2. In addition, organisational characteristics, member profiles and types of collaboration, community success factors and their relationship to social impact appeared during data analysis.

2.4.1 Process of Development

The analysis showed that the Coronavirus Makers community is undergoing a lifecycle. More specifically, five phases were identified: Needs Identification, Makers Mobilisation, Community Activation, Community Hibernation and Reactivation (Table 2.1). This cycle is intrinsically related to the outside events and the community members' actions.

Table 2.1 Phases in the Coronavirus Makers community's lifecycle

Phase	Characteristics	Example
Needs Identification	Emergence of a social or environmental crisis Public and private institutions and organisations' capacity to provide a rapid response to the contingency is limited.	Paco Rojas, a colleague from ITAINNOVA, and E. Borao discussed what was happening in Italy and the limitations of healthcare systems to respond to the COVID-19 patients' needs due to the lack of ventilators (interview with E. Borao, July 24, 2020). That afternoon E. Borao had spoken with Raul Olivan, general director of open government and social innovation at the government of Aragon. Olivan commented on the needs that people were going to have at home and how society could help. They discussed the possibility of creating a "Wallapop"-type platform to connect people with resources and people in need of them (interview with E. Borao, July 24, 2020). The movement was set up in response to a need (interview with A. Jansa, august 7, 2020).
Maker Mobilisation	Use of digital platforms to convene the development of technological solutions to address the need. Technical consensus Technical and operational organisation	That night, a tweet by Irish engineer Colin Keogh called on doctors, engineers and designers to join an interesting project to develop a low-cost ventilator, donating time and expertise. This tweet inspired E. Borao to create the coronavirus makers group on telegram that very night. Later, she also created the coronavirus-ITA group to contribute technical solutions for ventilators (interview with E. Borao, July 24, 2020).

(*continued*)

Table 2.1 (continued)

Phase	Characteristics	Example
Activation	Product design and production begins	"FabLab" creates a manufacturing and distribution node for Sant Cugat (interview with A. Jansa, august 7, 2020).
Hibernation	Contingency control	It is the people united who will achieve change if they stick together (...). The pot keeps boiling at first, but the dough will eventually collapse. And it is this core of people left who will be useful in the end, it is a matter of time (interview with A. Jansa, august 7, 2020). This does not mean that it is not alive, but that there is a change in the external circumstances: The end of the state of alarm, reasonable control of the health situation (despite the current outbreaks) and return to the "new normal". This has led many participants to return to their "new routines" (similar to those of the past: Work, family logistics, etc.), diluting one of the main collective incentives: Doing something to get out of the situation (interview with E. Borao, July 24, 2020).
Reactivation	Re-emergence of contingency or appearance of new challenges	In this regard, Esther suggests that the huge size achieved will not be repeated unless a new and similar threat to the previous one appears (interview with E. Borao, July 24, 2020).

Source: Author's own work

The Needs Identification phase took place on March 12 and refers to the detection of a social or environmental contingency. For example, Jansa (2020) points out the limitations of institutions and other public or private organisations to address the crisis. However, Borao (interview 24-07-2020) highlights the makers' institutional links and their involvement in the search for quick and effective solutions. Both conclude that the movement was born out of the makers' desire to provide a technological solution (Borao interview 24-07-2020; Jansa interview 07-08-2020).

In the Maker Mobilisation phase, the power of convening legitimate profiles within the community and the use of digital platforms to disseminate the challenge of creating a technological solution in a short time is evident. Active participation in different maker forums is fundamental in this phase. In this case, both makers were part of broad networks connected through Twitter, Facebook or WhatsApp (Borao interview 24-07-2020; Jansa interview 07-08-2020). In the words of Borao (interview 24-07-2020), "magic happened": in 48 hours more than 900 people had joined, and after ten days there were more than 10,000. This quote shows what Jansa (interview 07-08-2020) describes as the maker's own "curiosity".

The Community Activation phase is defined by the organisation of the community and the production of personal protection equipment. The manufacturing and distribution nodes were set up according to national coordination and local management structure, as is the case of "FabLabs". As pointed out by Jansa (interview 07-08-2020), the connection between makers and different professional profiles began based on their geographical proximity or their direct relationships with other members. The role of volunteer citizens in operational activities such as manufacturing of parts, disinfection and distribution (Jansa interview 07-08-2020) is also noteworthy.

The Community Hibernation and Reactivation phases were apparent when discussing the organisation's future. Hibernation is the suspension or reduction of activity. That is to say, the maker network groups remain active, but their scope has more to do with the activity of innovation communities than that of a social phenomenon (Borao interview 24-07-2020). This happens by the positive results obtained when facing the contingencies, their complexity or risk having been reduced.

Finally, the Community Reactivation phase is a future but latent stage. It is suggested that the emotional ties established between the makers at the moments of greatest activity are likely to endure and be activated in a much more organised way in the case of a new collective emergency (Borao interview 24-07-2020).

2.4.2 Maker Profile and Types of Collaboration

The members of this innovation community are characterised by versatile profiles working in a collaborative environment to reach their goals. It is observed that the makers' main attributes are professional and have a moral dimension. On the one hand, professionally speaking, Borao (interview 24-07-2020) and Jansa (interview 07-08-2020) state that the makers are highly specialised individuals, although not necessarily in technical matters; they are passionate about technology and innovation; a problem-solution approach characterises their activity; they are flexible and adaptable, and they are highly entrepreneurial. On the other hand, the moral dimension of the makers' profile is characterised by their interest in the common good, collective responsibility and social change. Their actions are based on the values of altruism, solidarity and collaboration (Borao interview 24-07-2020; Jansa interview 07-08-2020).

However, elements were identified that suggest that makers play different roles within the community. Borao (interview 24-07-2020) classifies community members by what they could contribute. Coronavirus Makers involved both people who could contribute knowledge (doctors, psychologists, engineers, scientists) and people who, having learned about the programme, wanted to contribute whatever they could: time, supplies, equipment and so on.

From this classification, a typology of makers called *facilitators* emerges. We can differentiate between strategic, technical, operational and resource facilitators (Table 2.2). Borao (interview 24-07-2020) also points out that one single person could have all four attributes or only one of them. We can, therefore, assume that one individual may play different roles within the community.

Table 2.2 Maker types within the Coronavirus Makers community

Maker types	Characteristics
Strategic	Makers with the capacity to mobilise and Institutional legitimacy.
Technical	They have nonmaterial resources and contributed their knowledge to create, learn and teach.
Operational	They were part of the group of "links" aimed at solving operational issues such as connecting producers with receivers.
Resources	They have material resources like 3D printers and were asked to work while there was still a need. This type of collaborator includes individuals as well as organisations such as companies and technological institutes.

Source: Author's own work

2.4.3 Innovation Community Success Factors: The Strategic Facilitator, Institutional Relations and the Environment

The factors that define the success of an innovation community are not apparent since, as explained by Borao (interview 24-07-2020), we are not dealing with a formalised movement in which it is possible to perform cost-benefit analyses and measure results. However, both interviewees agree that Coronavirus Makers can be considered successful due to (i) internal factors (within the community) such as the role of strategic facilitators, productive capacity and the organisation of members; and (ii) external factors such as relationships with institutions. In general terms, the main indicators on which they base their perception of success refer to the level of knowledge achieved by the community and the organisational capacity of the network itself (Table 2.3).

The first success factor is the so-called *strategic facilitators*: makers that are highly entrepreneurial, especially proactive and innovative, legitimised by public and private institutions, and with the capacity to mobilise many makers. Thanks to them, a community's developmental process is triggered, and close collaborative relationships are woven with public and private institutions. The second success factor is associated with the regulatory requirements of the institutions themselves. A clear example is the approval process before public health agencies, showing the

Table 2.3 Success factors

Success factors		Perception of success indicators	
		Organisational	Technical
External	Institutional Relations	Collaboration opportunities support from private organisations (e.g. NGOs or companies) Legitimacy from other agents	Developing prototypes that meet regulatory requirements
Internal	Strategic facilitators	Emergence of latent leadership capabilities	High technical specialisation in R&D project leadership.
	Organisation of members	Network size (20,000 makers)	Manufacturing and logistics for over 2 million products at Country scale.
	Organisation of members	Coordination of such a large community in such a short time	Information access and management

Source: Author's own work

Table 2.4 Health supplies produced by Coronavirus Makers as of June 2020

Product	Visors	Ear guards	Door opener
Units	992,409	373,956	134,784

Source: www.coronavirusmakers.org 06/09/20

relationship between institutional regulation and the phases of Community, Hibernation and Deactivation.

Table 2.4 summarises the volume of health supplies produced and distributed by the network. The units of the three most outstanding products are detailed.

2.4.4 Innovation Communities, Companies and Social Impact: The Role of CSR

The relationship between innovation communities, companies and social impact is created by pursuing the same goal: to alleviate the crisis. The dynamics established between the community and the companies revolve around the role played by the latter, mainly as providers of material and nonmaterial resources or distributors of the product manufactured by the network's nodes. Companies are key to promoting social change through a paradigm shift (Jansa interview 07-08-2020). Their role as resource facilitators was performed by donating materials and means for product manufacturing (Borao interview 24-07-2020; Jansa interview 07-08-2020). Some cases were also identified where companies acted as technical facilitators, supporting community projects with their employees (Borao, 2020). In some cases, ONG as Ashoka Foundation contributed to the collection of donations for a certain period. Additionally, it should be noted that the designs of the makers, being open-source, were available and were used by some companies to manufacture personal protection equipment and contribute to a massive introduction of them into the market.

The effects of the COVID-19 pandemic have also been felt very significantly in terms of corporate social responsibility, business ethics and sustainable businesses. The pandemic is offering great opportunities for companies to engage with their CSR strategies and agendas actively. Therefore, an optimistic view is that the COVID-19 pandemic will accelerate the development of CSR, as more and more companies realise that their long-term survival and development depend on achieving a delicate balance between profitability and harmony with their stakeholders. The most relevant and pressing question is probably not whether to invest in CSR or not, but how to invest in CSR to achieve mutually beneficial and interdependent social/environmental and economic goals.

However, this relationship is conditioned by the reputational use of short-term CSR programmes and possible bad practices by companies (Jansa interview 07-08-2020). It is believed that in some cases, rather than projects for the future, they are used as "corporate slogans".

2.5 Discussion

The main goal of this chapter was to look in greater depth at innovation communities by analysing the Coronavirus Makers case. Through the experience of two individuals who considered themselves to be "makers", and who have both played a key role in the community's creation and coordination, we identified the development process of an innovation community, the maker profile and the roles they adopt within the organisation, the factors that made the community success and finally the relationship between the community and company's CSR initiatives.

At the organisational level, it should be noted that the main limitation on the communities' developmental process is their short existence in time, which makes it difficult to establish relations with other agents in the long term. In addition, these communities are directly influenced by the lack of consensus among members about what the identity of these organisations is or should be. The formalisation, through the legal constitution of an association, is strongly criticised by sectors of the community, making it difficult to professionalise the organisation and management.

Despite being perceived as a democratic organisation, there are hierarchical relations between the maker roles that are a consequence of the members' relational and intellectual capital. Because of the strategic facilitators' institutional legitimacy, public visibility, and material and technical resources, they tend to occupy strategic coordination positions, differentiating themselves from the rest by their capacity to mobilise not only people but resources as well.

A pertinent reflection would suggest that the establishment of innovation communities involve finding the critical elements required by a strategic facilitator to be legitimised by all the "factions" within the community.

Although conditioned by the uncertainty of current events, the community's success is reflected by its organisational and technical achievements. However, it is worth noting the factors that hinder their success, which is nearly related to the coordination in a record time of a very large, geographically disperse critical mass.

The social impact of the maker community has become apparent in the health and wellbeing fields, in the community and the political system. Indirectly, it is also helping to encourage a cultural change regarding the values that should define social change and allow the construction of a more open, equitable and sustainable society.

The health crisis is teaching us a lesson: *we are all in this together*. This will undoubtedly raise people's expectations for companies to be more socially responsible. We can, therefore, imagine that companies with a strong commitment to CSR and that develop and implement effective CSR strategies will thrive in the post-pandemic period. Rather than returning to the world as it was before, the United Nations (UN) has called for efforts to build more equitable, inclusive and sustainable post-COVID-19 economies and societies.

However, it should be noted that, despite this optimistic scenario regarding CSR, the paradigm shift will be brought about by the redefinition of current organisational cultures. The maker culture, as a mechanism of social innovation, could help structure organisations with a clear social focus, balancing the creation of financial profit and the generation of social impact. In some instances, the analysis of this case also shows how the use of the community/companies' relationship can be tinged by certain bad corporate practices and a "reputational" use of the donations made. This suggests that there is scope for improving the way companies incorporate new values that place sustainability and the common good at their core.

In other words, new ethics for sustainable development are required, shifting from creating value to debating what creates value. The need to respond to a social, health and economic crisis has arisen in the midst of a society undergoing a change of economic model, in which companies have an (even more) active and relevant role in society, so alliances and collaborations are necessary to tackle global problems.

2.6 Concluding Remarks

This chapter has analysed a unique network: the Coronavirus Makers network, which was created to respond to the health system's needs in the context of the COVID-19 health emergency. This network has become a successful initiative thanks to its flexibility and capacity to respond to the slower pace associated with the inertia of large organisations or government entities.

Innovation communities are groups of people united through a common technology or used condition, connected either online or face-to-face to share willingly and freely their problems and solutions to the various use conditions of that technology. This chapter's results suggest that an understanding of their nature is a key element for ensuring their success. In addition, depending on the roles they play within an innovation community and thanks to their versatile profiles, makers can take on one or more roles. On the one hand, the role of the strategic facilitator stands out for its relational capital which provides legitimacy; the technical facilitator for its intellectual capital; the resources facilitator, which includes companies, for its tangible capital and finally, the operational facilitators for their working capital. Success will be guaranteed by consensus, legitimacy gained by strategic facilitators in the eyes of the members and the ability to respond quickly and effectively to contingencies.

The business implications of this study are practical. The analysis brings out a particular contrast of models: the formalised CSR of companies versus the very short-term response capacity of makers' innovation communities: professionalisation versus volunteer maker; CSR as a protocol versus open-source social innovation developed by thousands of volunteers working collaboratively. And between these two models, the intermediate territory of cooperation between them. In this sense, it is suggested that innovation communities, as strategic allies for companies, could help to maximise the social impact of their CSR programmes. Finally, it is suggested that encouraging the maker profile or identifying them within organisations would entail potential benefits due to their relational capital, while they can also have an impact in terms of open innovation, institutional visibility and the encouragement of intrapreneurs.

Acknowledgements The authors acknowledge financial support from the following projects: Spanish Ministry of Economy and Competitiveness project ECO2013-48496-C4-3-R, and the DGA (Aragon Government-European Regional Development Fund) through the CREVALOR research group and the Spanish State Programme for Knowledge Generation project PGC2018-093971-B-100, funded by MCIU/AEI/FEDER, UE.

References

Baldwin, C., & Clark, K. (2006). The architecture of participation: Does code architecture mitigate free riding in the open source development model? *Management Science, 52*(7), 1116–1127.

Blowfield, M., & Frynas, J. G. (2005). Setting new agendas: Critical perspectives on corporate social responsibility in the developing world. *International Affairs (Royal Institute of International Affairs 1944-), 81*(3), 499–513.

CANVAS and Cristina Monge. (2020). *Ética empresarial y Agenda 2030 en tiempos de COVID-19. El compromiso de las empresas durante la pandemia.* CANVAS Estrategias Sostenibles. Madrid. https://bit.ly/etica-agenda2030.

Carroll, A. B. (2008). A history of corporate social responsibility: Concepts and practices. In A. Crane, D. Matten, A. McWilliams, J. Moon, & D. S. Siegel (Eds.), *The Oxford handbook of corporate social responsibility* (pp. 19–46). Oxford: Oxford University Press.

Crane, A., McWilliams, A., Matten, D., Moon, J., & Siegel, D. (2009). The corporate social responsibility agenda. In A. Crane, D. Matten, A. McWilliams, J. Moon, & D. Siegel (Eds.), *The Oxford handbook of corporate social responsibility* (pp. 3–18). New York: Harper & Row.

Defining Social Innovation. (2020). Retrieved December 13, 2020, from Stanford Graduate School of Business website: https://www.gsb.stanford.edu/faculty-research/centers-initiatives/csi/defining-social-innovation.

Dougherty, D. (2012). The maker movement. *Innovations: Technology, Governance, Globalization, 7*(3), 11–14.

Dufva, T. (2017). Maker movement: Creating knowledge through basic intention. *Techne Series: Research in Sloyd Education and Crafts Science, 24*(2), 129–141.

Eisenhardt, K. M. (1989). Building theories from case study research. *Academy of Management Review, 14*(4), 532–550.

Eisenhardt, K., & Graebner, M. (2007). Theory building from cases: Opportunities and challenges. *The Academy of Management Journal, 50*, 25–32.

EY Spain. (2020). Impacto del COVID-19 en las prioridades de la RSC y Sostenibilidad y en el rol de sus profesionales [YouTube Video]. In *YouTube.* https://www.youtube.com/watch?v=7pKPaw9Vdl0&feature=youtu.be.

Fauchart, E., & Foray, D. (2016). On the democratization of innovation through communal organizations. In D. Harthoff & K. R. Lakhani (Eds.), *Revolutionizing innovation: Users, communities and open innovation* (pp. 175–194). Cambridge, MA: MIT Press.

Fichter, K. (2009). Innovation communities: The role of networks of promotors in open innovation. *R&D Management, 39*(4), 357–371.

FORETICA. (2020). Futuro de la Sostenibilidad post COVID-19. *Macrotendencias & Disrupciones Futuro de la Sostenibilidad post COVID-19 2020–2030*. Retrieved from https://foretica.org/publicacion/futuro-de-la-sostenibilidad-post-covid-19-macrotendencias-disrupciones-2020-2030/.

Gates, B. (2014). The next outbreak? We're not ready. Retrieved December 13, 2020, from Ted.com website: https://www.ted.com/talks/bill_gates_the_next_outbreak_we_re_not_ready?language=dz.

Gioia, D. A., Corley, K. G., & Hamilton, A. L. (2013). Seeking qualitative rigor in inductive research: Notes on the Gioia methodology. *Organizational Research Methods, 16*(1), 15–31.

Giusti, J. D., Alberti, F. G., & Belfanti, F. (2020). Makers and clusters. Knowledge leaks in open innovation networks. *Journal of Innovation & Knowledge, 5*(1), 20–28.

Jamali, D. (2007). A stakeholder approach to corporate social responsibility: A fresh perspective into theory and practice. *Journal of Business Ethics, 82*, 213–231.

Lakhani, K. R. (2016). Managing communities and contests to innovate with crowds. In D. Harthoff & K. R. Lakhani (Eds.), *Revolutionizing innovation: Users, communities and open innovation* (pp. 175–194). Cambridge, MA: MIT Press.

Morreale, F., Moro, G., Chamberlain, A., Benford, S., & McPherson, A. P. (2017). Building a maker community around an open hardware platform. In *Proceedings of the 2017 CHI Conference on Human Factors in Computing Systems*. 6948–6959.

Mortara, L., & Parisot, N. G. (2016). Through entrepreneurs' eyes: The fab-spaces constellation. *International Journal of Production Research, 54*, 7158–7180.

Papavlasopoulou, S., Giannakos, M. N., & Jaccheri, L. (2017). Empirical studies on the maker movement, a promising approach to learning: A literature review. *Entertainment Computing, 18*, 57–78.

Porter, M., & Kramer, M. R. (2006). Strategy and society: The link between competitive advantage and corporate social responsibility. *Harvard Business Review, 84*(12), 78–92.

Porter, M., & Kramer, M. R. (2011). Creating shared value: How to reinvent capitalism- and unleash a wave of innovation and growth. *Harvard Business Review, 1*, 3–17.

SERES. (2020a). *Presentación del VI informe Deloitte-SERES sobre impacto social.* Web SERES/Encuentros. https://www.fundacionseres.org/Paginas/Encuentros/Encuen-trosDetalle.aspx?IDEvS=159.

SERES. (2020b). *SERESResponsables, impacto social. Informe del impacto social de las empresas frente a la COVID-19.* Fundación SERES-Deloitte. https://www2.deloitte.com/content/dam/Deloitte/es/Documents/acerca-de-deloitte/Deloitte-ES-impacto-seres-covid-19.pdf.

Unterfrauner, E., Hofer, M., Pelka, B., & Zirngiebl, M. (2020). A new player for tackling inequalities? Framing the social value and impact of the maker movement. *Social Inclusion, 8*(2), 190–200.

Vanclay, F. (2002). Conceptualising social impacts. *Environmental Impact Assessment Review, 22*(3), 183–211.

Vanclay, F. (2003). International principles for social impact assessment. *Impact Assessment and Project Appraisal, 21*(1), 5–12.

von Hippel, E. (1994). Sticky information and the locus of problem solving: Implications for innovation. *Management Science, 40*(4), 429–439.

von Hippel, E., & von Krogh, G. (2003). Open source software and the "private-collective" innovation model: Issues for organization science. *Organization Science, 14*(2), 209–223.

Wood, D. J., Logsdon, J. M., Davenport, K., & Lewellyn, P. G. (2006). *Global business citizenship: A transformative framework for ethics and sustainable capitalism*. New York: Taylor and Francis.

Yin, R. (2013). Validity and generalization in future case study evaluations. *Evaluation, 19*(3), 321–332. Sage.

3

Corporate Social Responsibility Response During the COVID-19 Crisis in Mexico

René Díaz-Pichardo and Patricia S. Sánchez-Medina

3.1 Introduction

The SARS-CoV2 pandemic and its corresponding disease, COVID-19, has drastically challenged both developed and emerging countries, provoking a variety of responses as there has been no observable international coordination, not even at a regional level as might have been expected. Beyond the extreme stress the pandemic has placed on health systems, the economic consequences of social distancing will transform the world for years to come. As the pandemic progressed globally Latin American countries had the opportunity to observe how China, Europe, and the United States reacted to the disease and thus had the potential to be better prepared for it. However, even this advantage was insufficient in allowing Latin America to develop an improved response to the pandemic.

R. Díaz-Pichardo (✉)
South Champagne Business School, Troyes, France

P. S. Sánchez-Medina
Instituto Politécnico Nacional - CIIDIR Unidad Oaxaca, Mexico City, Mexico

A. Sörensson et al. (eds.), *Corporate Responsibility and Sustainability during the Coronavirus Crisis*, Palgrave Studies in Governance, Leadership and Responsibility,
https://doi.org/10.1007/978-3-030-73847-1_3

Corporate social responsibility initiatives are designed to help organizations implement strategies that reflect a CSR philosophy. Companies implement this type of initiative to act ethically and improve their image, either in response to stakeholders' pressures or to improve customer satisfaction (Ortas et al. 2015). The COVID-19 crisis represents an opportunity for companies to demonstrate their commitment to CSR. This research aims to explore the CSR response of companies during the first six months of the pandemic in Mexico.

3.2 Context

Demographic context. Mexico is a Latin American country located in North America. In 2015, its population was estimated at almost 120 million people (INEGI 2020a) (126 million people in 2019), with a GNP per capita of 9763 USD (11,085 USD in 2019) (Statista 2020); the population on average had 9.2 years of schooling (INEGI 2020a). In 2018, more than 40% of the population was considered to be living in poverty, 7% in extreme poverty (Coneval 2020). In 2020, it was estimated that 6.6% of the population spoke at least one of the 68 Mexican indigenous languages and 364 variants (INEGI 2020b).

Economic context. Mexico was already in economic recession before the pandemic with a slowdown of industrial activity, a reduction in foreign investment, uncertainty with government economic policies, and a reduction of government jobs themselves due to austerity measures. In 2019, the country registered 6.4 million enterprises, 97.3% being micro, small, or medium-sized enterprises, with 63% in the informal economy (Excélsior 2020). With the pandemic, tourism, one of the main sources of jobs and foreign currency for the country, has collapsed (El Universal 2020a, 2020b). The fall of petroleum prices has worsened this crisis as Mexico depends to a great extent on the income generated by its state-owned oil company PEMEX. Mexico participates in supply chains connected to the United States, China, and other countries (El Universal 2020a); due to the interruption in world supply chains and reduction in global demand, the pandemic has triggered the most severe economic crisis in the history of Mexico with more people falling into sub-employment and poverty than ever before. In June 2020, it was estimated that COVID-19 left 11.3 million people in work suspension, with no income and uncertainty about their employment. Additionally, 3.5 million people lost their jobs or had to close their businesses. Approximately, 82% of people affected work in the informal economy (Ponce 2020).

Social context. As a result of Spanish colonialism, Mexican society is highly stratified, with the rich enjoying great privileges because of close relationships with political power. In contrast, the poor experience all kinds of privations, hunger, and discrimination, working in the informal economy with little or no access to education or health services. Mexican society is also based on strong ties within both the nuclear and extended family. Families frequently get together, especially in the case of strong need. Family parties and funerals are events that cannot be missed. During the first few months of the pandemic, information about the coronavirus and COVID-19 was distorted extensively in social networks; many people believed the coronavirus was not actually real. The fact that many people in the informal economy must go out every day to work, a strong family culture, and the distortion of COVID-19 information explain to a great extent why many people did not follow the recommendations issued by the federal government, particularly those urging people to stay at home and keep socially distanced. Consequently, the disease spread beyond the worst of expectations (El Universal 2020c).

Political context. Andrés Manuel López Obrador (AMLO), current president of Mexico for the period 2018–2024, entered the presidency with complete support from the unprivileged sectors and in clear rupture with the previous governments of PRI (2012–2018) and PAN (2000–2012). His political party, MORENA, controls the National Congress (Chávez 2018) and groups together many left-political interests. AMLO calls his period the Fourth Transformation (4T) in reference to the main milestones in Mexican history: Independence (1810–1821), Reform (1857–1861), and Revolution (1910–1917). The president has promised to fight corruption and criminality. His government has forced big corporations to pay taxes, an obligation many of them had been avoiding for years through lobbying former governments (Mendoza 2019). Privileges to the rich have been reduced and the relationship between the president and the "entrepreneurial cupola"[1] has become toxic as a result, with many entrepreneurs now forming part of the political opposition (Gómez 2020). The upcoming elections of governors, mayors, and congress members in 2021 (INE 2020) complicate the political scenario as the president wants to strengthen confidence in his electoral base while his political rivals try to undermine his position by emphasizing how badly he has managed the pandemic, the economy, national security, and the political process.

Environmental context. Even as the world trend is for renewable sources of energy in replacement of fossil sources, and the prices of petroleum reach a historical minimum, AMLO insists on restoring the past glory of PEMEX and pushes investment in petroleum exploration, extraction, and refinement. Recently, he has retracted some of the energy reforms of the previous government to impede private firms from investing in renewable energy sources such as electricity. This measure was taken because it was believed that the entrepreneurial sector had colluded with the past government to take over the energy sector. AMLO is in favor of government control of strategic natural resources, although he says he is not against entrepreneurial activity (El Universal 2020d).

Health system. Since the beginning of his presidency, AMLO has faced significant problems in Mexico's health system: insufficient hospital infrastructure, with unfinished and abandoned hospitals all over the country, major inequalities in the population's access to health care, and a lack of medicine, medical equipment, and medical staff, among other issues. In 2018, it was estimated that 16% of the Mexican population had no access to health care (Rodríguez 2019) and at the end of 2018 almost 10% of hospitals were still closed because of the 2017 earthquakes (El Universal 2018).

[1] Entrepreneurial cupola refers to the relevant associations and lobbies of the main large-scale private companies.

3.3 Method

Based on a content analysis of text news reports ordered chronologically from the beginning of the pandemic, this research aims to analyze the evolution of the CSR response in Mexico during the first six months of the pandemic throughout five periods: (1) before the first case was confirmed, (2) Phase I—imported cases confirmed, (3) Phase II—local spread and confinement, (4) Phase III—exponential spread and opening, and (5) adopting the "new normal". Figure 3.1 shows the accumulated cases, deaths, and periods of analysis.

News articles were obtained from the major online newspapers in Mexico according to website rankings. Table 3.1 shows the list of online newspapers with the number of news articles per period included in the sample. News articles were obtained after searching for the following keywords: "Responsabilidad Social Empresarial", "Empresa Socialmente Responsable", "COVID-19", and "Coronavirus". News articles obtained were then reviewed to evaluate their content for relevance. Those articles were then saved in .txt format to be imported into Weft QDA software for content analysis.

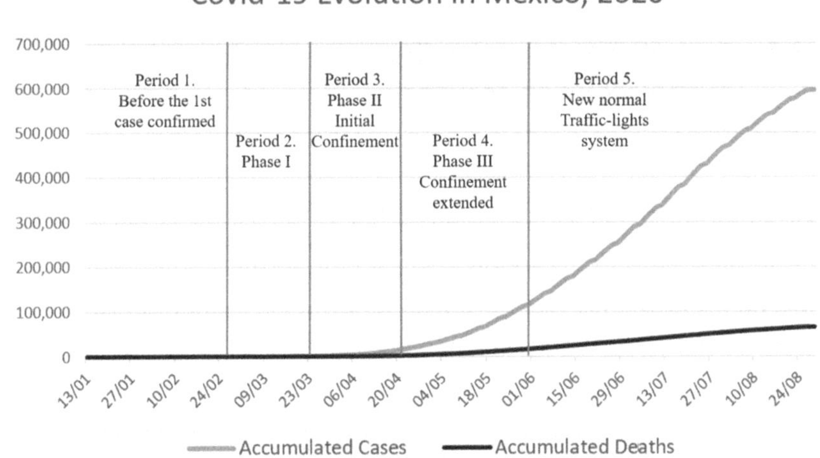

Fig. 3.1 COVID-19 Evolution in Mexico in 2020. Source: Authors' own work with data from https://coronavirus.gob.mx/datos/#DownZCSV

Table 3.1 Newspapers and number of news articles describing CSR initiatives actually cited in this research

	Period					
Newspaper	1	2	3	4	5	Total
El Economista	0		1	1	12	14
Excélsior	0		1		2	3
El Universal	0	1	3			4
Milenio	0			1	4	5
El Financiero	0	1		1	2	4
Publimetro	0		1	2		3
La Jornada	0		1			1
Informador	0		1			1
Total	0	2	8	5	20	35

Source: Own research

Content analysis was performed to identify CSR initiatives implemented by companies in response to the pandemic. Codification was done by means of categorizing the information in the articles based on the declared objectives of the initiative as stated by the company according to the articles.

3.4 Results

3.4.1 Period 1: Before the first case confirmed in the Mexican territory.

This period starts with the discovery of COVID-19 and ends on February 28, the day the first case was reported in Mexico. During this period, no news articles discussing the disease and corporate social responsibility were identified. Even if certain CSR initiatives could have been anticipated based on the experience of China, Italy, or Spain, no actions were reported, not even from multi-national corporations operating in those territories.

3.4.2 Period 2: Phase I, imported cases confirmed.

This period starts when the first imported case of COVID-19 was confirmed in Mexico on February 28 and ends on March 24, when the government declared that most new infections occurred locally, and confinement began.

During this period, few news articles appeared reporting CSR initiatives in response to the pandemic. The entrepreneurial cupola, represented by the CCE (Consejo Coordinador Empresarial—Entrepreneurial Coordinator Council) made a call to the population to remain calm and avoid panic buying or cornering products as the entrepreneurial sector was committed to maintaining normal economic and social activity regardless of the public health measures that might be implemented (El Universal 2020e). However, the Ministry of Labor (Secretaría del Trabajo) reported that some companies began firing employees without justification (Guadarrama and Páramo 2020). One big company in the restaurant sector suggested its workers could stay at home for 30 days without any salary in order to protect their jobs (El Universal 2020f). One company in the Southeast of Mexico was reported as offering basic food products to people in marginalized zones, in cooperation with civil society organizations (Gallardo 2020).

3.4.3 Period 3: Phase II, local spread and confinement.

This period starts with the confinement established by the federal government on March 24 and ends on April 21 with the expected end of the "Jornada Nacional de Sana Distancia" (National Period of Health Distancing). Even if this period was extended until May 30 (Urrutia and Jiménez 2020), we decided to maintain this phase in the analysis as it was originally planned because it created certain expectations that could have affected companies' decisions in terms of CSR initiatives. Confinement meant closing schools and all non-essential activities and staying home as much as possible, measures that were reinforced at different levels throughout the country (Enciso 2020).

At the time, confinement was seen as the most effective strategy to reduce contagion and ensure that the existing medical infrastructure could absorb a surplus of patients without collapsing. However, a few months later confinement was revealed to have been implemented too early (see Fig. 3.1), provoking enormous economic consequences.

During this period, CSR initiatives started to appear throughout Mexico. These initiatives can be classified in five types: (1) related to protecting the health and wellbeing of employees and their families, (2) related to helping the population in need, (3) related to protecting the natural environment, (4) related to assuring the supply of their own products and services, even in challenging conditions, and (5) related to expanding the hospitals' capacity to face the pandemic.

Initiatives of the first type include: working from home when possible (especially for workers in vulnerable groups—with pre-existing diseases or older than 60 years), staggered working hours, adaptation of work facilities to reduce social contact and exposure, sanitizing gel in work areas, use of masks and social distancing, private transportation to reduce exposure, and a declared commitment to preserving jobs and salaries (El Universal 2020g, 2020h).

Initiatives of the second type include: offering basic food products to people in marginalized zones, media campaigns to better inform poor people and reduce the spread of the disease, offering food and hygiene kits for small children living in poverty, digital technology for medical services for poor people with diabetes, and facilitating crowdfunding for specific needs (La Jornada 2020; El Universal 2020i).

As for the third type, it was reported that an organization of plastic recycling companies developed a recycled and recyclable body bag to be used during the pandemic. These companies offered a source of income for poor and homeless people that collected plastic from the streets. One producer mentioned that in case the bags were not needed, they could be reprocessed to produce garbage bags (Informador 2020).

With regard to the fourth type of initiative, some companies in the food sector adopted the compromise of maintaining prices and assuring the supply of their products to help families attend to their basic needs (El Universal 2020i). Another company committed to offering financial services to the poor (Díaz 2020a).

As for the fifth type, one initiative brought together the efforts of companies, educational institutions, government institutions, and civil society organizations to adapt available spaces to receive and treat COVID-19 patients (Publimetro 2020).

In many cases, these initiatives were developed in coordination with civil society organizations and the local government at different levels. Micro and small companies were praised by the Mexican president for protecting employment and salaries, giving an example of responsibility to larger corporations (Guadarrama and Páramo 2020).

Anti-CSR initiatives were also detected during this period: companies firing employees simply for sneezing or because a relative had the disease, not allowing vulnerable people to work from home even when it was possible, and unobserved measures of containment or social distancing. Shamefully, several physicians and nurses reported being insulted, threatened, and battered by public officials, companies, and neighbors (Toribio and Nava 2020).

3.4.4 Period 4: Phase III, exponential spread and opening.

This period starts with the extension of the "Jornada Nacional de Sana Distancia" on April 21 and ends on May 30, when the government declared its end.

Paradoxically, this period was characterized by the initial exponential spread of COVID-19 and at the same time the opening of the economy after the end of the social distancing campaign. During this period, confinement was substituted with a "traffic lights" system that aimed to indicate the degree of seriousness of the disease in every state and region. In this system, containment measures would be designed and adapted according to the local situation (Gobierno de México 2020).

During this period, CSR initiatives spread throughout the nation. These initiatives can be classified in four types: (1) related to protecting the health and wellbeing of customers, employees, and their families, (2) related to helping the population in need, (3) related to helping the supply chain when it is composed of small businesses at risk, and (4) related to supporting the activities of first-line pandemic fighters.

For the first type, some companies put up barriers to separate customers from workers in local stores, implemented sanitary protocols established by health authorities, and reorganized their activities to reduce social contact. Some companies allowed workers from vulnerable groups to stay at home and keep their jobs and salary (Curiel 2020).

For the second type, companies in the restaurant sector offered their food products through food banks to reach relatives of hospitalized people, indigenous communities, and poor children. Other companies offered support for elderly people with chronic diseases in rural communities through civil society organizations. Some companies offered food and training to construction workers that lost jobs because of the pandemic. One company, in association with a university, offered psychological support by telephone. Other companies donated money and food to civil society organizations that were active in various sectors (Mireles 2020; Campos 2020).

For the third type, one beverage company offered gift cards to be exchanged for its products in restaurants and bars (Campos 2020). A big bakery company offered support to small grocery stores by providing masks and reinforcing its credit policy. It also offered IT services so small businesses could receive credit cards and food vouchers, sell mobile telephony credit, and receive payments for services. A company in the cosmetic industry offered coupons to be exchanged in beauty salons, they also offered online training and sanitizing gel, and withheld payments until reopening. An association created an initiative to allow small businesses to offer their products to hospitals to protect jobs and salaries (Curiel 2020).

For the fourth type of CSR initiative, some companies donated their products to help medical staff and police officers. Some transformed their production processes to make this possible. For instance, a brewery produced cans of water for police officers and antibacterial gel derived from non-alcoholic beer (Sánchez 2020). A company in the car industry started producing medical equipment to be donated to public hospitals. A beverage company started producing recycled plastic masks to be donated to different institutions and, in association with another company in the alcoholic beverages industry, donated sanitizing alcohol (Campos 2020). A company in the cosmetics industry started producing sanitizing gel to be donated to public hospitals (Curiel 2020). Companies donated ventilators to public hospitals as well as medical equipment for hospitals in rural areas. In different sectors, companies donated their own products to medical staff of public hospitals, such as food, writing devices, personal health products, antibacterial gel, and masks (Mireles 2020; Curiel 2020).

3.4.5 Period 5: Adopting the "new normal".

This period starts on May 30, when the government declared the end of social distancing. During this period the "traffic lights" system was still in operation even if some state governments (from the opposition parties) saw the system as a tool of political control and influence in advance of the 2021 elections. This period ends on August 30 when our search for newspaper articles was closed.

The CSR initiatives in this period can be classified in six types: (1) related to protecting the health and wellbeing of customers, employees, and their families, (2) related to helping the population in need, (3) related to protecting the natural environment, (4) related to helping the supply chain when it is composed of small businesses at risk, (5) related to supporting the activities of the first-line fighters, and (6) related to preparing people in need to reactivate their own economy.

For the first type, companies have implemented the recommendations of health authorities including: working from home when possible; workplace sanitization; use of antibacterial gel; masks during working hours; information in the workplace; gloves; adaptation in circulation within the workplace; no use of meeting rooms; expanding e-commerce; hygiene protocols to protect clients, workers, and their families; and a commitment to protecting jobs and salaries. Using their databases and a questionnaire, some companies detected potential COVID-19 patients and put them in contact with medical specialists (Mata 2020).

For the second type, companies donated money through civil society organizations to offer hygiene kits, food, and education for children in poverty (Ramírez 2020a). Some companies offered digital technology to people with diabetes. Other companies donated money to provide basic food products for people in need in rural communities. Through specialized organizations some companies offered support to youth to prevent criminal activity (Ramírez 2020b). Some initiatives coordinated different companies to offer solidarity cards to people that lost their jobs with up to 3000 pesos to buy products in supermarkets; these cards were sent with the help of local delivery companies (De la Rosa 2020). Creatively, a football club invited its fans to pay for a cardboard silhouette with their photograph to be located in the stadium and donated the proceeds (El Financiero 2020).

In the third type, one company donated the profits from its ice cream made for dogs to feed abandoned dogs and cats, a population that has grown significantly during the pandemic (Díaz 2020b). A company in the packaging industry donated modular spaces for medical treatment made of recycled materials (Díaz 2020c).

In relation to the fourth type, helping the supply chain when it is composed of small businesses at risk, some companies prioritized contracts with local suppliers to protect jobs. Others donated food and beverage products to bars and restaurants so they could reopen. They also offered to pay part of the delivery costs of their products. Some companies offered training to restaurant staff so they could amplify their talents and improve commercial strategies through social networks. A major brewery created an initiative to offer tickets to consumers in a buy one get one free scheme (Díaz 2020d, 2020e).

For the fifth type, some companies offered their own food products to medical staff (Ramírez 2020c), other companies offered to sanitize hospitals and public spaces in zones of high risk using their own equipment and materials (Méndez 2020). One company in the print business donated printers, paper, and ink so that physicians and nurses treating COVID-19 patients could show their faces and build a human connection with their patients (Díaz 2020f). Some companies offered flexible modular solutions to public hospitals so they could increase their bed capacity (Díaz 2020g). Other companies have donated thousands of medical kits through different foundations. Some companies offered monetary donations to the Mexican Red Cross. Others offered millions of pesos to acquire specialized medical equipment for public hospitals (Ramírez 2020d). An alliance of different companies created a crowdfunding campaign that multiplied the donations of their customers by a factor of four so they could buy protection medical equipment for public hospitals (Ramírez 2020d). Some non-manufacturing institutions started producing masks to be donated to hospitals (Santinelli 2020). An alliance of several companies, public institutions, and universities quickly developed a ventilator that is practical and efficient. Ventilators were acquired by other companies and then donated to public hospitals (Del Pozo 2020). A packaging company donated recycled material as well as instructions for building modular dormitories for medical personnel in public hospitals (Díaz 2020c).

For the sixth type, some companies offered food and training for construction workers who had lost their jobs because of the pandemic. Others offered crowdfunding assistance to emerging artists so they could reach new online audiences (El Economista 2020). In association with education institutions, large companies offered training to women entrepreneurs so they could grow and improve their small businesses (EF Branded Media 2020).

Figure 3.2 summarizes our research findings and the evolution of CSR initiatives as the pandemic expanded in Mexico. We can observe that CSR initiatives multiplied and diversified during this period, starting from offering basic food products to the poor and protecting the health

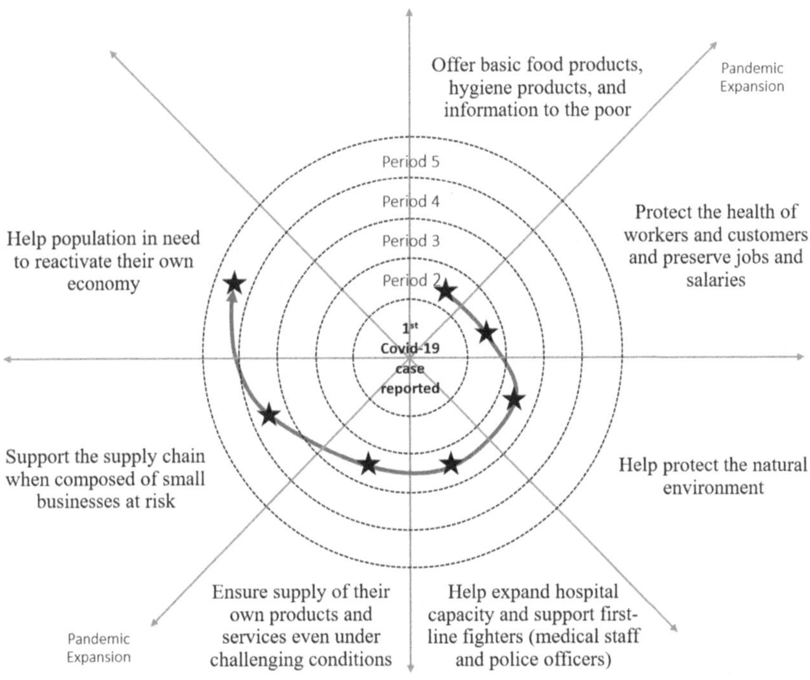

Fig. 3.2 Evolution of CSR initiatives during the first six months of the SARS-CoV2 in Mexico (February 28–August 30). Source: Authors' own work

of workers and customers and preserving jobs and salaries in Period 2 to helping the population in need to reactivate the economy in Period 5. In the graph, initiatives are registered in the period they were identified for the first time; however, in most cases, initiatives were expected to last more than one period.

3.5 Conclusions

This research analyzes the CSR response of companies during the first six months of the SARS-CoV2 pandemic in Mexico, and particularly, the evolution of these initiatives through five periods: (1) before the first confirmed case, (2) Phase I—imported cases confirmed, (3) Phase II—local spread and confinement, (4) Phase III—exponential spread and opening, and (5) adopting the "new normal". Enterprises have shown an evolution in the number and type of initiatives they have undertaken.

While no CSR initiatives in response to COVID-19 were reported in period 1, in period 2 one company undertaking this type of action was identified. In the following periods, an important growth of CSR initiatives was observed not only in the number of companies and initiatives but also in the diversification of such initiatives, from helping poor people meet their immediate needs to helping people in need reactivate the economy. This diversification includes seven different types after a relatively short period of time, as shown in Fig. 3.2. This trend in company behavior might indicate that companies will continue developing a greater number of CSR initiatives, perhaps oriented to other aspects not observed here.

Many companies have disappeared with the corresponding loss of jobs and a drastic decline in economic and social welfare. Most enterprises in a fragile financial position have focused only on survival and put aside any effort on CSR. The pandemic has detonated the worst economic crisis in the history of Mexico but also a renewed interest in humanitarian and environmental actions. It is expected that the economy might recuperate to the level of 2018 within six years. The Canada-US-Mexico Agreement (CUSMA), a renegotiation of NAFTA that was enacted on July 1, 2020, is expected to play a significant role in this endeavor (Forbes

México 2020). Social consequences of the pandemic are still to be seen beyond the thousands of deaths. However, some positive effects can also be observed, such as the capacity to act in an organized manner and bring together enterprises, government, and non-government institutions, in the pursuit of superior objectives.

3.6 Limitations and Recommendations for Future Research

Our primary limitation in this research is the use of newspapers as our main source of information. Newspapers might have their own interests and consequently present facts in a non-objective manner, as is the case when articles are paid for by companies. Also, the use of only a few free-access online newspapers imposes a limit to the possibility of having a wider variety of information and perspectives. Finally, information about different initiatives was not validated (by triangulation, for instance) to confirm if those initiatives were carried out or not. Further research on the topic could include additional sources of information such as more online newspapers, specialized magazines and websites, company websites, and those of civil society organizations and the government.

References

Campos, I. (2020). La solidaridad empresarial se deja sentir para sacar adelante al país. Publimetro, 14 May. Retrieved August 30, 2020, from https://www.publimetro.com.mx/mx/coronavirus-covid-19/2020/05/14/la-solidaridad-empresarial-se-deja-sentir-sacar-adelante-al-pais.html.

Chávez, V. (2018). AMLO tendrá mayoría en las dos cámaras. El Financiero, 3 July. Retrieved August 30, 2020, from https://www.elfinanciero.com.mx/elecciones-2018/morena-pt-pes-tendran-mayoria-absoluta-con-312-diputados.

Coneval. (2020). Medición de la pobreza. Pobreza en México. Retrieved August 30, 2020, from https://www.coneval.org.mx/Medicion/Paginas/PobrezaInicio.aspx.

Curiel, R. (2020). Bimbo al rescate de las tienditas y misceláneas. Publimetro, 13 May. Retrieved August 30, 2020, from https://www.publimetro.com.mx/mx/opinion/2020/05/13/bimbo-al-rescate-las-tienditas-miscelaneas.html.

De la Rosa, E. (2020). Empresarios de NL apoyarán a 17 mil personas afectadas por Covid-19. Milenio, 26 August. Retrieved August 30, 2020, from https://www.milenio.com/negocios/empresarios-nl-apoyaran-17-mil-personas-afectadas-coronavirus.

Del Pozo, M. (2020). Más barato y seguro: diseñan ventilador mexicano para pacientes con Covid-19. Milenio, 6 August. Retrieved August 30, 2020, from https://www.milenio.com/politica/ventilador-vsz-20-2-conoce-diseno-mexicano-seguro-barato.

Díaz, V. (2020a). Fundación Dondé, modelo ganar-ganar. El Economista, 13 April. Retrieved August 30, 2020, from https://www.eleconomista.com.mx/empresas/Fundacion-Donde-modelo-ganar-ganar-20200413-0111.html.

Díaz, V. (2020b). Neverías Frody impulsa la adopción de mascotas y ayuda a lomitos callejeros. El Economista, 20 July. Retrieved August 30, 2020, from https://www.eleconomista.com.mx/empresas/Neverias-Frody-impulsa-la-adopcion-de-mascotas-y-ayuda-a-lomitos-callejeros-20200720-0052.html.

Díaz, V. (2020c). Crean dormitories para médicos con empaques de Tetra Pak. El Economista, 29 June. Retrieved August 30, 2020, from https://www.eleconomista.com.mx/empresas/Crean-dormitorios-para-medicos-con-empaques-de-Tetra-Pak-20200629-0088.html.

Díaz, V. (2020d). Apoyan a bares y restaurants en medio de la pandemia. El Economista, 22 June. Retrieved August 30, 2020, from https://www.eleconomista.com.mx/empresas/Apoyan-a-bares-y-restaurantes-en-medio-de-pandemia-20200622-0086.html.

Díaz, V. (2020e). Con bonos gastronómicos, impulsan al sector restaurantero. El Economista, 15 June. Retrieved August 30, 2020, from https://www.eleconomista.com.mx/empresas/Con-bonos-gastronomicos-impulsan-al-sector-restaurantero-20200615-0089.html.

Díaz, V. (2020f). Un puente entre paciente y medico. El Economista. 1 June. Retrieved August 30, 2020, from https://www.eleconomista.com.mx/empresas/Un-puente-entre-paciente-y-personal-medico-20200601-0114.html.

Díaz, V. (2020g). Fabrican clínicas de diagnóstico modulares. El Economista, 1 June. Retrieved August 30, 2020, from https://www.eleconomista.com.mx/empresas/Fabrican-clinicas-de-diagnostico-modulares-20200601-0108.html.

EF Branded Media. (2020). Hablemos de mujeres en tienditas. El Financiero, 19 August. Retrieved August 30, 2020, from https://www.elfinanciero.com.mx/mundo-empresa/hablemos-de-mujeres-en-tienditas.

El Economista. (2020). Apoyan a artistas en medio de Covid. 10 August. Retrieved August 30, 2020, from https://www.eleconomista.com.mx/arteseideas/Apoyan-a-artistas-en-medio-de-Covid-20200810-0078.html.

El Financiero. (2020). Apoya Fundación Sonigas a comunidades rurales: Salvador Oñate. 4 June. Retrieved August 30, 2020, from https://www.elfinanciero.com.mx/nacional/apoya-fundacion-sonigas-a-comunidades-rurales-salvador-onate-barron.

El Universal. (2018). Más de 90% de hospitals dañados por sismos operan con normalidad: SSA. 19 September. Retrieved August 30, 2020, from https://www.eluniversal.com.mx/nacion/sociedad/mas-de-90-de-hospitales-danados-por-sismos-operan-con-normalidad-ssa.

El Universal. (2020a). ¿Cuál es el impacto real del coronavirus sobre la economía? 20 March. Retrieved August 30, 2020, from https://www.eluniversal.com.mx/cartera/covid-19-mexico-cual-es-el-impacto-real-del-coronavirus-sobre-la-economia.

El Universal. (2020b). ¿Cómo pueden actuar las Pymes ante la contingencia del Covid-19? 23 March. Retrieved August 30, 2020, from https://www.eluniversal.com.mx/cartera/como-pueden-actuar-las-pymes-ante-la-contingencia-del-covid-19.

El Universal. (2020c). Se cumple "escenario catastrófico" de López-Gatell con 60 mil muertes por Covid-19 en México. 22 August. Retrieved August 30, 2020, from https://www.eluniversal.com.mx/nacion/coronavirus-22-de-agosto-mexico-llega-escenario-catastrofico-de-60-mil-muertes-por-covid-19.

El Universal. (2020d). La política energética de México regresa a la dependencia del petróleo de los años 70. 22 May. Retrieved August 30, 2020, from https://www.eluniversal.com.mx/english/la-politica-energetica-de-mexico-regresa-la-dependencia-del-petroleo-de-los-anos-70.

El Universal. (2020e). Comercio está preparado para la pandemia de Covid-19: CCE. 16 March. Retrieved August 30, 2020, from https://www.eluniversal.com.mx/cartera/comercio-esta-preparado-para-afrontar-la-pandemia-de-covid-19-cce.

El Universal. (2020f). De ser necesario, se constuirán hospitales para attender coronavirus: AMLO. 21 March. Retrieved August 30, 2020, from https://www.eluniversal.com.mx/nacion/de-ser-necesario-se-construiran-hospitales-para-atender-coronavirus-amlo.

El Universal. (2020g). Las empresas ante el Covid-19. 24 March. Retrieved August 30, 2020, from https://www.eluniversal.com.mx/opinion/editorial-el-universal/las-empresas-ante-el-covid-19.

El Universal. (2020h). Bimbo no aumentará el costo de sus productos. 9 April. Retrieved August 30, 2020, from https://www.eluniversal.com.mx/cartera/bimbo-no-aumentara-el-costo-de-sus-productos-por-crisis-de-coronavirus.

El Universal. (2020i). Bimbo dará más de 2 millones de box luch a médicos. 17 April. Retrieved August 30, 2020, from https://www.eluniversal.com.mx/cartera/coronavirus-mexico-grupo-bimbo-donara-mas-de-2-millones-de-box-lunch-personal-medico.

Enciso, A. (2020). Comienza la Jornada Nacional de Sana Distancia. La Jornada, 23 March. Retrieved August 30, 2020, from https://www.jornada.com.mx/ultimas/politica/2020/03/23/comienza-la-jornada-nacional-de-sana-distancia-1056.html.

Excélsior. (2020). Covid-19 afectó economía del 91.3% de empresas: Censo Económico. 13 August. Retrieved August 30, 2020, from https://www.excelsior.com.mx/nacional/covid-19-afecto-economia-del-913-de-empresas-censo-economico/1399629.

Forbes México. (2020). ¿Qué es el T-MEC y por qué es importante para México? 1 July. Retrieved August 30, 2020, from https://www.forbes.com.mx/economia-que-es-el-t-mec-y-por-que-es-importante-para-mexico/.

Gallardo, M. (2020). Nuevos entornos, nuevos retos, nuevos compromisos. El Financiero, 31 July. Retrieved August 30, 2020, from https://www.elfinanciero.com.mx/opinion/miguel-gallardo/nuevos-entornos-nuevos-retos-nuevos-compromisos.

Gobierno de México. (2020). Semáforo Covid-19. Retrieved August 30, 2020, from https://coronavirus.gob.mx/semaforo/.

Gómez, M. (2020). El tigre y el Covid-19. El Universal, 17 April. Retrieved August 30, 2020, from https://www.eluniversal.com.mx/opinion/marcela-gomez-zalce/el-tigre-y-el-covid-19.

Guadarrama, J., & Páramo, A. (2020, April 9). México pierde 346 mil 878 empleos; las empresas pequeñas resisten la crisis. Excélsior, 9 April. Retrieved August 30, 2020, from https://www.excelsior.com.mx/nacional/mexico-pierde-346-mil-878-empleos-las-empresas-pequenas-resisten-la-crisis/1375009.

INE. (2020). Calendario electoral. Retrieved August 30, 2020, from https://www.ine.mx/voto-y-elecciones/calendario-electoral/.

INEGI. (2020a). México en cifras. Retrieved August 30, 2020, from https://www.inegi.org.mx/app/areasgeograficas/.

INEGI. (2020b). Estadísticas a propósito del día internacional de los pueblos indígenas (9 de agosto). Retrieved August 30, 2020, from https://www.inegi.org.mx/contenidos/saladeprensa/aproposito/2020/Indigenas2020.pdf.

Informador. (2020). Empresa mexicana de bolsas de basura fabrica ahora sacos para cadáveres. 16 April. Retrieved August 30, 2020, from https://www.informador.mx/economia/Empresa-mexicana-de-bolsas-de-basura-fabrica-ahora-sacos-para-cadaveres-20200416-0127.html.

La Jornada. (2020). Libre Abordo entrega ayuda humanitarian en Chiapas por Covid-19. 24 March. Retrieved August 30, 2020, from https://www.jornada.com.mx/ultimas/estados/2020/03/24/libre-abordo-entrega-ayuda-humanitaria-en-chiapas-por-covid-19-8940.html.

Mata, A. (2020). Así preparan corporativos regreso a la "nueva normalidad". Excélsior, 5 August. Retrieved August 30, 2020, from https://www.excelsior.com.mx/comunidad/asi-preparan-corporativos-regreso-a-nueva-normalidad/1398218.

Méndez, E. (2020). Empresario regiomontano llega a Coparmex, tras campaña contra Covid-19. Excélsior, 14 August. Retrieved August 30, 2020, from https://www.excelsior.com.mx/nacional/empresario-regiomontano-llega-a-coparmex-tras-campana-contra-covid-19/1399972.

Mendoza, J. L. (2019). AMLO obliga a pagar impuestos a grandes contribuyentes. El Rincón de Maquiavelo, 21 May. Retrieved August 30, 2020, from https://elrincondemaquiavelo.com/amlo-obliga-a-pagar-impuestos-a-grandes-contribuyentes/.

Mireles, B. (2020). Acciones de empresas contra el coronavirus. El Economista, 27 April. Retrieved August 30, 2020, from https://www.eleconomista.com.mx/empresas/Acciones-de-empresas-contra-el-coronavirus-20200427-0157.html.

Ortas, E., Álvarez, I., Jaussaud, J., & Garayar, A. (2015). The impact of institutional and social context on corporate environmental, social and governance performance of companies committed to voluntary corporate social responsibility initiatives. *Journal of Cleaner Production, 108*, 673–684.

Ponce, K. (2020). Virus aniquila 12.5 millones de empleos; sector informal, el más golpeado. Excélsior, 2 June. Retrieved August 30, 2020, from https://www.excelsior.com.mx/nacional/virus-aniquila-125-millones-de-empleos-sector-informal-el-mas-golpeado/1385588.

Publimetro. (2020). Centro Citibanamex se convierte en unidad temporal Covid-19. 15 April. Retrieved August 30, 2020, from https://www.publimetro.com.mx/mx/coronavirus-covid-19/2020/04/15/centro-citibanamex-se-convierte-unidad-temporal-covid-19.html.

Ramírez, J. (2020a). American Express dona 6 mdd a nivel global. El Economista, 22 June. Retrieved August 30, 2020, from https://www.

eleconomista.com.mx/empresas/American-Express-dona-6-mdd-a-nivel-global-20200622-0085.html.

Ramírez, J. (2020b). AT&T en México, en pro de la comunidad. El Economista, 1 June. Retrieved August 30, 2020, from https://www.eleconomista.com.mx/empresas/ATT-en-Mexico-en-pro-de-la-comunidad-20200601-0111.html.

Ramírez, J. (2020c). Subway reconoce a héroes mexicanos durante la pandemia. El Economista, 27 July. Retrieved August 30, 2020, from https://www.eleconomista.com.mx/empresas/Subway-reconoce-a-heroes-mexicanos-durante-la-pandemia-20200727-0060.html.

Ramírez, J. (2020d). Grupo Coppel ayuda a quienes salvan vidas. El Economista, 15 June. Retrieved August 30, 2020, from https://www.eleconomista.com.mx/empresas/Grupo-Coppel-ayuda-a-quienes-salvan-vidas-20200615-0088.html.

Rodríguez, M. (2019). Sector salud inicia 2019 con rezagos. El Sol de México, 2 January. Retrieved August 30, 2020, from https://www.elsoldemexico.com.mx/mexico/sociedad/sector-salud-2019-imss-issste-secretaria-de-salud-2868014.html.

Sánchez, C. (2020). Heineken México dona 22 mil latas de agua y 50 caretas al Gobierno de Nuevo León. El Financiero, 30 April. Retrieved August 30, 2020, from https://www.elfinanciero.com.mx/monterrey/heineken-mexico-dona-22-mil-latas-de-agua-y-50-caretas-al-gobierno-de-nuevo-leon.

Santinelli, M. A. (2020). ¿Cuál será el future de la Responsabilidad Social? Milenio, 21 August. Retrieved August 30, 2020, from https://www.milenio.com/sustentable/el-futuro-de-la-responsabilidad-social-frente-al-covid-19.

Statista. (2020). México: product interno bruto per cápita a precios actuales desde 2010 hasta 2020. Retrieved August 30, 2020, from https://es.statista.com/estadisticas/635224/producto-interior-bruto-pib-per-capita-de-mexico-en-2020/.

Toribio, L., & Nava, A. (2020). Crece discriminación por Covid-19; CDMX lidera número de quejas. Excélsior, 7 April. Retrieved August 30, 2020, from https://www.excelsior.com.mx/nacional/crece-discriminacion-por-covid-19-cdmx-lidera-numero-de-quejas/1374504.

Urrutia, A., & Jiménez, N. (2020). La Jornada Nacional de Sana Distancia se extiende al 30 de mayo. La Jornada, 17 April. Retrieved August 30, 2020, from https://www.jornada.com.mx/2020/04/17/politica/002n1pol.

4

What Are the Outcomes of Corporate Social Irresponsibility (CSI)? The Disconnect Between CSI *Theory* and CSI *Practice*

Irina Surdu and Giulio Nardella

4.1 Introduction

Over the past four decades, management scholarship has been concerned with examining corporate social responsibility (CSR) opportunities, as well as understanding what may curtail corporate irresponsibility (CSI) and wrongdoing. Studies tend to discuss how irresponsible behavior can be defined (e.g., Lange and Washburn 2012; Lin-Hi and Müller 2013), what drives some firms to behave irresponsibly (see Kim et al. 2018), and, most relevantly, what the outcomes of corporate irresponsibility are (e.g., Jones and Rubin 2001; Karpoff et al. 2005; Nardella et al. 2020). Interest

I. Surdu (✉)
University of Warwick, Coventry, UK
e-mail: Irina.Surdu@wbs.ac.uk

G. Nardella
Loughborough University, Loughborough, UK

A. Sörensson et al. (eds.), *Corporate Responsibility and Sustainability during the Coronavirus Crisis*, Palgrave Studies in Governance, Leadership and Responsibility,
https://doi.org/10.1007/978-3-030-73847-1_4

in CSI as an area of research has increased to the point where corporate social irresponsibility itself has become referred to as a "grand challenge" in strategic and international management (see: Brammer et al. 2019; Buckley et al. 2017; Mellahi et al. 2021). Within this stream of research on CSI, studies agree that CSI has a negative effect on the associated organization's reputation in the eyes of its many domestic and international stakeholders, followed by a swift decline in organizational performance (notably: Coombs 2004; Coombs and Holladay 2009; Fombrun and Shanley 1990; Highhouse et al. 2009; Lange et al. 2011).

In practice, however, organizations continue to engage in irresponsible behavior, with examples ranging from the tax avoidance scandals involving companies such as Google and Amazon to ongoing human rights abuses associated with the global value chains of fashion companies such as Primark, GAP, and H&M, the child labor controversies associated with international companies such as Nike and Nestlé, or the environmental and public health harm caused by organizations such as Dow and DuPont. These examples suggest that a firm's reputation and subsequent performance are not necessarily eroded when the firm becomes associated with, or accused of, CSI. Recent evidence has therefore started to emerge, depicting a more nuanced process of when and how stakeholders penalize (or not) organizations which behave irresponsibly (e.g., Bae et al. 2020; Nardella et al. 2020; Wans 2020). The discrepancy between theoretical assumptions and observations of business practice is important (Jackson et al. 2014) in order to gain a better understanding of the managerial and policy decisions needed to curtail CSI and encourage more CSR activities.

Increasingly, multinational enterprises (MNEs) are among those firms accused of irresponsible behavior, both at home and abroad (Nardella and Brammer 2021). MNEs provide a nuanced and complex context to study the relationship between CSI and organizational outcomes due to the scope of their operations and the diversity of home as well as host market stakeholders whose expectations these firms need to manage (Rabbiosi and Santangelo 2019; Wang and Li 2019). News of MNE irresponsibility together with current changes in home, as well as host regulatory processes, are expected to place increasing pressures on multinational firms to behave more responsibly in the different locations in which they serve their international customers, as well as to manage their global value chains more sustainably and effectively. Although we are yet to see the effects of firms behaving more responsibly across the different markets in which they operate, crises and disruptions—such as the COVID-19 pandemic—tend to shed light on the sustainability of business operations (Juergensen, Guimón and Narula 2020) but also on the prevalence of irresponsible behavior by MNEs. The COVID-19 pandemic—as explained later in the chapter—has made the disconnect between what the theory assumes (i.e., that firms are penalized for CSI) and what actually happens in business practice (i.e., when financial pressures increase, firms do not take care of their key partners and stakeholders). In this context, it has become apparent that the role of nuanced host market policies is crucial to curtail MNE irresponsibility.

The overall aim of this chapter is to provide an overview of the key literature on CSI with a particular focus on CSI's main outcomes, namely organizational reputation and performance. Throughout the chapter, we discuss the managerial and policy implications associated with irresponsible corporate behavior. We zoom in on multinational firms, which face, on the one hand, pressures to reduce costs and adapt to host market consumer demand and keep up with technological advancements and, on the other hand, pressures to better monitor, and upgrade the capabilities of, their global value chains. Significant progress has been made to increase investment in sustainable practices driven by international organizations such as the World Bank, Organization for Economic Co-operation and Development (OECD), the International Labor Organization (ILO), and the World Trade Organization (WTO). Even so, this chapter sheds light on the fact that changes to become more socially responsible will come with managerial effort and other costs which many firms cannot, or wish not to, bear post-crises such as post-COVID-19 pandemic. This means that regulating and penalizing irresponsible behavior is becoming ever more important to continue the progress made to curtail CSI.

The remaining of this chapter is organized as follows. The next section will summarize some of the core as well as more recent studies on the main outcomes of CSI, such as the decline in organizational reputation and market performance. Then, we move on to explain that there are also key factors that may moderate this complex relationship between CSI and performance, and notable among them is the role of stakeholder expectations. Lastly, the chapter discusses the broader role of crises and disruptions such as, but not limited to, the COVID-19 pandemic, on making the disconnect between CSI theory and CSI practice more visible to a wider range of both home market and international organizational stakeholders.

4.2 What We Know About the Outcomes of CSI

Corporate irresponsibility has been associated with two broad and interrelated outcomes, namely (1) decline in corporate reputation; and (2) decline in organizational performance. In the earlier studies examining the relationship between CSI and organizational reputation—"a perceptual representation of a company's past actions and future prospects that describes the firm's overall appeal to its key constituents" (Fombrun 1996: 72)—authors have broadly theorized that CSI leads to reputation decline (see also Fombrun and Shanley 1990; Karpoff and Lott 1993), as stakeholders act to penalize those firms which are associated with acts of irresponsible behavior. Over the years, the increased popularity and relevance of CSI research has led to the idea that CSI renders organizational reputation fragile and that firms are expected to be constantly vulnerable to being penalized by stakeholders (Lange et al. 2011) following CSI disclosure (Karpoff et al. 2005; Karpoff et al. 2008). The idea that reputations of those associated with CSI are "fragile" has been proliferated over the years as the media and business press have increasingly disclosed and debated CSI.

To understand the relationship between CSI and organizational reputation, scholars have conducted numerous experiments, generally concerned with the perceptions of stakeholder groups such as existing or potential customers of the firm; these studies focus on measuring stakeholder perceptions of the firm following an act of wrongdoing; for example, Coombs and Holladay (2009) found that customer trust decreases when firms are perceived to behave irresponsibly, which is translated into customers being less likely to continue purchasing the firm's products and services. Kim later (2014) suggested that news of CSI behavior tend to lead to customers blaming the associated organization for causing the CSI event, which is expected to also lead to a decrease in purchase intention, as well as negative word-of-mouth (see also Sweetin et al. 2013).

Notwithstanding the contribution of these studies, there is little evidence that consumer perceptions will, indeed, endanger the reputation of a firm and lead to changes in their purchase behavior toward the firm following CSI. For instance, in July 2013, UK fashion retailer—Primark—experienced a 20% increase in sales, after having avoided a consumer boycott over one of their plants in Bangladesh which collapsed in April of the same year and claimed around 1129 workers' lives (The Guardian 2013). In July 2020, Nike and Apple were warned to monitor their Chinese suppliers more closely as international organizations suspect the companies to have used "forced labour" of Chinese ethnic minorities (BBC 2020); again, we observe stakeholder attention and pressure, but this does not translate in decreased reputation or reduction in performance. Using large-scale secondary data, studies reveal a complex CSI-reputation-performance relationship (Breitinger and Bonardi 2019; Nardella et al. 2020; Zyglidopoulos 2001), whereby CSI does not always affect reputation (Nardella et al. 2020) and moreover, there may be a CSI reputational gain (Nardella et al. 2020; Zyglidopoulos 2001).

Extant research has also examined specific performance outcomes following CSI disclosure. For instance, by examining the short-term decline in stock market value, scholars have, again, proposed that CSI has a significant and negative impact on performance (e.g., Ertimur et al. 2012; Karpoff et al. 2008), and this impact may be greater than actual litigation (Karpoff and Lott 1993; Engelen 2010). In other words, investor perception of the firm's involvement in a CSI event is proposed to lead to greater performance decline than outcomes following the actual decision made by the court concerning the firm's culpability; such findings point to the subjective and socially constructed nature of reputation and its performance impact (Ravasi et al. 2018). Overall, scholars have associated a short-term decline in stock market price following the disclosure of a CSI event in the media, with negative long-term performance outcomes for the associated firm.

While the stock market reaction to CSI may be an indicator of investor perception, and thus, short-term performance; we know that markets overreact to CSI news (Gillet et al. 2010); and after a few days have passed following the event disclosure, companies and markets recover, and may even benefit from the CSI event. Take for instance, the share price of Samsung following product recalls due to faulty batteries in the Galaxy Note 7 (Tech Times 2017); or that of Apple, following child labor and human rights controversies involving Foxconn, their main Chinese supplier (The Guardian 2011): the losses in share price which incurred soon after the CSI activities were disclosed, were recouped in a very short time frame. In other instances, the market even reacts positively, particularly when the outcomes of CSI are less penalizing than expected (The Conversation 2020); for example, in 2017, DuPont agreed to pay the amount of US$671 million in order to settle the class-action lawsuit whereby the company was accused of, and found culpable for, highly toxic spills; notably, since the final settlement amount was below Wall Street expectations, the company's share price increased by 1% on the day of the announcement, and continued to increase by over 4% in the following days.

Consequently, measuring performance by simply examining stock market reactions contributes to the overly simplistic and naïve view that CSI leads to negative performance outcomes, and thus, firms will be disincentivized to engage in CSI. There may be an opportunity cost for stakeholders to significantly alter their behavior toward the organization. For instance, in the case of companies such as Apple, there is a degree of uniqueness of the company's offering and position in the marketplace which makes their reputation and performance more resilient. The expected impact of CSI may also matter; as per the DuPont example, when the impact of CSI on the firm is less significant than previously expected, firms may even benefit from engaging in CSI, or at the very least, not be massively hindered by CSI media disclosure.

4.3 Stakeholder Expectations, CSI, and Organizational Outcomes

In this chapter, we emphasize that, in order to truly understand the nature of the relationship between CSI and outcomes such as reputation and performance, we must understand what factors moderate these complex relationships. A key moderating factor, we propose, is the role played by *stakeholder expectations*. We know by now that expectations influence perceptions and subsequent behavior (Lange and Washburn 2012; Mishina et al. 2012). Stakeholder expectations of a given firm may therefore influence the extent to which stakeholders will penalize the firm (or not) in light of CSI. For instance, companies which have built good reputations over time, may benefit from stakeholder good-will and be protected against reputation damage (e.g., Brammer and Pavelin 2005; Nardella et al. 2020). This is because firms which have been known to be "good social actors" are often afforded the benefit of the doubt when associated with, or accused of, CSI. Scholars even suggested that stakeholders may choose to ignore, or pay little attention to, CSI news, when the information provided by the media does not meet their own expectations about the company (see Love and Kraatz 2009; Pfarrer et al. 2010). Similar studies found that the stock market prices of well-reputed firms suffered less as a result of disclosed CSI compared to counterparts with weaker reputations (Raithel et al. 2010). In general, a good reputation may be expected to act as a buffer against the potential negative effects of CSI on the organization. This is particularly important in times of crises, when firms are likely to already experience performance challenges that may threaten their survival.

In a recent study, Nardella et al. (2020) further examined the role of stakeholder expectations and found that firms with a past reputation for high social performance may also carry the burden of high stakeholder expectations; these expectations, in turn, become violated when the firm is associated with CSI. Stakeholder expectancy violations may have an even stronger negative reputational effect when firms have a strong reputation for certain characteristics (Janney and Gove 2011; McDonnell and King 2018; Rhee and Haunschild 2006). Firms which build their reputations around product and service excellence are likely to be more severely penalized by stakeholders following product recalls or product harm (Rhee and Haunschild 2006), whereas firms which build their reputations around superior governance are more severely penalized when associated with CSI events such as executive compensation controversies, earnings mismanagement, taxation, or fraud (Janney and Gove 2011). McDonnell and King (2018) added that when the well-reputed firms were associated with CSI in the media, the reputation penalty was great, irrespective of actual litigation, yet again drawing attention to the difference between stakeholder expectations and law-determined culpability (Nardella et al. 2020). When stakeholder expectations are violated, stakeholders may perceive firm behavior as being hypocritical and deceitful and thus, penalize previously well-reputed firms even more in light of CSI. Therefore, reputations are not always "fragile", but some reputations are more fragile than others, as a result of the stakeholder expectations.

From a managerial perspective, the abovementioned findings illustrate the importance of managing stakeholder expectations. Organizational responses to CSI range from admitting culpability to scapegoating strategies, firing CEOs and executive teams, or compensating for the harm caused by investing significantly in CSR initiatives. Extant research on the types of organizational responses needed to manage stakeholder expectations suggests that the effectiveness of communication strategies depends on the prior reputation of the accused firm (Coldwell et al. 2012; Fennis and Stroebe 2014). This may mean that, for instance, organizations can self-disclose acts of CSI if they benefit from a superior reputation and, thus, are likely to elicit stakeholder trust (Fennis and Stroebe 2014). Stakeholder trust is important when organizations invest in CSR post a CSI-crises, whereby their responses may be interpreted as a strategy to distract from the harm caused. Alternatively, firms may opt for shorter-term fixes; a recent example is that of Rio Tinto, whose top executives have resigned following the scandal whereby the mining company destroyed a 46,000-year-old aboriginal site in Australia to extract natural resources from that site (S&P Global 2020). Yet, we observed with the example of Rio Tinto, and the many policy and media debates that this scandal has elicited, that the worldwide political upheaval triggered to some extent by the COVID-19 pandemic has increased stakeholder emotions and awareness of the activities of global firms.

4.4 How Crises and Disruptions May Act as Catalysts to Changing Stakeholder Expectations

We know by now that crises and disruptions—economic recessions, climate changes, wars, terrorist attacks, and, of course, pandemics—cause shifts in patterns of consumption, investor behavior, and policies and, subsequently, changes to firm activities and long-term performance (Klassen and McLaughlin 1996). But, how are stakeholder expectations changing? Stakeholder expectations may have shifted during the COVID-19 pandemic, as people are becoming more aware of, and invested in understanding about, aspects linking business and society. For instance, in the midst of the onslaught caused by the pandemic, the higher death toll in certain communities in the UK has been associated with race, injustice, poorer working and living standards, and air pollution (The Guardian 2020a). In the same vein, the deepening of economic problems for firms in developing countries, such as Bangladesh, is associated with the irresponsible practices of foreign retailers which, following the COVID-19 pandemic, have withheld billions in payments that should have been made to their suppliers, resulting in millions of job losses (Forbes 2020). Parallel to these issues, domestic and international firms are becoming more focused on reducing costs and making strategic decisions aimed at recovering the losses incurred due to the demand shocks of the pandemic.

The challenges of reconciling economic and social goals are even greater for MNEs which have suffered both demand and supply shocks due to the spontaneous reactions of home and host governments to implement national lockdowns and impose trade restrictions. Given the international scope of their operations, MNEs have also been associated with CSI, particularly activities conducted by firms within the MNE-controlled global value chains. An MNE's global value chain—defined as the collection of governance arrangements that utilize geographically dispersed activities of the supply chain (see Buckley 2009)—consists of hundreds and even thousands of firms which are contracted to produce, assemble, or deliver goods for the lead firm. Notable examples associated with CSI in global value chains include worker rights controversies, the use of child labor, and the lack of appropriate health and safety conditions for factory workers in the developing world. The fashion industry, in particular, has come under scrutiny over the years, due to the poor working conditions that often characterize their developing market factories (Narula 2019). In many instances, the blame for CSI has been passed on to the lead firm's main suppliers who are contractually responsible with managing those parts of the value chain. The COVID-19 pandemic has seen MNEs reneging on their supplier contracts, under-paying workers or firing without compensation; in this context, the fashion industry's exploitative business model has been placed under scrutiny (Forbes 2020). Lead MNE power over developing market suppliers (often located in Bangladesh, Cambodia, Vietnam) leads to the latter accepting orders below cost (a common practice in the industry), undermining supplier ability to offer decent working conditions to employees. These irresponsible practices did not begin with COVID-19, but the emotionality caused by the pandemic, we argue, has brought MNE CSI to global stakeholder attention.

Here also, there is a discrepancy between what the literature proposes and examples from business practice. On the one hand, for an MNE, reputation is a key source of competitive advantage which the firm can leverage in different international markets. In fact, a firm's international growth is expected to be primarily driven by its ability to exploit superior firm-specific resources such as organizational reputation in the host markets targeted (Rugman et al. 2011). Negative stakeholder assessment of MNE behavior can therefore increase the legal and other transaction costs associated with managing and protecting reputation-based advantages (Rugman et al. 2011; Maggioni et al. 2019; Wang and Li 2019). Reputation damage following media disclosure of CSI in a host market is expected to spread globally and damage the reputation of the firm in its home and host markets; as such, firms are expected to benefit from reducing ownership of those host market operations which are associated with CSI to avoid global reputational damage and financial risk (Kölbel et al. 2017; Wang and Li 2019).

On the other hand, the examples of CSI behavior suggested earlier indicate that there are many benefits to being irresponsible. When pressures to reduce costs increase, we are likely to see more of these firms divesting their operations and reneging on their international orders with little to no notice. Furthermore, despite the increased stakeholder scrutiny observed recently, there is a real possibility that the reputation of the MNE at home and in its key markets is likely to remain unaffected because stakeholders have become accustomed to these firm practices and often associate unfair employee treatment with lack of effective host market legislation. Customers, in turn, may, in theory, support better practices, and rise against CSI behavior, but have been historically unwilling to pay more for sustainable and responsible products, which companies could produce if they were to make value chain decisions beyond raw material costs and cheap labor considerations (White et al. 2019). Similarly, investors understand the potential cost savings that often come with exploiting factor markets in developing countries (Ke et al. 2010). The role of policy in curtailing CSI has never been so important. In mid-2020, together with Nike and Apple, Boohoo (UK fashion retailer) was associated with labor exploitation scandals in China, an investigation which resulted in no visible outcomes. At the same time, Boohoo and their suppliers were accused of inappropriate labor conditions at a factory in their home market in Leicester, UK (The Guardian, 2020b); this home-based CSI event, however, resulted in PWC resigning as their main auditor and a 20% decline in shares.

Specifically, the role of policy is particularly important in order to mediate the relationships between lead MNEs (which are often developed market players) and their (generally non-developed market) partners and suppliers (Narula 2019). When disruptions and crises occur, the losses are unevenly distributed among global value chain partners (Crane et al. 2014). This is reflected in the further shocks delivered to informal sectors in developing economies, whose market players will continue to struggle (Narula 2020). In these contexts, global stakeholders tend to substitute the media hype around societal issues with the actual measures taken to curtail CSI. Due to the institutional and cultural distance between the MNE's main markets and stakeholders (Campbell et al. 2012) (which tend to be the US or other developed Western markets) and those harmed by CSI in the different host markets, social regulation triggered by the media alone is unlikely to lead to CSI practices becoming reduced (see the study by Surdu and Nardella 2020). In fact, we are yet to see significant, large-scale evidence that either the global reputation or performance of MNEs associated with irresponsible practices in host markets has been impacted by CSI disclosure of those practices (also illustrated by the example of Boohoo earlier, whereby only CSI in the home market was shown to have an impact on the company's performance). Without appropriate measures taken by home but also host market policymakers, there is little incentive for lead MNEs to invest time, managerial capabilities, and financial resources in upgrading the working conditions of factory workers and improving labor standards. This could be achieved with better control over key suppliers who are responsible for curtailing irresponsible practices in the global value chains—but again, control and coordination of these partners come at a cost.

Importantly, there are examples where MNEs, through socially responsible initiatives, have been able to increase their reputation and legitimacy following crises and disruptions. During times of crisis, some firms may, indeed, benefit from having positive reputations, but at the same time, crises and disruptions could be an opportunity to build reputation and legitimacy by increasing involvement in societal issues. A study by Mithani (2017) showed that philanthropy can mitigate the liability of foreignness that many firms experience when entering international markets, in the aftermath of crises such as natural disasters; the social restructuring that comes with these natural disasters may provide MNEs with opportunities to establish strong local ties and gain acceptance by contributing to recovery efforts. This indicates that major crises and disruptions can frame or reframe social perceptions of firms, in their home as well as host markets (e.g., Baron 2013; Mithani 2017). CSR activities offer opportunities for firms to build legitimacy with relevant market players and institutions, increase trust in their operations, and reduce the tendency of stakeholders to view the firm as distant from society and merely profit driven.

4.5 Conclusions

What are the outcomes of corporate social irresponsibility? And why is this question a "grand challenge" of international business and management research? CSI research has, for many years, taken for granted that socially irresponsible behavior results in reputational penalties and performance decline for firms associated with it. However, this chapter discussed why some firm characteristics, such as a firm's prior reputation, may buffer against negative CSI outcomes. In this way, we showed that CSI outcomes are much more complex and nuanced, and in some cases, they do not occur, as irresponsible behavior remains unpenalized. The discrepancy between theory and practice is also reflected in the context of multinational firms, as their irresponsible behavior in host markets appears to rarely impact home market reputation or performance. In times of crises and disruptions, stakeholders become more aware of, and actively interested in, societal issues, but again, it is important to avoid substituting stakeholder interest with actual negative CSI outcomes for the firm accused. We discuss the managerial implications and role of policy in managing and curtailing corporate social irresponsibility.

References

Bae, J., Choi, W., & Lim, J. (2020). Corporate social responsibility: An umbrella or a puddle on a rainy day? Evidence surrounding corporate financial misconduct. *European Financial Management, 26*(1), 77–117.

Baron, D. P. (2013). *Business and its environment.* Boston: Pearson Education.

BBC. (2020). Apple and Nike urged to cut "China Uighur ties". Retrieved from https://www.bbc.co.uk/news/business-53481253.

Brammer, S. J., & Pavelin, S. (2005). Corporate reputation and an insurance motivation for corporate social investment. *The Journal of Corporate Citizenship, 20*(Winter), 39–51.

Brammer, S., Branicki, L., Linnenluecke, M., & Smith, T. (2019). Grand challenges in management research: Attributes, achievements, and advancement. *Australian Journal of Management, 44*(4), 517–533.

Breitinger, D., & Bonardi, J.-P. (2019). Firms, breach of norms, and reputation damage. *Business & Society, 58*(6), 1143–1176.

Buckley, P. (2009). Internalisation thinking: From the multinational enterprise to the global factory. *International Business Review, 18*(3), 224–235.

Buckley, P. J., Doh, J. P., & Benischke, M. H. (2017). Towards a renaissance in international business research? Big questions, grand challenges, and the future of IB scholarship. *Journal of International Business Studies, 48*(9), 1045–1064.

Campbell, J. T., Eden, L., & Miller, S. R. (2012). Multinationals and corporate social responsibility in host countries: Does distance matter? *Journal of International Business Studies, 43*(1), 84–106.

Coldwell, D. A. L., Joosub, T., & Papageorgiou, E. (2012). Responsible leadership in organizational crises: An analysis of the effects of public perceptions of selected SA business organizations' reputations. *Journal of Business Ethics, 109*, 133–144.

Coombs, W. T. (2004). Impact of past crises on current crisis communications: Insights from situational crisis communication theory. *Journal of Business Communication, 41*(3), 265–289.

Coombs, T. W., & Holladay, S. J. (2009). Further explorations of post-crisis communication: Effects of media and response strategies on perceptions and intentions. *Public Relations Review, 35*(1), 1–6.

Crane, A., Palazzo, G., Spence, L. J., & Matten, D. (2014). Contesting the value of "creating shared value". *California Management Review, 56*(2), 130–153.

Engelen, P. J. (2010). What is the reputational cost of a dishonest CEO? Evidence from US illegal insider trading. *CESifo Economic Studies, 58*(3), 1–24.

Ertimur, Y., Ferri, F., & Maber, D. A. (2012). Reputation penalties for poor monitoring of executive pay: Evidence from option backdating. *Journal of Financial Economics, 104*(1), 118–144.

Fennis, B. M., & Stroebe, W. (2014). Softening the blow: Company self-disclosure of negative information lessens damaging effects on consumer judgment and decision making. *Journal of Business Ethics, 120*(1), 109–120.

Fombrun, C. J. (1996). *Reputation: Realizing value from the corporate image*. Cambridge, MA: Harvard Business School Press.

Fombrun, C., & Shanley, M. (1990). What's in a name? Reputation building and corporate strategy. *The Academy of Management Journal, 33*(2), 233–258.

Forbes. (2020). Bangladesh threatens to ban these UK brands, escalating battle to get factories paid. Retrieved from https://www.forbes.com/sites/elizabethl-cline/2020/05/27/bangladesh-threatens-to-ban-these-uk-brands-escalating-battle-to-get-factories-paid/#184d967015c4.

Gillet, R., Hübner, G., & Plunus, S. (2010). Operational risk and reputation in the financial industry. *Journal of Banking & Finance, 34*(1), 224–235.

Highhouse, S., Brooks, M. E., & Gregarus, G. (2009). An organizational impression management perspective on the formation of corporate reputations. *Journal of Management, 35*(6), 1481–1493.

Jackson, G., Brammer, S., Karpoff, J. M., Lange, D., Zavyalova, A., Harrington, B., & Deephouse, D. L. (2014). Grey areas: irresponsible corporations and reputational dynamics. *Socio-Economic Review, 12*(1), 153–218.

Janney, J. J. & Gove, S. (2011). Reputation and corporate social responsibility aberrations, trends, and hypocrisy: Reactions to firm choices in the stock option backdating scandal. *Journal of Management Studies, 48*, 1562–1585.

Jones, K. & Rubin, P. H. (2001). Effects of harmful environmental events on reputations of firms. *Advances in Financial Economics, 6*, 161–182.

Juergensen, J., Guimón, J., & Narula, R. (2020). European SMEs amidst the COVID-19 crisis: Assessing impact and policy responses. *Economia e Politica Industriale, 47*(3), 499–510.

Karpoff, J. M., & Lott, J. R., Jr. (1993). The reputational penalty firms bear from committing criminal fraud. *Journal of Law and Economics, 36*(2), 757–802.

Karpoff, J. M., Lott, J. R., Jr., & Wehrly, E. W. (2005). The reputational penalties for environmental violations: Empirical evidence. *Journal of Law and Economics, 48*(2), 653–675.

Karpoff, J. M., Lee, D. S., & Martin, G. S. (2008). The cost to firms of cooking the books. *Journal of Financial and Quantitative Analysis, 43*(3), 581–611.

Ke, D., Ng, L., & Wang, Q. (2010). Home bias in foreign investment decisions. *Journal of International Business Studies, 41*(6), 960–979.

Kim, S. (2014). What's worse in times of product-harm crisis? Negative corporate ability or negative CSR reputation?. *Journal of Business Ethics, 123*, 157–170.

Kim, K. H., Kim, M., & Qian, C. L. (2018). Effects of corporate social responsibility on corporate financial performance: A competitive-action perspective. *Journal of Management, 44*(3), 1097–1118.

Klassen, R. D., & McLaughlin, C. P. (1996). The impact of environmental management on firm performance. *Management Science, 42*(8), 1199–1214.

Kölbel, J. F., Busch, T., & Jancso, L. M. (2017). How media coverage of corporate social irresponsibility increases financial risk. *Strategic Management Journal, 38*(11), 2266–2284.

Lange, D., & Washburn, N. T. (2012). Understanding attributions of corporate social irresponsibility. *Academy of Management Review, 37*(2), 300–326.

Lange, D., Lee, P. M., & Dai, Y. (2011). Organizational reputation: A review. *Journal of Management, 37*(1), 153–184.

Lin-Hi, N., & Müller, K. (2013). The CSR bottom line: Preventing corporate social irresponsibility. *Journal of Business Research, 66*(10), 1928–1936.

Love, E. G., & Kraatz, M. S. (2009). Character, conformity, or the bottom line? How and why downsizing affected corporate reputation. *Academy of Management Journal, 52*(2), 314–335.

Maggioni, D., Santangelo, G. D., & Koymen-Ozer, S. (2019). MNEs' location strategies and labor standards: The role of operating and reputational considerations across industries. *Journal of International Business Studies, 50*, 948–972.

McDonnell, M. H., & King, B. (2018). Keeping up appearances: Reputational threat and impression management after social movement boycotts. *Administrative Science Quarterly, 58*(3), 387–419.

Mellahi, K., Meyer, K., Narula, R., Surdu, I., & Verbeke, A. (2021). *The Oxford handbook of international business strategy*. Oxford: Oxford University Press.

Mishina, Y., Block, E. S., & Mannor, M. J. (2012). The path dependence of organizational reputation: How social judgment influences assessments of capability and character. *Strategic Management Journal, 33*(5), 459–477.

Mithani, M. A. (2017). Liability of foreignness, natural disasters, and corporate philanthropy. *Journal of International Business Studies, 48*, 941–963.

Nardella, G., & Brammer, S. (2021). Corporate social responsibility, irresponsibility, and the multinational enterprise environment. In K. Mellahi, K. Meyer, R. Narula, I. Surdu, & A. Verbeke (Eds.), *The Oxford handbook of international business strategy* (pp. 401–420). Oxford University Press.

Nardella, G., Brammer, S., & Surdu, I. (2020). Shame on who? The effects of corporate irresponsibility and social performance on organizational reputation. *British Journal of Management, 31*(1), 5–23.

Narula, R. (2019). Enforcing higher labor standards within developing country value chains: Consequences for MNEs and informal actors in a dual economy. *Journal of International Business Studies, 50*, 1622–1635.

Narula, P. (2020). Policy opportunities and challenges from the COVID-19 pandemic for economies with large informal sectors. *Journal of International Business Policy, 3*, 302–310.

Pfarrer, M. D., Pollock, T. G., & Rindova, V. P. (2010). A tale of two assets: The effects of firm reputation and celebrity on earnings surprises and investors' reactions. *Academy of Management Journal, 53*(5), 1131–1152.

Rabbiosi, L., & Santangelo, G. D. (2019). Host country corruption and the organization of HQ–subsidiary relationships. *Journal of International Business Studies, 50*(1), 111–124.

Raithel, S., Wilczynski, P., Schloderer, M. P., & Schwaiger, M. (2010). The value-relevance of corporate reputation during the financial crisis. *The Journal of Product and Brand Management, 19*(6), 389–400.

Ravasi, D., Rindova, V., Etter, M., & Cornelissen, J. (2018). The formation of organizational reputation. *Academy of Management Annals, 12*(2), 574–599.

Rhee, M., & Haunschild, P. R. (2006). The liability of good reputation: A study of product recalls in the U.S. automobile industry. *Organisation Science, 17*(1), 101–117.

Rugman, A. M., Verbeke, A., & Nguyen, Q. T. K. (2011). Fifty years of international business theory and beyond. *Management International Review, 51*(6), 755–786.

Surdu, I., & Nardella G. (2020). What happens abroad, stays abroad? Reputation risks of MNE irresponsibility in home and host markets. *Academy of Management Proceedings*. https://doi.org/10.5465/AMBPP.2020.13213abstract.

Sweetin, V. H., Knowles, L. L., Summey, J. H., & McQueen, K. S. (2013). Willingness-to-punish the corporate brand for corporate social irresponsibility. *Journal of Business Research, 66*, 1822–1830.

Tech Times. (2017). Samsung shares hit new record high despite Galaxy Note 7 recall. Retrieved from https://www.techtimes.com/articles/191899/20170109/samsung-shares-hit-new-record-high-despite-galaxy-note-7-recall.htm.

The Conversation. (2020). Dark waters: What DuPont scandal can teach companies about doing the right thing. Retrieved from https://theconversation.com/dark-waters-what-dupont-scandal-can-teach-companies-about-doing-the-right-thing-132480.

The Guardian. (2011). Life and death in Apple's forbidden city. Retrieved from https://www.theguardian.com/technology/2017/jun/18/foxconn-life-death-forbidden-city-longhua-suicide-apple-iphone-brian-merchant-one-device-extract.

The Guardian. (2013). Primark sales rise 20% despite Bangladesh factory disaster backlash. Retrieved from https://www.theguardian.com/business/2013/jul/11/primark-sales-rise-despite-bangladesh-factory.

The Guardian. (2020a). Omission of air pollution from report on Covid-19 and race "astonishing". Retrieved from https://www.theguardian.com/environment/2020/jun/07/omission-of-air-pollution-from-report-on-covid-19-and-race-astonishing.

The Guardian. (2020b). "Just get out of here": How Leicester's factories went to war with Boohoo. Retrieved from https://www.theguardian.com/business/2020/aug/28/boohoo-leicester-factories-went-to-war.

Wang, S. L., & Li, D. (2019). Responding to public disclosure of corporate social irresponsibility in host countries: Information control and ownership control. *Journal of International Business Studies, 50*, 1283–1309.

Wans, N. (2020). Corporate social responsibility and market-based consequences of adverse corporate events: Evidence from restatement announcements. *Journal of Accounting, Auditing and Finance, 35*(2), 231–262.

White, K., Hardisty, D. J., & Habib, R. (2019). *The elusive green customer. Harvard Business Review.*

Zyglidopoulos, S. (2001). The impact of accidents on firms' reputation for social performance. *Business & Society, 40*(4), 416–432.

Part II

CSR, SMEs and COVID-19

5

Effects of the Coronavirus Pandemic on Swedish Tourism Firms and their Sustainability Values

Anna Sörensson, Maria Bogren, and Ulrich Schmudde

5.1 Introduction

The outbreak of the coronavirus (COVID-19) in late 2019 in Wuhan, China, has changed the way a large amount of firms operate around the world, with firms in the tourism industry being particularly hard hit. The coronavirus pandemic has led to a societal crisis that has radically changed conditions for Swedish businesses and their employees (the Swedish Agency for Economic and Regional Growth 2020). The pandemic and its consequences are described as the largest crisis ever experienced for tourism globally and it has affected virtually the whole industry on a global

A. Sörensson (✉) • U. Schmudde
Mid Sweden University, Östersund, Sweden
e-mail: anna.sorensson@miun.se

M. Bogren
Mid Sweden University, Östersund, Sweden

Nord University, Bodø, Norway

A. Sörensson et al. (eds.), *Corporate Responsibility and Sustainability during the Coronavirus Crisis*, Palgrave Studies in Governance, Leadership and Responsibility,
https://doi.org/10.1007/978-3-030-73847-1_5

scale (Farzanegan et al. 2020; Gössling et al. 2020; Hoque et al. 2020). Within the space of only a few weeks in March/April of 2020, international travel almost completely came to a halt, before slowly re-emerging in a new, severely limited form in June 2020. During the northern summer, tourists travelled domestically and during the autumn, travel slowed down again as fewer people had holidays and the spread of coronavirus gained pace again.

Tourism was one of the fastest growing industries in Europe before the pandemic struck and it has been a prioritised area for the European Commission since the 1990s. The tourism sector is Europe's largest industry dominating over 60 per cent of all tourism activity in the world, and further growth had been expected (EU 2020). Growth was steady as the trend has been for people to travel more and more. The shock to the tourism industry has been experienced as particularly dramatic as the crisis came with almost no warning after many years of uninterrupted global growth in a sector that generally has weak economic sustainability (Cotterell et al. 2019). Since the emergence of the coronavirus pandemic, tourism has been one of the industries most severely impacted by travel restrictions and lockdowns, making the sector lose both customers and revenues. Some parts of the tourism industry have been hit extra hard, with travel agencies, airlines, bus firms, and cruise lines as well as the events sector and gastronomy such as restaurants being clear examples. During this crisis, some industries made strategic adjustments to create "new" customer value and are therefore experiencing less problems.

In these times, tourism firms should be aware of sustainability dimensions and how they can contribute to a higher value for customers (Iniesta-Bonillo et al. 2016). Sustainability dimensions are often defined as covering three areas, namely economic, social, and environmental sustainability. Nowadays, the majority of Swedish tourism firms are aware of these dimensions and some include them in their everyday work. Previous studies have shown that European tourism firms have a tendency to focus on only one of these dimensions at a time (Sörensson 2011; Sörensson 2014). Other studies have shown that firms often see sustainability as a pyramid with economic sustainability as the base, social sustainability as the next step, and environmental sustainability on the top (Sörensson et al. 2019). There are also studies that show that different types of tourism firms seem to focus on different aspects (Sörensson and Jansson 2016). However, it is important to consider that previous studies have been conducted prior to the global pandemic taking place. Here, the aim is to discuss how Swedish tourism firms have been affected by the coronavirus pandemic, with a special focus on their sustainability values.

The structure of this article is as follows: Firstly, sustainability as a value for tourism firms is discussed. Then the methodology for the study is presented. After this, the context of tourism in Sweden and the coronavirus outbreak is introduced. This is followed by the findings of the study before the study's conclusions are presented.

5.2 Sustainability as a Value for Tourism Firms

Sustainability can be seen as a value for many tourism firms. The three dimensions of sustainability (economic, social, and environmental) can add value for customers in different ways. Previous research has shown that sustainability is seen from different perspectives. Some argue that the dimension has three pillars that are dependent on each other (Hall 2019). Others discuss the complexity of the contraction between economic growth and environmental protection. How can there be sustainability as well as development (Sörensson 2011)? This seems particularly difficult for firms during the COVID-19 crisis, since many tourism-related firms need to increase their prices due to lockdowns and the financial challenges they have caused. This also means that firms need to deliver excellent services and value in order to keep their customers and attract new ones. For more than 15 years, the concept of value has been gaining importance both in academia and among businesses (Vargo & Lusch, 2004) including businesses in the tourism industry. Value is defined in different ways, for instance, as a mixture of the price and the quality of a product (Aaker 2010). In this chapter, value is defined as making an actor, such as the customer, better off (Grönroos 2017).

The pandemic has affected tourism businesses primarily by greatly reducing demand for the services they offer. The survival and growth of tourism firms depend on satisfied tourists that are offered unique values and memorable experiences. Tourists' expectations are constantly changing and tourist firms must find ways to anticipate and respond to these expectations (Chathoth et al., 2013). Hotels are regarded, for instance, as critical to the customer experience and valuable insights can be made by applying this new emerging conceptual framework, Service-dominant logic (S-D logic), to the tourism industry (Fitzpatrick et al., 2013). In S-D logic, the co-creation of tourist experiences involves experiences customised by the tourists and includes the sharing of experiences between each other (Wang, Li & Li, 2013).

Since the pandemic started, sustainability has been discussed by governments, organisations such as the WHO and the European Union, and non-governmental organisations (The Swedish Agency for Economic and Regional Growth 2020; WHO 2020). Economic sustainability has been on the agenda for most tourism firms during the pandemic due to their struggle to survive financially. It has also influenced social sustainability as people are losing their jobs, yet have hope that tourism firms will get back on their feet as soon as the pandemic is over. Tourism firms also influence the social life of inhabitants of the destinations they work in since many events they organise have been cancelled. Environmental value may also be dropping in priority since tourism firms are choosing cheaper alternatives that are less environmentally friendly such as not prioritising eco-friendly food at restaurants, in order to survive. Tourism firms therefore need to think about their business models to attract customers during the pandemic. The sustainability pyramid (see Fig. 5.1) visualise that sustainability can be seen as a pyramid with three layers of value.

The base of the pyramid is the economic dimension since all firms need economic survival. They need a stable economic ground to stand on. The next layer is the social dimension with a focus on both the staff in the firm or organisation as well as the surrounding society. The top layer is the environmental dimension. This layer is becoming more and more important and many tourists request that tourism firms address environmental issues. These three layers are different values of importance for both the tourism firms as well as their tourists. Whittington et al. (2020) argue that if value should be seen as a business model for tourism firms, there are three areas that cooperate: namely (1) value creation, (2) value configuration, and (3) value capture.

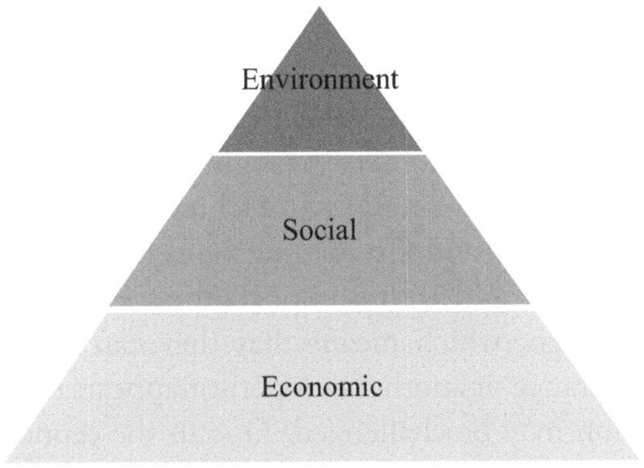

Fig. 5.1 The sustainability pyramid. Source: Own work

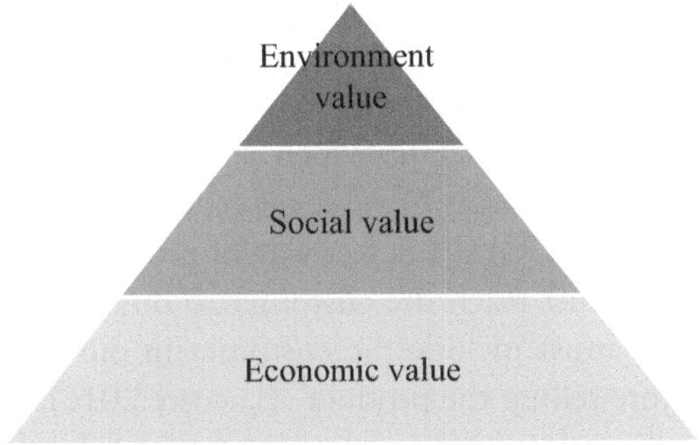

Fig. 5.2 Based on the sustainability pyramid. Source: Own work

It is to say that the value process starts from the so-called value proposition, which is the concept of where products (including goods and services) and experiences lead to value (Kotler and Armstrong 2010). Here is the focus on the products in connection to the benefits and experiences, which products create (value creation). Value configuration is the ongoing process from the value proposition over the value creation until the value capture. Thereby, the processes overlap each other continuously (Whittington et al., 2020). These three linked parts in the value business model presented in Fig. 5.2 will be discussed further in the sections below.

5.3 Value Creation

Value creation can be seen as the value that firms create in the process of buying by awakening customers' recognition and commitment to changes, which improves their ability to achieve their goals. Every interchange with a customer is important and should have value as the major goal (Osterwalder et al. 2014). It is important to be aware of the fact that services come and go, which means that they can be out of demand tomorrow. For instance, if another competitor appears tomorrow, a firm's dominant position may be challenged. Due to the economic crisis triggered by COVID-19, it is even more crucial for firms to have a positive bond with their customers, as they are particularly dependent on them. On the other hand, being customer-centric, suppliers need to put a lot of effort into the customer buying and implementation process, which leads to maximisation in value creation (Eletxigerra et al. 2018). Since monetary maximisation is not sustainable (Mori and Yamashita 2015), it is important to focus on sustainability when capturing values as a firm. This already leads to the complexity of value co-creation.

Value co-creation (VCC) is a newer way of moving as a firm from the one-way-stage "we must teach the customer to buy our product" to the two-way-stage "we must include the customer in our product development process before selling the product" (Lacoste 2016). The study conducted by Beritelli et al. (2014) emphasises that one should consider not focusing on all actors, but rather on the ones who commonly contribute to long-term development. Nevertheless, to create value it is important to think and act outside the box. This means that actors have to work together across industries (Brown et al. 2013; Gulati et al. 2006). Payne et al. (2008, p. 88) argue: "*Co-creation opportunities are strategic options for creating value. The types of opportunity available to a supplier are largely contingent on the nature of their industry, their customer offerings and their customer base. While customer research and innovation within the supplying organization should drive opportunity analysis, we suggest that suppliers consider at least three significant types of value co-creation opportunity*"; opportunities provided by technological breakthroughs, opportunities provided by changes in industry logics, and opportunities provided by changes in customer preferences. For tourism firms, it is necessary to adjust and find new opportunities during this pandemic since business logic is changed by government decisions and regulations as well as customers' new behaviour. Often, people build relationships with brands in similar ways they build other social relationships. Through these relationships, people develop strong emotional attachments to brands, which are reflected in behaviour that is favourable from tourist firms' perspectives such as commitment or support (Kim et al. 2014).

5.4 Value Configuration

The value configuration of tourism firms outlines the entire set of interdependent activities to profitably deliver value and create a competitive advantage (Fjeldstad and Ketels 2006). More simply said, value configuration is the question "what does a firm concretely offer to its customers?" Thereby, it is necessary that tourism firms ask "how do we operate and deliver?", which leads us at the same time to value proposition in the context of collaboration with other firms and whether the firms outline it due to its key competencies. In general, value proposition is the concept where products (including goods and services) and experiences lead via the value process to value outcome (Vargo & Lusch, 2004; Kotler and Armstrong 2010). This also might apply to and include individuals, places, ideas, and non-profit organisations. In this article, it means that more attention is directed to the product or service itself in connection to benefits and experiences, which the product creates (value co-creation). As a result of the "what" and "how" question, the process leads further to value capture.

5.5 Value Capture

The concept of value capture is found in many discussions and theories about management and organisational issues (Lepak et al. 2007). It is the process in which value capture results are based on value creation and the idea that value comes from resources (Lepak et al. 2007; Bowman and

Ambrosini 2000). Then once again: What is value creation? The concept can be explained by various processes in which the purpose is to create value for stakeholders. Lepak et al. (2007) believe that depending on the theory applied, some stakeholders have more or less to gain from value creation.

Value capture is the phenomenon that describes the benefits of value creation, as a final step in the process. Nationally, in different countries and societies, there are mechanisms that provide value (where it is not lost later), through competitiveness. It can be, for example, through unique resources to natural raw materials and resources, through strong demand patterns, and through characteristic industries in the country that can be seen as advantages over other countries, in this case the treatment against the pandemic in other countries with strong lockdowns compared with Sweden with no lockdown. Countries with these assets more often tend to be unique, which means that they have succeeded to a greater extent in creating and retaining their value. Depending on the source of value creation, as well as the degree of competitiveness and isolating mechanisms that exist, the process will create a varying amount of value (Lepak et al. 2007). Bowman and Ambrosini (2000) address an important difference between "creating value" and "capturing value"—"resources may be capable of producing profits, but if the resource owner, not the firm, is able to capture this exchange value, firm profitability will suffer" (ibid., p. 8).

In value capture, two major directions need to be differentiated: pro-profit firms (e.g. Hart 1989), where focus is on reducing the cost of short-term contracts in the marketplace for the sake of value capture or appropriation is the ultimate goal (Agafonow 2015; James et al. 2013); and a second and newer direction is the anti-profit firm or a firm that delivers back benefits and services to the locals and/or society (Bhattacharjee et al. 2017). For these firms, monetary maximisation is not the first priority; rather it is a loyal customer who will give positive word-of-mouth (Aaker 2010). In pandemic times, it is crucial to realise that a loyal customer contributes to a positive long-term relationship and this is mirrored by value capture, which also increases the monetary part, but focus is on achieving customers' needs and wants in the long run (Osterwalder et al. 2015; Wohlfart 2002). Management science is instrumental for combining into a single unit of production those transactions that would reduce or prevent profitability if carried out on the open market. That is it attempts to harness the process of value creation for the sake of value capture, on behalf of the residual claimant of profits (e.g. Alvarez and Barney 2004; Jacobides et al. 2006; King and Slotegraaf 2011; Mizik and Jacobson 2003; Santos 2012; Wagner et al. 2010). Before value capture takes place, value must be created, which requires complex forecasting of future demand and the investment of capital to fuel a production process that results in outputs (Agafonow 2015; James et al. 2013). Nevertheless, these outputs must pass the test of marketability before rendering any profit (ibid.). With COVID-19, such marketability is impossible to predict, especially when it comes to the tourism-related industry, where various customers are staying away.

5.6 Tourism in Sweden and the Coronavirus Pandemic

Tourism in Sweden had a turnover of SEK 337 billion in 2018, up by 6 per cent from 2017. The value added to Sweden's GDP was SEK 108 billion, which corresponds to 2.6 per cent of Sweden's total GDP. Tourism is growing at the same pace as the Swedish economy at large, but has shown a stronger development over time in terms of exports and employment (The Swedish Agency for Economic and Regional Growth 2020). Swedish visitors' consumption amounted to SEK 193 billion, which corresponds to an increase of 5 per cent on the previous year, while the consumption of foreign visitors increased by 8 per cent to a total of SEK 144 billion. Foreign visitors accounted for 43 per cent of tourists' total consumption expenditure of SEK 337 billion. This share has gradually risen since 2000, when the proportion was 27 per cent. Tourism is nowadays an industry of great importance for Sweden.

As tourism is an important industry for Sweden, as well as for many countries around the globe, the pandemic in 2020 will have had effects. The virus was confirmed to have reached Sweden on January 31, 2020, when a woman returning from Wuhan, China, tested positive for the

COVID-19 virus. By February 26, following outbreaks in Italy and Iran, multiple travel-related clusters had appeared in Sweden (primarily in Stockholm). Community transmission was confirmed on March 9 in the Stockholm region. Since then, individuals in every county have tested positive for COVID-19. The first death in Sweden was reported on March 11 in Stockholm and was a case of community transmission. By December 2020, more than 7000 people had died from coronavirus in Sweden. Deaths caused by the coronavirus in Sweden are among the highest in the world per capita of population. Sweden has employed a strategy to minimise the impact of the virus that differs from the majority of countries, as it does not involve lockdowns. The Public Health Agency of Sweden is responsible for national public health issues and works to ensure a high standard of public health (Folkhälsomyndigheten 2020a). The Public Health Agency of Sweden has strongly promoted three things as being of primary importance—hand washing, staying home if sick, and practising social distancing from other people (two metres).

In addition to these recommendations, people over 70 and people with underlying health conditions should avoid all unnecessary contact with other people. Furthermore, people who can work from home are recommended to do so and people are recommended not to use public transportation. During the spring of 2020, the government closed all universities and upper secondary schools in Sweden and students engaged in distance learning. The argument behind this was that these students were old enough to manage distance studies and it would prevent students from travelling around the country. On March 14, the Swedish government decided that any unnecessary travel would be banned. Unnecessary travel included visitor and tourist travel, but the Ministry of Foreign Affairs fought for important business travel, which was not banned. "Due to the widespread spread of the new coronavirus and the rapidly changing and uncertain situation that prevails for travelers, the Ministry of Foreign Affairs advises against unnecessary travel to all countries. In countries or areas where the Ministry of Foreign Affairs already advises against travel, these decisions apply," the Minister of Foreign Affairs wrote in a press release. This travel ban was updated numerous times during the summer and the list of countries it applies to is constantly changing.

> Sweden's strategy to keep large parts of society open is widely backed by the public. It has been devised by scientists and backed by government, and yet not all the country's virologists are convinced. There is no lockdown here. Photos have been shared around the world of bars with crammed outdoor seating and long queues for waterfront ice cream kiosks, and yet it is a myth that life here goes on "as normal". On the face of it little has shut down. But data suggests the vast majority of the population have taken to voluntary social distancing, which is the crux of Sweden's strategy to slow the spread of the virus. Usage of public transport has dropped significantly, large numbers are working from home, and most refrained from travelling over the Easter weekend. The government has also banned gatherings of more than 50 people and visits to elderly care homes. Around nine in ten Swedes say they keep at least a metre away from people at least some of the time, up from seven in ten a month ago, according to a major survey by polling firm Novus. (BBC 2020)

The Swedish government has, on the advice of the Swedish Public Health Agency, decided to ban public events and public gatherings with more than 50 participants and later on with more than 8 participants. These include demonstrations, lectures, theatre performances, sports competitions, dance performances, markets, and fairs (Folkhälsomyndigheten 2020b). During the spring of 2020, Swedes were told not to travel more than two hours from their homes (to stay close to their local hospital). This regulation was lifted in the early summer of 2020.

Due to Sweden's unique strategy to combat the coronavirus, Swedes have been banned from travelling to other countries, and inhabitants of these countries are not allowed to travel to Sweden without spending 14 days in quarantine upon their return. For some parts of Sweden this ban on foreign travellers has had a huge effect on tourism. The municipality of Åre has the highest proportion of employees in the tourism sector in Sweden at around 20 per cent and is known for having Northern Europe's largest ski resort. Other highly impacted municipalities are Strömstad with 10 per cent and Borgholm (on the island of Öland) with 9 per cent (Travelnews, 2020) of employees in the tourism sector. Strömstad, like Åre, is located close to the Norwegian border and is highly dependent on Norwegian visitors coming to Sweden to shop.

5.7 Methodology

This study was designed with a qualitative and interpretative approach. Data were collected during the period of June–August 2020 from 100 tourism firms in Sweden. The selection process was based on a strategic selection targeting different types of tourism firms in Sweden. Awareness of the struggle of certain segments within the tourism sector caused by restrictions led to them being selected. The research process followed certain steps. Firstly, the database www.allabolag.se was used. This website lists every limited firm in Sweden. It enables the selection of firms based on different criteria. The selection of firms was focused on three tourism segments: (1) Accommodation and Restaurants (AR),[1] (2) Culture and Entertainment (CE),[2] and (3) Travel agencies (TA).[3] The selected firms were categorised according to staff headcount. Small and medium-sized enterprises (SMEs) are defined by The European Commission (2020) based on staff headcount and turnover or balance sheet total (see Table 5.1):

SMEs represent 99 per cent of all businesses in the EU (European Commission 2020). Table 5.2 shows the tourism firms included in this study, divided into three different groups.

The mean turnover and employee figures for the different groups were the following: AR was SEK 79.6 million turnover and 69 employees, CE SEK 331 million turnover and 209.3 employees, and TA SEK 1.6748 billion turnover and 103.5 employees.

Table 5.1 Definitions of small and medium-sized enterprises (SMEs)

Firm category	Staff headcount	Turnover	(or) Balance sheet total
Medium-sized	< 250	≤ €50 m	≤ €43 m
Small	< 50	≤ €10 m	≤ €10 m
Micro	< 10	≤ €2 m	≤ €2 m

Source: Own creation

[1] Bransch: Hotell & Restaurang

[2] Bransch: Kultur, Nöje & Fritid

[3] Bransch: Resebyrå & Turism

Table 5.2 The studied tourism firms based on size

Firm category	Staff headcount	Turnover	Number of AR (based staff headcount)	Number of CE (based staff headcount)	Number of TA (based staff headcount)
Medium-sized	< 250	≤ €50 m	22	8	6
Small	< 50	≤ €10 m	17	1	1
Micro	< 10	≤ €2 m	29	8	8
Total number of studied firms from each group			68	17	15

Source: Own work

Table 5.3 Selection for the studied cases

	Total number limited firms in Sweden	Number of firms based on our selection criteria		Number of firms in the study
AR	36,740	15,407	88%	68%
CE	7671	1042	6%	17%
TA	3832	1088	6%	15%
		17,537	100%	N=100 100%

Source: Own work

The number of tourism firms in each sector in the study is approximately representative of the number of firms in each sector in Sweden; see Table 5.3:

Data for these firms were collected from the firms' annual reports through the website www.allabolag.se. Data were also collected through the firms' websites, social media, and Swedish television and newspaper articles. The results were categorised into the three different groups (Accommodation and Restaurants; Culture and Entertainment; and Travel Agency) and related to the themes of sustainability and value. The analysis is based on an interpretative approach.

5.8 Findings

The tourism firms included in the study have been hit hard financially by the pandemic and their economic sustainably value has been severally affected. During a pandemic, it becomes clear that economic sustainability becomes the top priority as firms struggle to survive. Regardless of type of tourism firm, the vast majority have struggled due to a major decrease in revenue. It has clearly been shown that the tourism industry does not have the financial sustainability required to cope with longer periods of no or greatly reduced income, and that the majority of firms do not have the buffer required to survive for longer than a short period without income. Tourism firms that are dependent on international tourists have been highly economically impacted by the coronavirus pandemic. For instance, AR40 has laid off all staff due to no events and no tourists visiting from Norway (SVT 2020f). Many countries have endured lockdowns but Sweden has avoided these; however, Sweden has had among the highest number of people per capita infected in the world. This has resulted in Sweden being seen as a country with a high rate of infection of the virus resulting in foreign tourists avoiding travelling to Sweden for summer holidays this year. In particular this can be clearly seen among Norwegian tourists who often visit Sweden to shop for products that have lower prices due to Sweden's tax system. This is also seen in restaurants such as AR14 and AR15 that usually have a high number of Norwegian tourists visiting them. The Norwegian government had initially forbidden Norwegians from travelling to Sweden but in the late summer of 2020 they allowed visits to some parts of Sweden, while visiting other parts resulted in mandatory self-isolation at home for ten days on their return. Since September 2020, the border has been closed to Sweden. The results of the study clearly show that economic sustainability is the foundation for these firms.

This loss of income leads to firms being forced to make employees redundant in order to survive. This means that the social sustainability value regarding the working environment is influenced and degraded. In the same way, tourism firms must use their resources carefully which means that environmental values decrease in priority. Some tourist firms think that the long-term effect of the pandemic could lead to a larger environmental concern. "*Will this create a new pattern of behaviour among business travelers who do not want to fly domestically or take high-speed trains when they get used to video meetings. We run video-conferences like many firms are doing right now. This week we have had training for all destination managers, 40 people in a video meeting using Microsoft Teams, it worked really well. As people get used to this, it could negatively affect the entire travel industry in the long run*" (Travelnews 2020c). This change in behaviour may lead to increased environmental concern and the possibility that environmental gains will exceed the advantages of travelling for business purposes.

Furthermore, below are the results from the three studied groups in the tourism industry: first, Accommodation and Restaurants, then Culture and Entertainment, and finally Travel Agencies.

5.8.1 Accommodation and Restaurants

The hotel and restaurant industry stands out as being particularly hard hit by the pandemic, with half of the firms in this category having lost more than 75 per cent of their revenue (The Swedish Agency for Economic and Regional Growth 2020). A total of 78 per cent of firms in the hotel and restaurant sector state that there is a risk of being forced to shut their doors. The corresponding figure in the service sector as a whole is 40 per cent. The hotel and conference industry has been the first part of the Swedish business community to be hard hit by the effects of the coronavirus pandemic. Comprehensive notice has already arrived in the hotel industry (Visita, 2020) with many hotels and restaurants now empty. Conferences have been cancelled along with concerts and other large events. The effects of this will be noticeable for a long time to come (Travelnews 2020b). The government limit of 50 people at gatherings has greatly influenced many tourism firms. The majority of events have been cancelled, which has influenced the firms participating in this study as people attending events often stay at accommodation providers and eat in restaurants in the area they were visiting for the event.

AR65's CEO does not deny that the coronavirus pandemic has made the situation very difficult for the hotel industry. Reducing the price of long-term housing is a way for hotels to earn income in order to retain their staff and survive this. For the entire industry, this is a huge challenge. It is important to adopt strategic change quickly and find new customers and opportunities (SVT 2020a). One example of strategic change is hotels offering staycations (AR, 92).

The hotel industry has been hit hard by the current pandemic. Travelling and, as a result, overnight stays have also fallen sharply. A hotel chain has chosen to close down their hotels in the region of Västernorrland (AR66-67). Heavy reductions in bookings and many cancellations due to the spread of COVID-19 are stated to be the reason. "*We have, like many others in our industry, unfortunately experienced an extreme fall in revenue during the last period due to the virus. We see that the support measures you can get are not enough and may be too late* (Swedish Director for the chain AR66-AR67)." The closure is considered necessary in order to save money that will help save the hotels in the long term. The affected hotels have 10 and 20 employees respectively and all employees have been notified of their redundancy. According to Swedish regulations, there is no other option other than to dismiss the staff. There will also be a loss of social sustainability since the hotels will lose a lot of experienced employees, and there is no guarantee that they will be available for rehiring if the hotels can open again after the pandemic (SVT 2020b).

There are no figures available yet on how the pandemic will ultimately affect the hotel industry. Some think that it will take a long time to get back on track as people are expected to avoid travelling until a vaccine is available. In April 2020, the number of guest nights in commercial accommodation in Sweden decreased by 69 per cent compared with the equivalent month in 2019. The share of foreign guest nights was down to 13 per cent, which was a decrease of 82 per cent from 2019, while Swedish guest nights lost 65 per cent during the month. Guest nights in Asia and North America plunged, with some markets ending up near zero (The Swedish Agency for Economic and Regional Growth 2020).

Another part of this group is commercial holiday parks that offer accommodation. Many camping sites in Sweden have had more Swedish tourists than previous years but less international tourists from Norway,

Germany, and Denmark, for example. The travel and hotel industries have suffered terrible losses since the pandemic started, but the number of bookings at holiday parks in Sweden has increased. "We are seeing an increased number of Swedish travellers and firms (AR68)." The Coronavirus outbreak has benefited camping chains as they have seen a 25 per cent increase on normal capacity. One example is guests who have moved from hotels to holiday parks as they feel safer. Holiday park cabins have their own entrance and it is easier to practise social distancing since you have your own toilet and kitchen and there is no interaction with other guests (SVT 2020d).

Another adjustment that many accommodation firms have introduced is free cancellation before arrival policies. Firms have recognised that during these times, it is important for guests to feel secure with their bookings and that they have as much flexibility as possible. Another strategic decision has been to offer long-term monthly stays at hotels (AR, 66).

Restaurants have suffered from the same problems as hotels with a huge reduction in guest numbers. Some municipalities offered their school students studying from home the opportunity to pick up a takeaway lunch from different restaurants in their neighbourhoods. This was a way for the municipalities to support students with a nutritious lunch that will certainly help when studying from home, while also supporting local restaurants, which risk losing large revenues due to the pandemic. Students have a personal QR code sent to their private mobile phone that can then be scanned at the restaurant when they pick up a lunch box (SVT 2020e).

Some food stores have started collaborations with restaurants during the pandemic. Instead of having their own salad bars, restaurants in the city have been selling their salads as takeaways. This is an example of social value being of importance. The food store does not make any earnings but the value is that customers see a social value of collaboration and support for other businesses in need (e.g. loss of all their customers). The coronavirus crisis has had major financial consequences on the restaurant industry. Restaurants are empty as more and more people choose to stay at home, so many of them now offer take-away options. On Facebook, local residents show their commitment by creating start-up groups with the aim of supporting local restaurants, cafes, and shops. Another adjustment that many restaurants have started with since the start of the pandemic is home delivery services. Many restaurants did not offer home delivery before the pandemic, but now customers can order their food to be delivered to their doorstep. This is adding value for customers who should not leave their homes but who still can get food and support local restaurants. "The commitment shown by our customers is enormous, many have changed their consumption habits and collect food now instead of eating out" (AR8).

5.8.2 Culture and Entertainment

Different tourism firms have experienced different problems as a result of the pandemic. Some of them are winter destinations while others are summer destinations, which influences how they have been affected. Ski resorts in Sweden closed for the season on Sunday April 5, 2020 (CE16), after being advised by the Public Health Authority to close due to the risk of overload in the health care system in the regions concerned. The decision meant that firms did not have any guests in their accommodation after the ski lifts closed (Skistar 2020). Skistar, which owns several large ski resorts, had no plans to close their ski resorts in the mountains. It was only after a conversation with the Director General of Public Health Johan Carlson that the firm heeded the "advice" to close its Swedish facilities, in an attempt to encourage people to stay home during the Easter break. "*The fewer people who move out of the cities, the less the risk of infection spreading*," says the Director General of Public Health (Expressen 2020) (https://www.expressen.se/dinapengar/konsument/ kritikstormmen-skistar-haller-oppet-in-i-det-sista/). This decision placed the major tourism firms in controversy. The local community did not want tourists coming since many of them would be travelling from larger cities situated many hours away. Social sustainability had an impact on the firm and divided the inhabitants for and against a closure of the ski resorts. This affected the social sustainability value of tourism firms.

Another example is amusement parks in Sweden. Due to the regulation of a maximum of 50 people being allowed to gather in one place, they are unable to open, as the economic sustainability of opening is not economically viable. This means that these parks have been closed for the entire summer season (CE 9, 11, 13, 14). Zoos in Sweden are not covered by the regulations for public gatherings and public events with the limit of 50 people and have focused on being responsible when being allowed to be opened. Some parts of zoos have been closed such as roller coasters and entertainment shows where people sit close together. Zoos have also limited the amount of people allowed into the park to enable responsible social distancing and have introduced new cleaning routines (CE17).

5.8.3 Travel Agencies

The Swedish Ministry for Foreign Affairs has advised against all non-essential travel outside Sweden. As a result, a number of airlines have temporarily suspended or reduced their number of flights to a large number of destinations (Swedavia 2020). During the summer, this has led to an increase in domestic tourism, which has had consequences. At times, there have been problems with car parking by major hiking trails due to a large number of Swedish tourists. Since the government clearly communicated that you should not travel unnecessarily, a lot of trips have been cancelled both in Sweden and internationally (TA4, TA8 and TA14). In addition, people have been fearful of becoming infected with the virus away from their home hospital.

In the early summer, the government changed travel recommendations from a maximum of two hours from home to unrestricted travel in Sweden, claiming that travel itself is not a big problem as long as people practise safe social distancing. Most of the travel agencies included in this study work primarily with international travel, which has made this a very difficult summer for them as the majority of international trips have been cancelled (TA4, TA8 and TA14). A few of the included travel agencies working with domestic travel have experienced increased revenues due to Swedes spending their holidays in Sweden (TA1 and TA9). Swedish tourist numbers have increased while foreign tourist numbers have decreased sharply.

The Swedish Agency for Economic and Regional Growth (2020) states that on May 11, 2020, Swedavia announced that the number of passengers using state-owned firm airports had decreased by 98 per cent in April 2020 when compared to April 2019. On April 14, IATA estimated that passenger revenue globally is expected to decrease by 55 per cent in 2020 compared with 2019, which corresponds to approximately 7.7 million jobs in the aviation industry. As a direct consequence, airports and other aviation-related activities have been greatly impacted. During this period, some airlines have filed for bankruptcy, while others have been bailed out by government crisis packages and ownership contributions. The travel ban has had a major positive effect on the environmental sustainability due to the vast decrease in emissions.

5.9 Conclusions

This study is a snapshot of tourism firms during the early stages of an ongoing pandemic. The results may look different when the pandemic has progressed and again when it is over. The primary conclusion drawn from this study is that it has been very hard to be a tourism firm during the coronavirus pandemic, which is an unprecedented, ongoing situation and we do not know how long it will last. It is interesting to see how sustainability as a value has been affected by the pandemic.

One conclusion is that economic sustainability value has been the key perspective for the studied cases, as their main focus has become economic survival. Normally, many consider that the three sustainability dimensions are equal. In this study, during a global pandemic, it has become clear that the focus has shifted to economic survival and social and environmental sustainability is being subordinated. Surviving financially becomes the basis for the tourism firms. The Swedish Agency for Economic and Regional Growth (2020) raised the point that with drastic declines in visitor numbers, there is a risk that destinations will move away from their ambitious sustainability strategies and instead start to invest in the simplest and cheapest possible way to attract guests. If this happens on a large scale, it will be a severe blow to all the years and hard work that have been invested into creating a more sustainable global tourism industry. If tourism firms run out of economic resources, it will affect their social sustainability value as people will lose their jobs. It will also affect their environmental sustainability as investments are reprioritised due to a lack of economic resources. This study's results show that tourism firms from different sectors have been affected differently by the pandemic. Some firms have made strategic decisions and tried to add value for their customers as well as attract new customers. Some firms have focused primarily on their core businesses, while others have been forced to adjust and find new business opportunities to create value for their customers. Many restaurants have also changed their focus from in-house dining to home deliveries. The results have shown that there has been a shift in how sustainability values are seen by tourism firms. One important conclusion is that firms with strong relationships with their customers have benefited as loyal customers have supported them, for example, by using their home delivery service.

This study has shown that tourism firms need to develop customised values during the corona pandemic. The values that are created are not the same as before the pandemic. Economic sustainability is a basic precondition for surviving when tourists are not allowed to travel as normal. Both tourist firms and tourists work together to capture values during the pandemic, firms have to adapt to the current situation through value configuration. It is not just making money but the long-term relationships become a key value. Swedish tourism firms have been affected by the pandemic and the conclusion is that the sustainability values are not equal. During this pandemic, the economic values are of key importance for the tourism firms to survive.

References

Aaker, D. A. (2010). *Building strong brands*. London: Simon & Schuster UK Ltd..

Agafonow, A. (2015). Value creation, value capture, and value devolution: Where do social enterprises stand? *Administration & Society, 47*(8), 1038–1060.

Alvarez, S. A., & Barney, J. B. (2004). Organizing rent generation and appropriation: Toward a theory of the entrepreneurial firm. *Journal of Business Venturing, 19*, 621–635. https://doi.org/10.1016/j.jbusvent.2003.09.002.

BBC. (2020). Retrieved September 20, 2020, from https://www.bbc.com/news/world-europe-52395866.

Bhattacharjee, A., Dana, J., & Baron, J. (2017). Anti-profit beliefs: How people neglect the societal benefits of profit. *Journal of Personality and Social Psychology, 113*(5), 671–696. https://doi.org/10.1037/pspa0000093.

Beritelli, P., Reinhold, S., & Laesser, C. (2014). Prozessorientierung im Destinationsmanagement (process orientation in destination management). *Marketing Review St. Gallen, 6*, 34–46.

Bowman, C., & Ambrosini, V. (2000). Value creation versus value capture: Towards a coherent definition of value in Strategy1. *British Journal of Management, 11*, 1–15. https://doi.org/10.1111/1467-8551.00147.

Brown, R. R., Farrelly, M. A., & Loorbach, D. A. (2013). Actors working the institutions in sustainability transitions: The case of Melbourne's stormwater management. *Global Environmental Change, 23*(4), 701–718.

Chathoth, P., Altinay, L., Harrington, R. J., Okumus, F., & Chan, E. S. (2013). Co-production versus co-creation: A process based continuum in the hotel service context. *International Journal of Hospitality Management, 32*, 11–20.

Cotterell, D., Hales, R., Arcodia, C., & Ferreira, J. A. (2019). Overcommitted to tourism and under committed to sustainability: The urgency of teaching "strong sustainability" in tourism courses. *Journal of Sustainable Tourism, 27*(7), 882–902.

Hart, O. (1989). An economist's perspective on the theory of the firm. *Columbia Law Review, 89*, 1757–1774. https://doi.org/10.2307/1122818.

Eletxigerra, A., Barrutia, J. M., & Echebarria, C. (2018). Place marketing examined through a service-dominant logic lens: A review. *Journal of Destination Marketing & Management, 9*, 72–84.

EU. (2020). Retrieved September 20, 2020, from https://ec.europa.eu/eurostat/statistics-explained/index.php/Tourism_statistics.

European Commission. (2020). Retrieved September 17, 2020, from https://ec.europa.eu/growth/smes/sme-definition_en.

Expressen. 2020. Retrieved September 20, 2020, from https://www.expressen.se/dinapengar/konsument/kritikstorm-men-skistar-haller-oppet-in-i-det-sista/.

Farzanegan, M. R., Gholipour, H. F., Feizi, M., Nunkoo, R., & Andargoli, A. E. (2020). International Tourism and Outbreak of Coronavirus (COVID-19): A Cross-Country Analysis. Journal of Travel Research, 0047287520931593.

FitzPatrick, M., Davey, J., Muller, L., & Davey, H. (2013). Value-creating assets in tourism management: Applying marketing's service-dominant logic in the hotel industry. *Tourism Management, 36*, 86–98.

Fjeldstad, Ø. D., & Ketels, C. H. (2006). Competitive advantage and the value network configuration: Making decisions at a Swedish life insurance company. *Long Range Planning, 39*(2), 109–131.
Folkhälsomyndigheten. (2020a). Retrieved September 20, 2020, from https://www.folkhalsomyndigheten.se/the-public-health-agency-of-sweden/.
Folkhälsomyndigheten. (2020b). Retrieved September 20, 2020, from https://www.folkhalsomyndigheten.se/smittskydd-beredskap/utbrott/aktuella-utbrott/covid-19/verksamheter/information-till-arrangorer-av-evenemang/.
Grönroos, C. (2017). On value and value creation in service: A management perspective. *Journal of Creating Value, 3*(2), 125–141.
Gulati, R., Nohria, N., & Zaheer, A. (2006). Strategic networks. In *Strategische Unternehmungsplanung—Strategische Unternehmungsführung* (pp. 293–309). Berlin, Heidelberg: Springer.
Gössling, S., Scott, D., & Hall, C. M. (2020). Pandemics, tourism and global change: A rapid assessment of COVID-19. *Journal of Sustainable Tourism, 1*, 1–20.
Hall, C. M. (2019). Constructing sustainable tourism development: The 2030 agenda and the managerial ecology of sustainable tourism. *Journal of Sustainable Tourism, 27*(7), 1044–1060.
Hoque, A., Shikha, F. A., Hasanat, M. W., Arif, I., & Hamid, A. B. A. (2020). The effect of coronavirus (COVID-19) in the tourism industry in China. *Asian Journal of Multidisciplinary Studies, 3*(1), 52–58.
Iniesta-Bonillo, M. A., Sánchez-Fernández, R., & Jiménez-Castillo, D. (2016). Sustainability, value, and satisfaction: Model testing and cross-validation in tourist destinations. *Journal of Business Research, 69*(11), 5002–5007.
Jacobides, M. G., Knudsen, T., & Augier, M. (2006). Benefiting from innovation: Value creation, value appropriation and the role of industry architectures. *Research Policy, 35*, 1200–1221. https://doi.org/10.1016/j.respol.2006.09.005.
James, S. D., Leiblein, M. J., & Lu, S. (2013). How firms capture value from their innovations. *Journal of Management, 39*(5), 1123–1155.
Kim, K., Park, J., & Kim, J. (2014). Consumer–brand relationship quality: When and how it helps brand extensions. *Journal of Business Research, 4*, 591–597.
King, D. R., & Slotegraaf, R. J. (2011). Industry implications of value creation and appropriation investment decisions. *Decision Sciences, 42*, 511–529. https://doi.org/10.1111/j.1540-5915.2011.00321.x.
Kotler, P., & Armstrong, G. (2010). *Principles of marketing*. London: Pearson Education.

Lacoste, S. (2016). Sustainable value co-creation in business networks. *Industrial Marketing Management, 52*, 151–162.
Lepak, P. D., Smith, G. K., & Taylor, S. M. (2007). Value creation and value capture: A multilevel perspective. *Academy of Management Review, 32*(1), 180–194. https://doi.org/10.5465/amr.2007.23464011.
Mizik, N., & Jacobson, R. (2003). Trading off between value creation and value appropriation: The financial implications of shifts in strategic emphasis. *JournalofMarketing,67*,63–76.https://doi.org/10.1509/jmkg.67.1.63.18595.
Mori, K., & Yamashita, T. (2015). Methodological framework of sustainability assessment in City sustainability index (CSI): A concept of constraint and maximisation indicators. *Habitat International, 45*, 10–14.
Osterwalder, A., Pigneur, Y., Bernarda, G., & Smith, A. (2015). *Value proposition design*. Frankfurt: Campus Verlag.
Osterwalder, A., Pigneur, Y., Bernarda, G., & Smith, A. (2014). *Value proposition design: How to create products and services customers want*. New Jersey: John Wiley & Sons.
Payne, A. F., Storbacka, K., & Frow, P. (2008). Managing the co-creation of value. *Journal of the academy of marketing science, 36*(1), 83–96.
Santos, F. M. (2012). A positive theory of social entrepreneurship. *Journal of Business Ethics, 111*, 335–351. https://doi.org/10.1007/s10551-012-1413-4.
Skistar. (2020). Retrieved September 20, 2020, from https://www.skistar.com/sv/myskistar/kundservicesupport/information-om-corona/sverige-corona/.
SVT. (2020a). Retrieved September 20, 2020, from https://www.svt.se/nyheter/lokalt/vast/prisvart-for-bostadssokande-att-bo-pa-lyxhotell.
SVT. (2020b). Retrieved September 20, 2020, from https://www.svt.se/nyheter/lokalt/vasternorrland/first-hotels-stanger-ner-hela-sommaren.
SVT. (2020d). Retrieved September 20, 2020, from https://www.svt.se/nyheter/lokalt/helsingborg/fler-valjer-camping-pa-hemmaplan.
SVT. (2020e). Retrieved September 20, 2020, from https://www.svt.se/nyheter/lokalt/blekinge/gymnasieelever-erbjuds-take-away-fran-restauranger.
SVT. (2020f). Retrieved December 11, 2020, from https://www.svt.se/nyheter/lokalt/jamtland/gamla-teatern-i-ostersund-varslar-samtliga-anstallda.
Swedavia. (2020). Retrieved September 20, 2020, from https://www.swedavia.com/arlanda/travel-information-related-to-the-coronavirus/?_ga=2.175563498.914296058.1590098837-225858067.1590098837.
The Swedish Agency for Economic and Regional Growth. (2020). Retrieved September 20, 2020, from https://tillvaxtverket.se/download/18.95c36ee173f23b8c3d159cf/1597752062988/MASTER%20Turism%20och%20

bes%C3%B6ksn%C3%A4ring%20efter%20Corona%20Rapport%20juni%202020_rev08_18.pdf.

Sörensson, A. (2011). Sustainable mass tourism: Fantasy or reality? *International Journal of Environmental, Cultural, Economic and Social Sustainability, 7*(5), 325–334.

Sörensson, A. (2014). *Can tourism be sustainable?: Service experiences from tourism destinations in Europe*. Åbo: Åbo Akademy University. Dissertation.

Sörensson, A., Bogren, M., & Schmudde, U. (2019). How do cities of different sizes in Europe work with sustainable development? *International Journal of Design & Nature and Ecodynamics, 14*(4), 287–298.

Sörensson, A., & Jansson, A. M. (2016). Sustainability reporting among Swedish tourism service providers: Information differences between them. *WIT Transactions on Ecology and the Environment, 201*, 103–113.

Travelnews. (2020b). Retrieved September 20, 2020, from https://www.travelnews.se/sverige/turism/har-drabbas-turismen-varst-av-corona/.

Travelnews. (2020c). Retrieved September 20, 2020, from https://www.travelnews.se/sverige/camping/campingen-kan-bli-en-vinnare-i-corona-epidemin/.

Vargo, S. L., & Lusch, R. F. (2004). Evolving to a new dominant logic for marketing. *Journal of marketing, 68*(1), 1–17.

Visita. (2020). https://visita.se/visitas-arbete-under-coronakrisen-covid-19/, accessed 2021-02-08

Wang, D., Li, X. R., & Li, Y. (2013). China's "smart tourism destination" initiative: A taste of the service-dominant logic. *Journal of Destination Marketing & Management, 2*(2), 59–61.

Wagner, S. M., Eggert, A., & Lindemann, E. (2010). Creating and appropriating value in collaborative relationships. *Journal of Business Research, 63*, 840–848. https://doi.org/10.1016/j.jbusres.2010.01.004.

Whittington, R., Regnér, P., Angwin, D., Johnson, G., & Scholes, K. (2020). Exploring Strategy: Text and Cases. Pearson Education Limited.

Wohlfart, U. (2002). Zur Geschichte interorganisatorischer Netzwerke. (History ofinter-organisationalnetworks).DIEZeitschriftfürErwachsenenbildung,1,39.

WHO. (2020). Retrieved September 20, 2020, from www.who.int.

6

Managing the COVID-19 Crisis. A Case Study of Entrepreneurship and Social Responsibility in Swedish SMEs

Besrat Tesfaye and Anders Lundström

6.1 Introduction

On March 11, 2020, the World Health Organization (WHO) declared the coronavirus disease (COVID-19) a pandemic. The outbreak, which originated in China, has spread rapidly across the world with devastating effects on societies. Governments have adopted various measures, including social distancing to mitigate its effects. Social distancing includes a wide range of restrictions: for example, self-isolation, physical distance to others, closing of schools, universities, community centers, prohibition of mass gatherings, and travel restrictions. Lockdown measures have been imposed in many countries.

B. Tesfaye (✉)
Södertörn University, Huddinge, Sweden
e-mail: Besrat.Tesfaye@sh.se

A. Lundström
Mid Sweden University, Östersund, Sweden

A. Sörensson et al. (eds.), *Corporate Responsibility and Sustainability during the Coronavirus Crisis*, Palgrave Studies in Governance, Leadership and Responsibility,
https://doi.org/10.1007/978-3-030-73847-1_6

The economic, social, and psychological impact of COVID-19 and the ensuing government response have had severe impact on global business but not equally distributed. Allowing for the spectrum of measures adopted by different governments, social distancing has a particularly shattering effect on small businesses (Fairlie 2020; Brown and Rocha 2020; Belghitar et al. 2020). Nonetheless, the effects of this unprecedented and unique global crisis on businesses vary widely across nations, regions, industries, and enterprises (Bapuji et al. 2020; Kraus et al. 2020). Some industries are thriving while others are waning. The understanding of and the responses to the COVID-19 crisis are also differential. Some businesses perceive the crisis as a threat to their survival. Others see opportunities for new solutions for their businesses and communities, for creativity and innovation. We daily witness how some enterprises are being pushed into liquidation and bankruptcy while others are struggling to maintain operational continuity. Yet others are repurposing their expertise and resources in order to meet a sudden upsurge in the demand for their products and services or adjust to the expectations of their stakeholders. In Sweden, for example, Absolut Vodka, Elite Hotels, and Essity are among the many companies that are repurposing their resources to deliver products and services to health care institutions such as hospitals and pharmacies or provide temporary homes for self-isolation (SvD, March 26, 2020). It is important to gain an understanding of the different ways in which the crisis affects specific industries and enterprises in order to make informed policy decisions.

In this context, more attention needs to be placed on entrepreneurship. Entrepreneurs can play a key role in generating new ideas and solutions to mitigate the impact of the pandemic and contribute to the efforts of communities to survive and recover from the crisis (Haeffele et al. 2020). In particular, more focus needs to be placed on small and medium-sized enterprises (SMEs), that is, businesses with less than 250 employees. SMEs are a source of innovation and entrepreneurship, new jobs, competitiveness, economic growth, and societal welfare in general (OECD 2019; EU Commission 2018; Gray 2004). Moreover, in sheer numbers, SMEs are the dominant form of enterprises and account for a higher proportion of employment and production of goods and services. According to the OECD (2019), SMEs constitute about 99 percent of all enterprises in the member countries and account for 50–60 percent of the value added. More than 65 percent of the labor force are employed in the SME sector. Furthermore, SMEs constitute a vehicle of innovation and entrepreneurship and contribute to the identity and cohesion of the communities in which they are embedded (OECD 2019). They play a key role in community welfare by providing needed goods and services, sustaining social networks, and in generating ideas and solutions to communities (Haeffele et al. 2020). The role of SMEs as a source of entrepreneurship and economic growth, job generation, competitiveness, and societal welfare in general is well acknowledged (EU Commission 2018).

Nevertheless, it is important to note that SMEs are highly heterogeneous, for example, in terms of entrepreneurial orientation, technology, age, size, industry, economy, and location. Furthermore, the majority of SMEs is very small. In Sweden, which is a member of the OECD for example, 96 percent of all 1.2 million enterprises have less than 10 employees (Swedish Agency for Economic and Regional Growth, 2010). A global pandemic can place many SMEs in a highly vulnerable position. Consequently, there is a growing concern that SMEs may not be getting the attention and support they desperately need (Belghitar et al. 2020).

Preliminary reports indicate that the concern for the situation of SMEs during the pandemic is legitimate. In a study of the impact of COVID-19 on SMEs in the US reported in the middle of April 2020, about 40 percent of the approximately 5000 enterprises in the sample had temporarily closed due to the crisis. Active employment had been reduced by 39 percent (Bartik et al. 2020; Cowling et al. 2020; Belghitar et al. 2020). Although the study indicated that most business were highly financially fragile, it indicated that the impact of the crisis varied widely across states, regions, and industries. Likewise, in a survey of European SMEs, 40 percent of the enterprises reported liquidity problems. Among those in the most affected areas including hospitality, retail, and construction, the figure was 50 percent (SMEsUnited, 2020).

Business organizations may be exposed to various types of crisis caused by internal or external events, such as the loss of key employees, conflicts, neighborhood riots, and natural disasters, for example, earthquakes or tsunamis (Doern 2016). However, the ongoing COVID-19 crisis is unique in many respects (Bapuji et al. 2020; Kraus et al. 2020; Juergensen et al. 2020; Kuckertz et al. 2020). The speed at which the pandemic is spreading globally, the many ambiguities surrounding the disease itself including its persistence, and its impact on the relationship between business and society pose unique challenges to businesses, particularly SMEs. The fact that the most natural practices of human interactions such as a handshake become a significant risk (Bapuji et al. 2020) underscores the unique challenges faced by SMEs, which are dependent on social interactions and personal networks. Against the background of the socio-economic importance, and the vulnerability of SMEs, it is important to understand how SMEs manage crises in the context of a unique COVID-19 pandemic.

How entrepreneurs perceive and respond to this crisis as it evolves is likely to be highly heterogeneous. From a study of the early months of onslaught of the COVID-19 pandemic, Wenzel et al. (2020) indicate that SMEs respond to the crisis in one of four strategic ways: retrenchment, perseverance, innovation, and exit. The study does not elaborate on the types of SMEs adopting the respective strategy or the output of the strategic choices of SME managers. There is little research to provide information about the perceptions, responses, outcomes, and expectations of SMEs during the crisis (Doern et al. 2019; Williams et al. 2017; Doern 2016; Herbane 2010). The existing research is based on experiences of crises that differ from the present crisis in almost all respects. In particular, the global character, scope, and duration of the crisis pose unique challenges to business and society: How smaller businesses are experiencing the COVID-19 crisis, how they are impacted by the pandemic, how they are responding to the crisis, how they are participating in the struggle to mitigate the impact of the crisis on society.

This study draws attention to this gap in research, for example: how do managers of SMEs perceive the crisis? What are the major economic, social, and psychological challenges faced by SMEs? How do the managers respond to these challenges? What practical measures (activities) do the managers undertake? Does the crisis influence their views and involvement in socially responsible activities? What are the short-term outcomes of their responses and measures taken? By putting the spotlight on the experiences, strategies, and managerial practices of Swedish SMEs' managers to mitigate the economic and social challenges posed by the ongoing COVID-19 crisis, the study hopes to bring these burning issues to the forefront. The study presented in this chapter focuses on only three main issues: (i) How do entrepreneurs, that is, the owner-managers of different SMEs, perceive the threat from the crisis? (ii) How do they respond to these threats? (iii) What are the outcomes and implications of their responses? The target group in the study is entrepreneurial SMEs, which refers to businesses that are in the startup phase and those that are pursuing new business opportunities in the wake of the pandemic. The aim is to gain some insight into SME managers' experiences of the COVID-19 crisis and identify the strategies and practices they employ in response to the challenges faced by their businesses and communities.

The remaining parts of the chapter are organized as follows. In the next section, the theories and findings of prior research are summarized. Then, the research strategy and data collection techniques are described. This is followed by a case study presentation and analysis. The findings of the study are discussed and commented on in the concluding section.

6.2 Entrepreneurship and Social Responsibility in SMEs in the Context of Crisis

Entrepreneurship is conceptualized in various ways and approached from different perspectives, for example, as an economic function, as an occupation, and as a structural phenomenon. Entrepreneurship as an economic function has been characterized in a multiplicity of ways, for example, judgmental decision making under uncertainty (Knight 1921), the introduction of an innovation (Schumpeter 1934), and alertness and opportunity recognition (Kirzner 2009; Shane and Venkataraman 2000). Entrepreneurship as an occupation is defined in terms of self-employment. Thus, the focus is on the attributes of self-employed individuals, for example, those who own and operate their own businesses (Kihlstrom and Laffont 1979). The structural approach relates entrepreneurship to the entry of entrepreneurial firms defined as new and small firms. The focus in this strand of research is on firm growth and industrial dynamics

(Aldrich 1990; Acs and Audretsch 1990). Furthermore, entrepreneurship in terms of new business creation is considered temporal, often extending over a few years before and after startup (Lundström and Stevenson 2005; Reynolds et al. 2001). Established companies do engage in entrepreneurial activities, which in some cases result in new corporate ventures or in strategic changes such as organizational rejuvenation and business model renewal (Covin and Kuratko, 2010). Examples of entrepreneurship in established businesses in line with this definition are found among the cases presented.

In this study, entrepreneurship is perceived as the process of opportunity recognition and exploitation (Shane and Venkataraman 2000). An entrepreneur is defined as the owner/manager of a small business in a startup phase or in the process of strategic renewal such as the pursuit of new markets, the expansion or extension of existing business areas, or the readjustment of the business model (Covin and Miles 1999). Opportunities may be discovered, created, or imagined (Klein 2008). Alvarez and Barney (2007) suggest that the opportunity discovery mode is related to entrepreneurial responses to exogenous shocks (crises) which involve assessing risks, crafting strategies, and procuring resources.

The response of SMEs may be related to strategies and managerial practices concerned with challenges that are specific to the businesses they operate, and/or those that relate to the communities in which they are located. Small enterprises have a symbiotic relationship with the communities in which they operate and they engage in socially responsible activities (CSR). However, the practice of socially responsible activities tends to be invisible. Lee et al. (2015) suggest that SMEs do not communicate their involvement in CSR. Others argue that CSR in the context of SMEs differs from that of large firms whereas the theories are based on the experiences of large firms (Spence and Rutherfoord 2003).

Therefore, extant theories may not be adequate in explaining CSR in the context of SMEs (Perrini 2006; Jenkins 2006; Spence and Rutherfoord 2003). Jenkins (2006), for example, contends that SMEs tend to consider socially responsible activities as an integral part of the way they manage themselves rather than as external add-ons. Santos (2011) reported that CSR in SMEs is informal and unstructured. SMEs' practices were also found to differ in that they prioritize CSR activities that are simple, cheap, visible, and commonly situated in the local communities in which they operate (Santos 2011). CSR activities may be aimed at an audience that is external to the organization such as sponsorship or target internal audiences, for example, the work environment (Hawn and Ioannou 2016). Some CSR activities may be targeting both external and internal audiences simultaneously. There is very little prior research on CSR in SMEs during crises but some promising work on the experiences of the COVID-19 crisis is emerging. Popovka et al. (2020) argue that the transition of entrepreneurship to remote forms of activities, which implies an online provision of goods and services, and the creation of remote employment of workers is a clear manifestation of social responsibility. This suggests that in the context of a crisis, boundaries dividing activities that relate to entrepreneurship and those concerned with the practice of social responsibility in SMEs are indistinct. The question is whether this situation is applicable to crisis management in the context of SMEs in general or specific to experiences from COVID-19.

6.3 Crisis Management and Entrepreneurship

The concept of crisis may refer to varying situations and phenomena such as disasters, emergencies, different types of contingencies, and catastrophes. However, the definitions share some specific aspects of the phenomena: crises are extreme, unexpected, unpredictable, challenging, and require an urgent response (Doern et al. 2019; Herbane 2010; Pearson and Clair 1998). Pearson and Clair (in Doern et al. 2019, p. 3), for example, define crisis in an organizational context as "a low-probability, high-impact situation that is perceived by critical stakeholders to threaten the viability of the organization". Others argue that even mundane events can culminate into a crisis and propose a process-based definition that captures the dynamic which is lacking in Pearson and Clair (Williams et al. 2017). A crisis has been categorized from its magnitude as major or minor, its location as internal or external, and its nature as techno-economic or people centric, which can relate to individuals, organizations, or communities (Mitroff and Shrivastava 1988). An example of a techno-economic crisis can be an industrial accident while a people-centric crisis may be caused by a disease such as the coronavirus. Research tends to be more focused on the impact of economically oriented major, external crises, and natural disasters (Williams and Vorley 2014; Smallbone et al. 2012; Monllor and Murphy 2017; Grube and Storr 2018). The effect of crises induced by people has received less attention (Doern et al. 2019; Doern 2016). Yet people-centric crises with a severe impact on social life and the economy are becoming more frequent and global. The AIDS pandemic from 1981 that has caused more than 250 million deaths, the AVIAN flu from 2009, and the most current COVID-19 are examples of ongoing people-centric crises (Baldwin and Weder di Mauro 2020).

Empirical research based on the experiences of people-centric crises is primarily focused on large organizations (Williams et al. 2017). There is a dearth of research on people-centric crises in the context of SMEs (Williams et al. 2017; Herbane 2010). Herbane, for example, observes that no articles on crisis management in SMEs have been published in the journals dedicated to entrepreneurship and smaller enterprises. However, there are a few exceptions in extant literature (Williams and Shepherd 2016; Williams and Vorley 2014; Smallbone et al. 2012; Runyan 2006). This stream of research is primarily concerned with the pre-crisis periods, resources possessed by the entrepreneurs, and the small enterprises' capability to withstand a crisis (Korber and McNaughton, 2017) in Doern et al. (2019). Less is known about the perceptions, strategies, and management practices of entrepreneurs in response to crises and their inter-relatedness. Moreover, experiences of a global crisis of the magnitude of the present pandemic are uncommon despite a rapidly growing literature on the subject (Kraus et al. 2020; Brown and Rocha 2020; Bartik et al. 2020; Fairlie 2020; Belghitar et al. 2020; Eggers, 2020; Haeffele et al. 2020; Kuckertz et al. 2020; Juergensen et al. 2020; Thorgren and Williams 2020; Donthu and Gustafsson 2020).

A cursory review shows that many SMEs are severely affected and that government support may not be reaching those most in need (Fairlie 2020; Juergensen et al. 2020). Nevertheless, the impact of the crisis is not only negative; it may also create opportunities for innovation and growth (Kraus et al. 2020; Wenzel et al. 2020). A study by Faulkner (2001) supports this view. Kraus et al. (2020) studied the experiences of the management of the corona crisis in the context of family businesses in five European countries and identified five overarching strategies: safeguarding liquidity, operations, communication, renewal of business models, and cultural changes. These findings imply that SMEs can experience both threats, for example, liquidity and disruption in communication, but also opportunities for cultural change. In terms of cultural change, they observed a stronger social cohesion and solidarity in spite of an increased digitalization of the businesses.

Thorgren and Williams (2020) illustrate how SMEs attempt to ward off the crisis by halting investments, by reducing costs and expenses, and by renegotiating contracts. From a review of literature on crisis management during COVID-19, Wenzel, et al. (2020, p. v9-v12) have identified four strategic choices that SME managers tend to employ in managing the crisis. The most common strategy is retrenchment. This strategic response implies that the company attempts to resist and survive a crisis by "shrinking" the scope of the business, for example, through cost reduction (Pearce II & Robbins, 1993, p. 614). Some SMEs adopt a persevering strategy, which implies that firms focus on measures that mitigate the effect of the crisis in order to maintain the firm's pre-crisis status quo. An example of such measures can be to allow employees to work from home in order to minimize absenteeism and decreased productivity. Others choose innovation as a crisis management strategy. This strategy involves reallocating resources in order to exploit opportunities brought about by the crisis (Reymen et al. 2015). This strategic renewal may include the transformation of the business strategy, reorganization, adjustment of a business model, and/or adjustment of the target market (Covin and Kuratko, 2010). Through strategic renewal, a business can transform itself in relation to its existing resources or the industry (Covin and Miles 1999). An example of innovation as a strategic response can be repurposing resources in order to meet a growing demand for a product on the market or from society. Exit implies the discontinuation of a firm in response to a crisis but is not considered in this study. This framework is used in structuring the strategic responses of the cases in this study. In the following section, the research design and the data collection processes are briefly discussed.

6.4 Research Design

The research design is a multiple case study (Yin 2003). Departing from prior research and using its findings, we conducted interviews with owner-managers of small entrepreneurial businesses in different sectors in Stockholm. The interviews were conducted in the last weeks of July up to mid-August. The recommendations for social distancing were observed in conducting the interviews. The case study method is a well-established strategy that has been widely applied in crisis management as well as small business research (Kraus et al. 2020; Herbane 2010; Yin 2003; Eisenhardt 1989). By employing a qualitative approach, we were able to make in-depth interviews that enabled us to get an insight into the entrepreneurs' perceptions, experiences, and decisions during the crisis. This approach was particularly useful in understanding the shifts in their perceptions, experiences, and decisions as the crisis evolved. The impact of COVID-19 on SMEs as well as their responses tend to vary widely (Juergensen et al. 2020). Multiple cases can be used to illustrate these variations and compare possible patterns (Yin 2003). The multiple case design enabled us to compare individual cases as well as sub-groups, for example, along market orientation, industry, size, or age of their businesses for similarities and differences. In doing so, we can illustrate the nature of differential perceptions, impacts, and responses.

A purposive sampling technique was employed in selecting the cases. Seven small enterprises were identified through referral and Google search. Three of the cases are startup enterprises that are oriented toward international markets, while three of the remaining four enterprises serve the local/domestic market. The seventh case is established on the local/domestic as well as the international market. All cases are share companies but vary in resource endowments, size, age, product/service, market, and industry. The interviews were conducted with the entrepreneurs, that is, owner-managers or managers of SME using an unstructured interview guide. The themes of the interview included: (i) pre-COVID-19 status and strategies of their businesses, (ii) their perceptions of the COVID-19 onslaught, (iii) their initial reactions and measures undertaken, (iv) strategies and practices to mitigate the impact and/or exploit opportunities, (v) their views on government support, (vi) their involvement in socially responsible causes, and (vii) their future outlook. A zoom video link was used and the conversations were recorded with the permission of the respondents. The interviews were conducted in Swedish and later translated into English by the authors. Quality aspects such as construct reliability and validity were considered in designing the case study (Yin 2003). Both within-case and cross-case comparisons have been conducted in analyzing the cases. Further, the indications from data from varying sources have been triangulated for convergence and divergence. The following section presents a brief case presentation followed by a detailed analysis of the data on the crisis management practices of the case companies.

6.5 The Case Study

The results of the case study are presented in two steps. First, the case companies are described in terms of age, size, and industry and main businesses. This is followed by a presentation and discussion of the experiences, views, and the future outlook of the respondents regarding various aspects of coping with the crisis (the main themes of the discussion are presented in the section on Research Design).

6.5.1 Demographic Description of the Case Companies

As stated in the preceding section, the cases are all different in almost all respects. Three of the cases share some common attributes in terms of their backgrounds in academic R&D, product innovation, orientation toward an international market, and stage of development. A common denominator for the remaining four businesses is perhaps the dominance of service in their offerings (Table 6.1). In two of the cases, staffing services are offered but to two different markets. Excluding the oldest case (registered 1994), the businesses are relatively young, one of which is still in its startup phase. In terms of size, five of the cases can be categorized as micro-firms (less than ten employees), while two of them are small

Table 6.1 Profile of the businesses of the cases

Case no.	Product/industry/ market	Year of registration	Size		Respondent
			Employees	Turnover	
C1	-product & R&D services -biotechnology -international market	2008	5	2.4 million	Co-owner CEO
C2	-product; R&D -medical technology -international market	2016	8	6.65 million	Co-owner CEO
C3	-product; R&D -diagnostic -international market	2017	10	5 million	Co-owner CEO
C4[a]	-transport services; recruitment/ staffing services; consultancy -transport and freight traffic sector -domestic/ Local market	2012	25	25.6 million	CEO
C5	-lighting products and services -wholesale -domestic market	2010	4	1.9 million	Founder-owner, CEO
C6	-staffing services -health care sector -domestic market	2014	6	7 million	CEO
C7	-trade in metals -alloying services -metallurgy -domestic & international market	1994	19	408 million	Co-owner, CEO

[a]The company consists of a coalition of three independent enterprises offering complementary services. Source: Own work

enterprises, one of which has the turnover of a medium-size business (OECD 2019). The turnover per employee also varies from 0.5 million up to over 20 million in one extreme case.

6.5.2 The Respondents, their Perceptions, Responses, Strategies, and Expectations

The respondents were six men and one woman. Two of them occupied a managerial post only (but had a significant investment in the company), while the remaining five were in co-owner-manager or owner-manager positions. Six of the seven respondents hold at least a university degree and all have several years of previous experience as employees in the industry. Five of them had families. Three are aged above 50. In spite of the disparities of the cases, their stories with regard to COVID-19 share many similarities. We use excerpts and direct quotes from the interviews to illustrate their views and arguments. The individual cases are briefly described in the following section.

6.5.3 Case C1

C1 is a new technology-based startup company in the area of medical technology with roots in academic research. The company was founded in 2008 by a research team at a university but its operations are still dominated by R&D activities. However, there are mature plans and steps to bring the product to the international market. It is financed by R&D resources and equity capital through business angels as well as private and state-owned venture capital firms. The target market includes medical technology companies, hospitals, and private practitioners. The founding team is still involved in the company but has recruited an external manager with experiences of international markets for innovations in the industry. At the outbreak of the pandemic, final tests to validate the product were being conducted in a laboratory located in another country. Preparations for an international launch of the business were well underway.

The entrepreneur did not initially consider the outbreak as a threat. He believed it to be yet another virus disease, some type of influenza that would likely pass soon. Reports of the rapid spread and increasing death tolls continued and the situation became highly worrisome. Soon after the outbreak, the company was hit hard by the travel restrictions at home and the lockdown in partner countries. These measures implied that their laboratory tests as well as their plans for marketing at international conferences and fairs were canceled. Social distancing and the fear and anxiety that accompanied it further aggravated the situation. "…*The COVID-19 pandemic has implied that the laboratories for tests are closed and potential customers are in crisis. We cannot market the product unless verified by those tests. Everything has slowed down to a standstill. We had no choice but to lay off staff. The rest work from home. The pandemic affects everything. It is a difficult situation for startup companies that need capital. It is difficult to attract financial capital. On the social side, digital meetings can work but we feel isolated. Something must happen soon!*" (CEO).

6.5.4 Case C2

The company was founded in 2015 by a team of researchers and professionals with a background in the industry. The product is based on an innovation developed by researchers in the area of 3D printing. This new technology has attracted external equity capital, but the majority of shares are still owned by the founders. The present manager was recruited to establish the company on international markets. The primary market for 3D printing technology is large industrial firms in various sectors such as producers of household appliances, energy, pulp and paper, and airplane manufacturing.

The COVID-19 outbreak was not initially felt as a serious threat. But it soon became clear that the situation may develop into a crisis. Government measures to mitigate the rapid spreading such as social distancing, travel restrictions, and lockdowns implied that the startup process was brought to a halt. "…*The immediate impact of the COVID-19 was on our marketing since all international platforms such as conferences and trade fairs were cancelled. All planned visits to customers were also cancelled. At present we work from home but we are a small team and the social isolation this implies is hard. I believe that our behaviors will change. Some of the changes are likely to have a positive impact in a longer perspective*" (CEO).

6.5.5 Case C3

The company has its roots in academic research at a university. It was founded in 2017 by a team of researchers in Life Sciences. It is owned by the founders and a number of equity capital investors. The company is run by a professional manager who was recruited externally. The target market of the company is public and private institutions such as hospitals and laboratories in life sciences. The company has not yet been seriously affected by the onslaught of the pandemic. "*...None of our employees have become affected and we have all been able to work from home. We have not experienced any difficulties. We continue to conduct most of our business digitally and by regular mail. We send our products to our customers by regular mail and our customers send us orders or requests or questions*" (CEO).

6.5.6 Case C4

The company has existed in the transport sector since 2012. It was started by a married couple who still own the company. Recently the company joined two other independent businesses to build a self-sufficient delivery service to meet a rapidly growing demand in the wake of the pandemic. Together the group provides services in the areas of road transport, freight traffic, transport consultancy, and staffing. The management did not have plans for any sudden change in the business environment. However, they perceived the rapid growth in demand for delivery and courier services, particularly in the private sector, and acted upon the opportunity to expand their business. They were able to collaborate with other small firms with complementary services and succeeded in building up a capacity that enabled them to benefit from the growing market. The manager believes that the market will continue to grow as online shopping by both businesses and private households is becoming a common practice.

> "*...We had not planned for a crisis. We should have had a cash buffer but we did not. This pandemic has taught us the importance of planning for a crisis, but perhaps more important it has taught us to be alert to changes in the business environment*" (CEO).

The company emphasizes the importance of socially responsible business practices and makes concrete efforts.

6.5.7 Case C5

The company was founded in 2014 by two professionals in health care. It offers staffing services to the health care sector, primarily hospitals and elderly care centers. It is specialized in professionals such as doctors and nurses (consultants) that work on contractual assignments, or want temporary or part-time jobs. The company has been growing rapidly since 2017. In the wake of the COVID-19, the demand for its services increased very rapidly. At the same time, this opportunity exposed businesses in this sector to increased competition because the supply of qualified health care professionals has not increased in proportion to the demand. This was coupled with growing health concerns, fear, and anxiety among employees. However, the concerns of the office staff and the consultants (health care professionals such as nurses and doctors) are different. The consultants were more troubled by the lack of information from customers about their policies, directives, and routines regarding work during COVID-19 whereas office workers were more concerned about the risk of infection. The management decided to immediately reorganize so that office employees could work from home and improve the consultants' access to information online in real time. "*…We understood at an early stage that technical accessibility is not the only competitive edge for business in this sector during this crisis. It is important to understand the psychology of the crisis, everybody is affected. With office workers, we talk a lot about the situation and how each of us feels about it. We are a small team and can understand and support each other. We had a continued dialog with our consultants and also our customers. They also need our support. Health care workers come to us and tell us that they want to work with COVID-19 patients and we have to understand and help them get there. Others want to work but are afraid of the disease and worried about the situation and we need to understand and support them too*" (CEO).

6.5.8 Case C6

The company was founded by the present manager who is driven by a personal commitment to environmentally friendly recycling businesses. It is owned by the founder and external investors. The business idea is to recycle discarded flat-screen hardware into a cheap and easily maintained lighting system. The company offers a service consisting of hardware, technology, and maintenance of a lighting system for large properties such as offices, schools, and community centers. It is still in its startup phase but has just managed to win a large municipal procurement. The primary customers are real estate companies, public sector authorities such as municipalities, and businesses occupying large office spaces and/or other facilities with high lighting costs. The organization is decentralized by outsourcing parts of the activities such as manufacturing.

The founder/manager perceives a potential in the rapid digitalization and home-based work ensuing the outbreak of the COVID-19. He assumes that the amount of empty office space will increase and the costs of lighting will be an important issue for all stakeholders. "*…This situation is likely to put the spotlight on our technology and services. We do not worry about the business. We had no cash buffer for a crisis and to abandon a planned financing scheme. The first challenge we faced was that of supply. But we have managed to complete our projects despite the difficulties we faced in terms of the supply chain. In addition, we were able to secure a procurement during COVID-19. We are hoping that this contract will catch the attention of other customers. We are very flexible and can adapt to new conditions very quickly. We are used to digitalization and have easily been able to adapt to the new working conditions. We have not made many more changes*" (CEO).

6.5.9 Case C7

This is a family business that was founded in 1994. In recent years, the founder has retired and the leadership has been transferred to a new generation in the family. The company's business includes three areas: sales of metal bars to investors, the supply of precious metals and machinery to goldsmiths, other manufacturers such as the telecom, and recycling and sales of metal refuse.

The management did not perceive the situation as serious at the initial stages of the outbreak of the pandemic. However, they soon noticed that many customers were facing problems and the situation was becoming serious. "… *We called the Company Board to a meeting to discuss the situation. Normally in this industry, prices go up during an economic crisis. This time too, the industry was doing quite well, especially in the areas of investment bars and metal refuse. The scary part was how to deal with customers/suppliers, and especially our employees*" (CEO). Another challenge was the increasing amount of metal refuse that was being offered for recycling. "…*Many manufacturers were looking into their business to locate resources that may generate value. Refuse is such a resource*" (CEO).

The company had to rapidly build up a capacity to meet the growing volume of metal refuse supplied by customers who needed their business to survive. Thus, the management decided to employee additional personnel and expand the recycling business. This was highly profitable because of the increase in the prices of metals: "…*investments in metals continue to escalate and the recycling business is the largest and most profitable at the moment. We have the good luck of an increasing supply of metal refuse combined with high prices of the processed products*" (CEO).

The findings of the case study on the perceptions, strategies, and managerial practices are summarized and discussed in the following. First, we focus on perceptions, strategies, and managerial practices specifically concerned with the challenges faced by the business. Second, we follow this with a corresponding analysis of the cases with regard to the companies' management of social responsibility during this pandemic.

6.5.10 Summary

The brief description of the cases shows that the managers of SMEs perceive the COVID-19 crisis in different ways (Table 6.2). One group perceives the crisis as a threat (C1 and C2), another group perceives new opportunities for the business (C4–7), while a third group observes neither threats nor opportunities (C3).

The group that perceives the COVID-19 crisis as a threat has similar backgrounds and shares a number of attributes: (a) lacks plans for a crisis,

Table 6.2 Perceptions of and experienced impacts

	Perception of the case Entrepreneurs		
Cases	Threat	Opportunity	Impact of COVID-19 on the businesses
C1	✓		*-disruption in operations* *-Canceled investment (capital acquisition)* *-disruption in networking* *-increased risk of loss of customers and markets* *-fall in productivity* *-social isolation— Dissatisfaction at work*
C2	✓		*-disruption in operation* *-disruption in international networking* *-fall in productivity* *-social isolation* *-uncertainty about the future*
C3	Neutral		*No impact reported*
C4		✓	*-increase in demand for transport services* *-opportunity for business expansion/growth* *-increased need for capital and human resources* *-increased risk to employee health and safety*
C5		✓	*-increased demand for the services of the company* *-increased competition in the sector* *-increased risk for employees' health* *-increased uncertainty about work environment conditions*
C6		✓	*-increased financial stress* *-opportunity/potential for increased demand and market expansion* *-increased risk of a supply chain breakdown*
C7		✓	*-rapid increase in the prices of products/ services* *-rapid increase in the demand for products/ services in some areas of the business* *-need for reallocation of resources* *-need for investments in capacity* *-risk for employees' health and safety*

Source: Own work

(b) has neither a buffer nor cash flow, (c) heavy investments in product research and development (R&D), (d) depends on access to international markets, (e) in need of financial capital, and (f) in the process of launching a new product. As a result, these businesses are unable to adapt to the crisis situation. However, the impact of the crisis on the respective business and their future outlook differs. One of the cases considers the impact of the crisis as manageable, and another considers it as a threat to survival.

The cases that perceive opportunities rather than threats (C4, C5, C6, and C7) have different backgrounds and operate in varying sectors. However, they exhibit some common characteristics: for example, (a) operate on the domestic market, (b) are in industries that are already thriving during the crisis or have the potential for growth in the wake of the pandemic, (c) are alert to opportunities, and (d) have the capacity to rapidly adapt to changes. They managed to repurpose and relocate their resources, collaborate with others, and/or initiate new networks. Although these companies are located in industries that are favorably impacted by the pandemic, their entrepreneurial behavior makes them interesting. The discovery and exploitation of opportunities require an alertness and willingness to take risks as well as flexibility.

The company constituting the third "group" (C3) shares many attributes with C1 and C2 but perceives neither threats nor opportunities and anticipates no major changes in its business environment. The company's operations are already digitalized and its business is not jeopardized by the travel restrictions imposed by governments.

The perceptions are not always objective. Therefore, it is important to relate these to actual conditions. Table 6.2 summarizes the perceptions of the entrepreneurs and the actual impact of the COVID-19 crisis that they have experienced during the first six months.

Entrepreneurs may perceive the crisis as a threat or an opportunity. However, the impact is not dichotomous. There can be opportunities in a situation that is perceived as a threat. C2, for example, perceives digitalization as a positive development that will benefit the businesses. On the other hand, in pursuing opportunities, companies face many challenges and risks. Moreover, entrepreneurial perceptions are not always "rational" but perceptions are important because these guide the strategic choices

Table 6.3 Strategic responses and managerial practices in the SME

Cases	Strategic response	Management practice
C1, C2	Retrenchment	-cost reduction -digital network capacity building
C3	Perseverance	-"business as usual" -digitalization
C4, C5, C6, C7	Innovation	-organizational renewal/change -business model adjustment -supply chain adjustment -new products/new offerings

Source: Own work

and practices in managing the crisis. Entrepreneurs who perceive the crisis as a threat are likely to engage in strategies that reduce the level of threat to their businesses. Those who perceive opportunities in a crisis and act upon them (C4–C7) do, at the same time, face new challenges such as competition, financial stress, and the risk of failure. Entrepreneurs who see neither threats nor opportunities are not exempted from the impacts of the crisis. In perspective these may need to find strategies to mitigate the impact of the crisis on their operations. The different strategies employed by the cases are discussed in the following section.

6.5.11 COVID-19 Responses and Management Practices of SMEs

The strategic responses of the cases to the pandemic are affected by several factors including the entrepreneur's perceptions, the severity of the crisis, firm-specific aspects, changes in the industry and the business environment, as well as entrepreneurial capacity. The actual capacity of the business to resist an onslaught of a pandemic impacts on the strategic response. Factors such as the phase of development, products/markets, liquidity, and resource dependency may limit the room for maneuver. For example, companies at the startup phase which are illustrated by cases C1 and C2 are highly vulnerable and have limited strategic options. Moreover, strategies and practices may change over time and depending on the intensity and duration of the ongoing crisis. However, having said that, the strategic responses to the initial phases of the crisis (March–August, 2020) can be related to three main strategies: retrenchment, perseverance, and innovation. A brief description and the arguments forwarded by the entrepreneurs follow.

Retrenchment: This strategic response is illustrated by cases C1 and C2. The two companies are in the startup phase, on the verge of a pending international launch. They have exhausted their financial resources and are in the process of raising fresh capital. Therefore, they were caught in a precarious situation and are highly vulnerable. In reality, they have no other strategic options: "*…the pandemic affects everything. We have to lay off staff, we cannot access the laboratories that we need, and we cannot attract funding and capita*" (C1). The situation is of less urgency in the case of C2. "*… We did not lose any orders and they have kept coming. But in view of the layoffs and the lockdown in many countries, the processes have slowed down and projects are not being finished nor are bills being paid on time. We had to lay off ourselves during the past 4 months at 60 percent of full time and plan to increase to 80 percent from the beginning of August. What we can see just now and in view of what we are doing and the projects that we are working on, the situation feels quite stable, but things can change very quickly" (CEO/C2).* This strategy maybe plausible in managing a crisis with a foreseeable end but may not be sustainable in a longer perspective.

Perseverance: C3 illustrates this strategy. In this case, the main business has been digitalized and the impact of social distancing and similar measures (lockdown) were thus mitigated and the impact of the crisis was perceived to be manageable. At this stage, it is "business as usual" but the company is as susceptible to the disease as the others and the staff are forced to work from home: "*…we have always conducted most of our business digitally and by regular mail but we work from home. Cancellations of conferences do have an impact but for us it is just a ripple on the surface. It is other factors that determine our development, for example, our growth ambitions and strategies. We are not planning any changes" (CEO/C3).*

Innovation: This strategic response requires combinations of different types of interrelated transformations of the businesses. For example, companies that reallocate their resources to benefit from COVID-19-driven demands need to renew their organization in order to effectively meet customer needs. Cases C4, C5, C6, and C7 illustrate the point.

Case C4, for example, created a new partnership, thus transforming the organization in order to create an effective supply chain that allows the company to compete on the rapidly growing market for its services. C5 found itself on a market with an accelerating demand but a limited supply of health care professionals. The company renewed the whole organization in order to accommodate a rapid digitalization that was needed in order to adjust to the new requirements and market conditions: "*...we have a flexible organization and it was not difficult to reorganize for digitalized work. Thus, the office employees could work from home which helped because they felt safe and saved time, thus becoming much more productive. The consultants were able to access information online in real time. This gave us a competitive age and we are benefiting from the increased demand in spite of the limitation in supply" (CEO).* C7 repurposed its resources and made an organizational renewal to accommodate an expanding manufacturing operation in the area of refuse, an intensified online trade, and increased customer service. This strategy appears to appeal to entrepreneurially oriented firms on the domestic market located in industries that are benefiting from the pandemic. Moreover, these companies had internal resources that enabled them to adapt to the new conditions and take moderate risks. One case, C7, differs in many respects, for example, the company had plans for a crisis, a cash buffer, and an entrepreneurially oriented management approach. "*...You always have to anticipate bad times. Initially, my parents did not have access to the welfare I have today. So, I am trained in being ready for different types of crisis. You have to plan. Since I became the CEO of the company, we have changed many things and redefined our business. It has been very successful. This crisis has been very good for us and we were ready to make the best of it" (CEO).* Case C6 has decentralized large parts of its business through outsourcing which enables the company to be flexible. However, the company faced serious supply chain challenges and was forced to find creative solutions. This required an organizational change and establishing new relations and networks: "*we are very flexible and can adapt to new conditions very quickly. We are used to digitalization and have easily been able to adapt to the new working conditions. We have not made many more changes*" (CEO).

In summary, the case companies which perceive that their survival is at stake respond with a retrenchment strategy. Their priorities are cost reduction and digitalization in order to sustain international networking and enable work from home. In these cases, downsizing is not an option because their employees are specialists in technology and product development.

Cases that do not perceive any immediate threat to their survival choose perseverance as a strategic response. Their priority is to maintain a status quo and thus, employee health and a digital infrastructure to continue to serve customers. Cases that perceive opportunities in the crisis respond with innovation as a strategy. This strategy primarily involves innovative changes and adjustments geared toward the organization, for example, structure, business model, and customer services. In doing these, they repurpose and relocate existing resources.

6.5.12 Social Responsibility in SMEs during the Crisis

The pandemic has changed the norms of social responsibility, but the new normal has not yet emerged. At present, the expectation is for society to intervene and support businesses rather than expect these to engage in social responsibility. Nonetheless, SMEs engage in socially responsible activities during the crisis, but there are variations in their views, priorities, and focus areas. This can be illustrated in the responses of some of the cases:

> "…first we have to survive and operate a profitable business. That is why we do this. Then if you are profitable, you can engage in social responsibility." (C5)

> "…during COVID-19 everybody has to help in every manner they can, it is not about profit." (C6)

> "…we consider our business to be a social mission. This product can change the lives of many patients. To bring this product to the market is a socially responsible act." (C1)

> "…my mission is to popularize environmentally friendly business. I need to make money to achieve my goal but that is not the reason for my involvement in entrepreneurship." (C6)

> "...we are committed to a socially responsible business. We have an inclusive staffing policy and we have invested in electricity driven cars. All our cars are electricity driven. The workplace environment has been more challenging because this involves customers. We have had discussions with clients about rules for contacts and so on. We try to make sure that everybody abides by the Public Health Agency. We have had no incidents of the Coronavirus so far. We try to help where we can, for example, with free transport of goods to hospitals." (C4)

> "...do the right thing! We employ people and pay taxes. In addition to that, we donate relatively large sums of money. We try to recycle and work in an environment friendly manner. During the COVID-19 we take care of our employees, we have employed additional personnel. We have a special post for philanthropy, for example, cancer research and continue to make the donations." (C7)

Entrepreneurs have different views about the priorities of a business during a crisis. Some argue that businesses should prioritize the fight against the pandemic, others emphasize the survival and resilience of their businesses. The latter argue that retaining and/or creating job opportunities during a crisis is an important and socially responsible action (C4, C7). Perhaps more intriguing are those cases that perceive the mission of their businesses as an act of social responsibility. They consider that the act of bringing technology/products that can improve the quality of life for patients is a clear example of CSR (C1, C2, C3, and C6). This is not to say that they consider themselves as social enterprises.

Another observation is in the areas of focus of the CSR involvement of SMEs. There is a shift toward internal CSR activities, particularly employee health but also social and psychological support in view of social distancing and isolation. Employees are a key resource to SMEs because they are small and cannot afford sick leave and absenteeism. Perhaps as important is that these are small teams who develop close relations and normally take care of each other. Some refer to the team as the "family". In practice, a socially responsible management primarily implies investment in digitalization to enable employees to work from home. It also implies offering employees support in following COVID-19 restrictions at work and at home. As employers, the companies need to support workers in their interaction with customers. Working from home can also affect the well-being of employees and the entrepreneurs need to find creative means to socialize. Most external CSR actions are sporadic and limited. Some of the cases offer digital/distance socialization events, joint coffee breaks, and so on. Two of the case companies have continued with their pre-crisis CSR commitments but believe that the focus will shift toward internal CSR in a longer perspective.

In summary, as exhibited in Table 6.4, the primary focus of socially responsible activities in the case companies is geared toward internal issues, specifically employee health and welfare. In practice, socially responsible employee health and welfare implies digitalization which makes it possible to work from home. This further involves the new workplace environment to mitigate isolation and social support that a normal workplace offers. Investment in digitalization also enables new forms of customer relations and care. Some sporadic involvement in external CSR in terms of free services and donations can also be observed. Taken together the practice of social responsibility among these companies suggests close relations between their strategic responses to the crisis, the status of their companies (e.g., economic, entrepreneurial), and their involvement in social responsibility.

Table 6.4 Strategies and managerial practices in social responsibility in the SME

Strategic responses	CSR priorities	CSR practices
Retrenchment	*Internal CSR*: -employee health and safety -team cohesion and welfare	-digitalization -work from home -distance socialization
Perseverance	*Internal CSR*: -employee health and safety	-digitalization -work from home
Innovation	*Internal and external CSR*: -employee health and safety -community outreach in a crisis -planned CSR	-digitalization -work from home -work environment safety assurance activities -donations to COVID-19 alleviation -sporadic involvements, for example, free services to health care sector -donations to pre-crisis projects

Source: Own work

6.6 Conclusions and Discussion

Our study only captures the first six months of the COVID-19 crisis and it is therefore difficult to draw any conclusions. However, we have learned some important lessons that can create a fruitful ground for further studies. One important lesson is that small businesses resembling those in our study are unlikely to anticipate a crisis or have plans for such an event. Second, the perceptions and beliefs of the entrepreneurs about the crisis and its impact on their companies and their business environment play a key role in how the crisis is managed in smaller SMEs. In this study, for example, the type of crisis management strategies and practices differ between entrepreneurs who perceive the pandemic as a threat and those who see opportunities. These perceptions are likely to guide the strategic choices and managerial practices of the entrepreneurs. Those entrepreneurs who perceive a threat rather than an opportunity are likely to craft strategies for survival (short term), for example, retrenchment or perseverance rather than innovation. Third, the impact of the COVID-19 pandemic on a specific SME is related to the state of the industry in which it is located, and its pre-crisis status. However, the ability to manage the crisis and capitalize on the opportunities brought about by the crisis depends on its entrepreneurial capacity, that is, the ability to recognize and transform opportunities into marketable products and services. Fourth, digitalization is the common denominator with regard to social responsibility. It is employed as a tool for implementing the restrictions imposed by the government and creating new ways of mitigating the impact on customers and employees. However, much of the CSR effort is geared toward internal social issues, primarily employee health and welfare. Finally, entrepreneurship is a critical resource in managing a crisis with longer duration. Our study shows that businesses which adopt innovation as a crisis management strategy are thriving and making contributions to combating the crisis by offering new solutions that mitigate the impact of the pandemic. Home delivery service to self-isolated households is a useful example. On the other hand, businesses trying to manage the crisis through cost-reduction and downsizing strategies are facing serious challenges as the pandemic continues. These strategies may not be sustainable in the context of SMEs in a longer perspective.

As mentioned above, our study only captures the first few months of the COVID-19 crisis and our knowledge of crisis management in SMEs in a longer perspective is thus limited. Although our study represents a specific category of businesses, namely entrepreneurial firms, the cases illustrate experiences from several industries. Therefore, we have been able to compare these varying experiences for similarities and differences and identify patterns. The strategic patterns are in line with the indications from prior research (Kraus et al. 2020; Wenzel et al. 2020). We elaborate on previous findings by relating perceptions to strategies and managerial practices. Our study also makes a contribution by extending the strategic responses to social responsibility as an integral part of SMEs' response to crisis. It is important to study crisis management in SMEs in a longer perspective. We have not discussed exit in this study. However, exit may become a norm for SMEs in a longer perspective, including those adopting survival strategies. It is important to study the characteristics, strategies, and managerial resources of resilient SMEs during a longer crisis such as the present pandemic. We hope to do a follow-up study of the cases in order to document their development as the pandemic evolves.

References

Acs, Z., & Audretsch, D. B. (1990). *Innovation and small firms.* Cambridge, MA: MIT Press.

Aldrich, H. E. (1990). Using an ecological perspective to study organizational founding rates. *Entrepreneurship Theory and Practice, 14*(3), 7–24.

Alvarez, S., & Barney, J. (2007). Discovery and creation: Alternative theories of entrepreneurial action. *Strategic Entrepreneurship Journal, 1*(1–2), 11–26.

Baldwin, R., & Weder di Mauro, B. (2020). Introduction. In R. Baldwin & B. Weder di Mauro (Eds.), *Economics in the time of COVID-19.* London: CEPR.

Bapuji, H., de Bakker, F. G. A., Brown, J. A., Higgins, C., Rehbein, K., & Spicer, A. (2020). Business and society research in times of Corona crisis. *Business & Society, 1*, 1–12.

Bartik, A. W., Bertrand, M., Cullen, Z., Glaeser, E. L., & Luca, M. (2020). The impact of COVID-19 on small business outcomes and expectations, *PNAS*, volume 117, No. 30, available at:www.pnas.org/cgi/10.1073/pnas.2006991117, downloaded 20200830.

Belghitar, Y., Moro, A., & Radic, N. (2020). When the Rainy Day is the Worst Hurricane Ever: The Effect of Governmental Policies on SMEs during COVID-19, https://ssrn.com/abstract=3661501

Brown, R., & Rocha, A. (2020). Entrepreneurial uncertainty during the Covid-19 crisis: Mapping the temporal dynamics of entrepreneurial finance. *Journal of Business Venturing Insights, 14*, e00174.

Covin, J. G., & Kuratko, D. F. (2010). 'The Concept of Corporate Entrepreneurship' in Narayanan, V.K. & O'Connor, G.C., (eds.), Encyclopedia of Technology and Innovation Management.

Covin, J., & Miles, M. (1999). Corporate entrepreneurship and the pursuit of competitive advantage. *Entrepreneurship Theory and Practice, 23*, 47–63.

Cowling, M., Bown, R., & Rocha, A. (2020). Did you save some cash for a rainy COVID-19 day? The crisis and SMEs, *International Small Business Journal*, vol. Online First. 0.1177/0266242620945102.

Doern, R. (2016). Entrepreneurship and crisis management: The experiences of small businesses during the London 2011 riots. *International Small Business Journal, 34*(3), 276–302.

Doern, R., Williams, N., & Vorley, T. (2019). Special issue on entrepreneurship and crises: Business as usual? An introduction and review of the literature. *Entrepreneurship and Regional Development, 31*(5–6), 400–412.

Donthu, N., & Gustafsson, A. (2020). Effects of COVID-19 on business and research. *Journal of Business Research, 117*, 284–289.

Eggers, F. (2020). Masters of Disasters? Challenges and opportunities for SMEs in times of crisis. *Journal of Business Research*, 116, 199–202.

Eisenhardt, K. M. (1989). Building theories from case study research. *Academy of Management Review, 14*(4), 532–550.

EU Commission. (2018). *Annual Report on European SMEs 2017/2018: The 10th anniversary of the Small Business Act, SME Performance Review* 2017/20188.

Fairlie, R. (2020). The Impact of Covid-19 on Small Business Owners: Evidence of Early-Stage Losses from the April 2020 Current Population Survey, *Permalink* https://escholarship.org/uc/item/89w827c9.

Faulkner, B. (2001). Towards a framework for tourism disaster management. *Tourism Management, 22*(2), 135–147.

Gray, C. (2004). Management development in European small and medium enterprises. *Advances in Developing Human Resources, 6*(4), 451–469. https://doi.org/10.1177/1523422304268381.

Grube, L. E., & Storr, V. H. (2018). Embedded entrepreneurs and post-disaster community recovery. *Entrepreneurship and Regional Development, 30*(1), 7–8. https://doi.org/10.1080/08985626.2018.1457084.

Haeffele, S., Hobson, A., & Storr, V. H., (2020). Coming Back from COVID-19: Lessons in Entrepreneurship from Disaster Recovery Research, *Mercatus Center or George Mason University, Policy brief, Special Edition.*

Hawn, O., & Ioannou, I. (2016). Mind the gap: The interplay between external and internal actions in the case of corporate social responsibility. *Strategic Management Journal, 37*, 2569–2588.

Herbane, B. (2010). Small business research: Time for a crisis-based view. *International Small Business Journal, 28*(1), 43–64.

Jenkins, H. (2006). Small business champions for corporate social responsibility. *Journal of Business Ethics, 67*, 241–256. https://doi.org/10.1007/s10551-006-9182-6.

Juergensen, J., Guimon, J., & Narula, R. (2020). European SMEs amidst the COVID-19 crisis: Assessing impact and policy responses. *Journal of Industrial and Business Economics, 47*, 499–510. https://doi.org/10.1007/s40812-029-00169-4.

Kihlstrom, R. E., & Laffont, J. J. (1979). A general equilibrium entrepreneurial theory of firm formation based on risk aversion. *Journal of Political Economy, 87*(4), 719–748.

Kirzner, I. (2009). The alert and creative entrepreneur: A clarification. *Small Business Economics, 32*(2), 145–152.

Klein, P. (2008). Opportunity discovery, entrepreneurial action, and economic organization. *Strategic Entrepreneurship Journal, 2*(3), 175–190.

Knight, F. H. (1921). *Risk, uncertainty, and profit.* New York: August M. Kelley.

Kraus, S., Clauss, T., Breier, M., Gast, J., Zardini, A., & Tiberius, V. (2020). The economics of COVID-19: Initial empirical evidence on how family firms in five European countries cope with the corona crisis. *International Journal of Entrepreneurial Behavior & Research, 26*(5), 1067–1092. https://doi.org/10.1108/IJEBR-04-2020-0214.

Kuckertz, L. B., Gaudig, A., Hinderer, S., Reyes, C. A. M., Prochotta, A., Steinbrink, K. M., & Berger, E. S. C. (2020). Startups in times of crisis – A rapid response to the COVID-19 pandemic. *Journal of Business Venturing Insights, 13*(2020), e00169.

Lee, K-H., Harold, D. M., & Yu, A-L. (2015). Small and Medium Enterprises and Corporate Social Responsibility Practice: A Swedish Perspective,

Corporate Social Responsibility and Environmental Management, Wiley Online Library. https://doi.org/10.1002/csr.1366.

Lundström, A., & Stevenson, L. (2005). *Entrepreneurship Policy. Theory and Practice, International Studies in Entrepreneurship,* Springer.

Mitroff, I. P. T., & Shrivastava, P. (1988). The social structure of man-made organizational crises: Conceptual and empirical issues in the development of a general theory of crisis management. *Technological Forecasting and Social Change, 33*(2), 83–107. https://doi.org/10.1016/0040-1625(88)90075-3.

Monllor, J., & Murphy, P. (2017). Natural disasters, entrepreneurship, and creation after destruction: A conceptual approach. *International Journal of Entrepreneurial Behaviour & Research, 23*(4), 618–637. https://doi.org/10.1108/IJEBR-02-2016-0050.

OECD. (2019). *SME and Entrepreneurship Outlook* 2019, OECD Publishing, Paris. https://doi.org/10.1787/34907e9c-en.

Pearce II, J. A., & Robbins, K. (1993). Toward improved theory and research on business turnaround. *Journal of management, 19*(3), 613–636.

Pearson, C. M., & Clair, J. A. (1998). Reframing crisis management. *Academy of Management Review, 23*(1), 59–76. https://www.jstor.org/stable/259099.

Perrini, F. (2006). SMEs and CSR theory: Evidence and implications from an Italian perspective. *Journal of Business Ethics, 67*, 1.

Popovka, E., Delo, P., & Sergi, B. S. (2020). Corporate social responsibility amid social distancing during the COVID-19 crisis: BRICS vs. OECD countries. *Research in International Business and Finance, 55*(2020), 101315.

Reymen, I. M. M. J., Andries, P., Berends, H., Mauer, R., Stephan, U., & van Burg, E. (2015). Understanding dynamics of strategic decision making in venture creation: A process study of effectuation and causation. *Strategic Entrepreneurship Journal, 9*(4), 351–379. https://doi.org/10.1002/sej.1201.

Reynolds, P. D. S., Camp, M., Bygrave, W. D., Autio, E., & Hay, M. (2001) *Global Entrepreneurship Monitor: Executive Report.* London Business School and Kaufman Center for Entrepreneurial Leadership.

Runyan, R. C. (2006). Small business in the face of crisis: Identifying barriers to recovery from a natural disaster. *Journal of Contingencies and Crisis Management, 14*(1), 12–26. https://doi.org/10.1111/j.1468-5973.2006.00477.x.

Santos, M. (2011). CSR in SMEs: Strategies, practices, motivations and obstacles. *Social Responsibility Journal, 7*(3), 490–508.

Schumpeter, J. (1934). *The theory of economic development.* Cambridge, MA: Harvard University Press.

Shane, S., & Venkataraman, S. (2000). The promise of entrepreneurship as a field of research. *Academy of Management Review, 25*(1), 217–226.
Smallbone, D., Deakins, D., Battisti, M., & Kitching, J. (2012). Small business responses to a major economic downturn: Empirical perspectives from New Zealand and the United Kingdom. *International Small Business Journal, 30*(7), 754–777. https://doi.org/10.1177/0266242612448077.
Spence, L. J., & Rutherfoord, R. (2003). Small business and empirical perspectives in business ethics: Editorial. *Journal of Business Ethics, 47*(1), 1–5.
Thorgren, S., & Williams, T. A. (2020). Staying alive during an unfolding crisis: How SMEs ward off impending disaster. *Journal of Business Venturing Insights, 14*, e00187.
Wenzel, M., Stanske, S., & Lieberman, M. B. (2020). Strategic responses to crisis. *Strategic Management Journal, 41*, V7–V18. https://doi.org/10.1002/smj.3161.
Williams, T. A., & Shepherd, D. A. (2016). Building resilience or providing sustenance: Different paths of emergent ventures in the aftermath of the Haiti earthquake. *Academy of Management Journal, 59*, 2069–2102.
Williams, T. A., & Vorley, T. (2014). Economic resilience and entrepreneurship: lessons from the Sheffield City Region. *Entrepreneurship and Regional Development*. https://doi.org/10.1080/08985626.2014.894129.
Williams, T. A., Gruber, D. A., Sutcliff, K. M., Shepherd, D. A., & Zhao, E. Y. (2017). Organizational response to adversity: Fusing crisis management and resilience research streams. *Academy of Management Annals, 11*(2), 733–769. https://doi.org/10.5465/annals.2015.0134.
Yin, R. K. (2003). *Case study research: Design and methods* (3rd ed.). London: Sage Publications.

7

Experiences of Small Businesses Due to the COVID-19 Pandemic

Håkan Boter, Anders Lundström, and Anna Sörensson

7.1 Introduction

The COVID-19 pandemic has affected firms' businesses around the world and caused crises in the corporate sector. Previous research on such crises is relatively limited. However, studies have focused on how future crises can be detected in advance and whether operations can be adapted to the conditions that apply during ongoing crises. Studies of crises have mainly been concerned with negative effects caused by economic downturns, financial crises or natural disasters. However, the current pandemic is in many respects radically different from previous crises. COVID-19 has so far led to major restrictions on the functioning of society, partly because the business community has been given limited opportunities,

H. Boter
Umeå University, Umeå, Sweden

A. Lundström • A. Sörensson (✉)
Mid Sweden University, Östersund, Sweden
e-mail: anna.sorensson@miun.se

A. Sörensson et al. (eds.), *Corporate Responsibility and Sustainability during the Coronavirus Crisis*, Palgrave Studies in Governance, Leadership and Responsibility,
https://doi.org/10.1007/978-3-030-73847-1_7

and partly because powerful obstacles have been created that prevent civil society from functioning effectively.

The initial weeks of the pandemic meant that both demand and supply in the corporate sector were suddenly significantly reduced, and it was essential for many companies to implement cuts in operations. For smaller companies with limited resource potential, it became necessary to generate a range of different complementary efforts to cope with the first phase of the crisis, such as using previously accumulated resources but also actively using their corporate network for resource exchange and increased collaboration. The perspective at this time, however, was that these would be efforts to survive in the short term and that everything would soon return to normal. It has now been shown that significantly more sustainable efforts were needed, such as postponing ongoing investment projects as well as utilizing the support programmes that were gradually established during the first six months of the pandemic (Wenzel et al. 2020; Thorgren and Williams 2020). The crisis has reduced the opportunities to run efficiently commercially oriented operations at full scale, but it has also opened up new business opportunities. An example of this is "effectuation", whereby companies that are in development processes do not necessarily have to adhere to an original business idea but can continuously develop the ability to change tracks and seek new business solutions, thus taking small steps to successfully manoeuvre in a turbulent and insecure environment (Sarasvathy 2001; Reymen et al. 2015).

This chapter reports on how companies have coped with the first six months of the COVID-19 pandemic. The basis for analyses consists of interviews with 1200 small companies from four different industry segments in Sweden. Some industry groups have suffered significant negative effects and continue to do so, while other categories have only been marginally affected. There is also a small group that has noticed growing sales and there are occasional signals from the market that new products and services are needed in the near future. It may even be the case that the industry repercussions of COVID-19 will open up new perspectives that affect and stimulate entrepreneurs, companies, customers and markets (Davidsson 2020).

7.2 Method and Selection

One objective in selecting the categories of companies to be included in this study was to cover the situation during the COVID-19 pandemic for small firms operating in both the manufacturing and service industries. The selection process followed Eurostat's classifications of industries (Eurostat 2016) and, with regard to manufacturing industries, chose the broad group of companies characterized by high or medium use of technology in their operations. This applies to companies whose staff have experience and higher education, giving the recipient the capacity to run their own innovation processes but also to use externally available knowledge. Examples of industries in this category are medicine, chemistry, computer equipment and other digital products and services, as well as the automotive and transport sectors. The second group in the manufacturing sector comprises firms that have lower requirements for the core technology used in the business. Development is driven here by experience-based learning, development in smaller steps and the use of mature technology. Examples of industries with lower requirements for technology levels include the manufacture of products from metal and plastic, food products and products linked to forestry and agriculture.

Eurostat also has a standard for classifying service-oriented industries where the two main groups are knowledge-intensive and less knowledge-intensive activities. In this study, we found it appropriate to select two service industries that faced special challenges during the first half of the coronavirus pandemic. The first is hotels and restaurants, SNI 55 and SNI 56, which have been the industries hardest hit by the pandemic: available statistics show that turnover for companies in this sector decreased by 30–50% and that over 40% of the workforce was laid off in the short term during the period March–June 2020 (Statistics Sweden 2020). On the one hand, the other selected service industry is retail, SNI 47, where the food trade has seen radically increased sales due to redundancies and the rise in working from home. On the other hand, there are also sub-sectors in the retail trade that have been negatively affected by the ongoing pandemic.

From the industry categories, four random selections were made, one in each industry. Only active smaller firms were included in the study—that is, firms with 5–49 employees. Companies with fewer than five employees were excluded because many of these smallest micro-companies are relatively young and thus still in a start-up phase, where the business has not had time to fully develop. Another reason to exclude these smallest firms is that a certain proportion of them are conducted as activities in addition to a full-time job or involvement in other companies, or as "extra cracker companies". Table 7.1 shows which sub-sectors were included, the total number of existing companies divided into two

Table 7.1 Selected companies

Stratum	Companies in manufacturing industries	Total number of companies 5–49 employees	Selection
A	**High and middle high technology** 20 chemicals 21 pharmaceutical products and medicines 26–30 computers, electronics, electricity, machinery, vehicles	5–9 employees—627 companies 10–49 employees—1016 companies **Total—1643 companies**	300
B	**Middle low and low technology** 10–19 food, textiles, clothing, rubber, plastics, forestry and agricultural products, graphic products 22–25 products of rubber, plastic, metal 31–33 furniture, other, machine repairs	5–9 employees—2836 companies 10–49 employees—3401 companies **Total 6236 companies**	300
C	**Companies in service industries** 47 retail	5–9 employees—3942 companies 10–49 employees—3210 companies **Total 7152 companies**	300
D	**Companies in service industries** 55, 56 hotel, restaurant	5–9 employees—4598 companies 10–49 employees—4124 companies **Total 8722 companies**	300
Total selection			1200

Source: Own work

Table 7.2 Distribution between women and men

	Women		Men		Total	
	Share	No.	Share	No.	Share	No.
Industry						
Manufacturing—High technology	**13**	39	**87**	236	25	300
Manufacturing—Low technology	**14**	42	**86**	258	25	300
Service—Retail	21	64	79	236	25	300
Service—Hotel/restaurant	**28**	84	**72**	217	25	301
	19	229	81	972	100	1201
Number of employees						
5–9 persons	**22**	138	**78**	502	53	640
10–19 persons	**16**	56	**84**	302	30	358
20–49 persons	17	35	83	168	17	203
	19	229	81	972	100	1201
Age of the interviewee						
40 years or younger	20	36	80	141	15	177
41–60 years	21	165	79	630	67	795
61 years or older	**13**	28	**87**	187	19	215

Note: Bold marks the significant difference within the group (with 95% probability)

size classes and the sample size per stratum and for the entire study. The three groups that were finally included in the study were firms with 5–9 employees, those with 10–19 employees and those with 20–49 employees.

The questionnaire was developed through a collaboration between the researchers, the scientific leader at Skandinavisk Opinion SKOP analysis and staff from Almi Företagspartner Ltd., who also ordered us as researchers of its research council to carry out this research project. A draft questionnaire was also examined in a special workshop with Almi's research council. This research council consists of 14 researchers from different universities around Sweden; see www.almi.se for further information. The data collection was carried out by SKOP, and the selected companies were contacted by telephone. The interviewees were contacted at different times of the day to fit into the companies' work schedules. In total, SKOP sought contact with 1537 business leaders, and the final number of interviews conducted was 1201. The staff at SKOP kept careful notes regarding the characteristics of the companies that dropped out (21%), but no distortions in the material occurred during the process. The companies contacted showed considerable interest in participating in the study, and reasons for not participating in many cases concerned temporary workloads. The strata that guided the random selection, with 300 companies in four different industry segments, were fully met. The answers have been weighted for processing, so that the four industry segments have an equal impact on the analysis. Our final assessment is that the size of the sample, the design of the survey and the implementation of the data collection create a data set that is representative of the population of companies in the four current industry segments and in the size range of 5–49 employees. With the aim of increasing the possibilities for a broader and in-depth analysis of the collected material, additional background information about the participating companies was also obtained and "docked" to the participating survey companies. This applies to key figures for these companies regarding the most recent years (2017–2019) before the pandemic struck in March 2020, such as number of employees, turnover, profitability and financial status.

7.3 Comparison of Women and Men as Operational Business Leaders

For several years, the Swedish Agency for Economic and Regional Growth, in partnership with Statistics Sweden, has mapped and analysed women in the business sector and shown that about 25% of all companies are led by women. The definition used is based on the term operational business manager, which is defined as "the person who handles the day-to-day management of a company with at least one gainfully employed person" (Statistics Sweden, 2019). This definition is not identical to the term entrepreneur, as the latter usually presupposes financial ownership, and the statistics show that 85% of women who are operational business leaders are also owners or partners in their companies. In this study, however, we have assumed that operational business management is nevertheless a useful definition for women with strategic management roles, especially considering that the object of the study is small firms with far-reaching entrepreneurial qualifications in business development and risk-taking. Seventy-nine per cent of these entrepreneurs are also owners or partners.

In the study, almost 20% (n = 229) of those who answered the survey represented women-led companies. An important reason why this share falls below the national norm of 25% is that we chose not to include the smallest micro-enterprises, those with 1–4 employees, which is a group that has a higher proportion of companies led by women. If the proportion of companies with women as business leaders is distributed between the four industries, then the two manufacturing categories had a lower proportion of women than expected, while the two service industries had a higher proportion of women in this role. When the material for this study is compared with other statistics, Statistics Sweden's data material shows that the percentage of female operational business leaders in manufacturing companies is 15%, while the retail industry and hotel and restaurant industry have 24% and 30%, respectively. During the selection process, the two latter service industries were also selected because they have a higher proportion of women in leading positions, as well as because these businesses are generally characterized by occupational categories that include a significant number of women.

More than half of the companies (53%) belonged to the smallest size class, measured by number of employees; 30% were included in the company group with 10–19 employees; and 17% were in the group with 20–49 employees. The difference between companies led by women and men shows that the proportion of women in the role of leaders was highest for micro-enterprises (i.e., companies with less than 10 employees).

The age of the company leader was included because existing research clearly indicates that this can affect leadership style and company culture and thus also the way a company is led. We believe that leadership style becomes particularly important when a society is faced with a global pandemic that results in genuine uncertainty. A recent study conducted during the ongoing pandemic shows that elderly people are better able than younger people to deal with stressors in the environment. These results thereby indicate that elderly people in the role of business leaders are a force that can be used to handle the advanced stresses created by a pandemic (Carstensen et al. 2020). Having elderly business leaders also means that their network connections, which are based on established contacts with a large amount of trust, come to the fore in situations of great stress, risk and uncertainty (Newman et al. 2018).

The selection of companies shows that the distribution between women and men regarding the companies' CEO positions mainly followed the 20–80 structure that applied to the basic selection. However, the group of companies having a female leader who is 61 years or older had a significantly lower share compared with the corresponding group on the male side.

The total proportion of women in the sample was 19%, and the proportion of men was 81%. The highest proportion of women was in the hotel and restaurant industry at 28%, with retail at 21%, and the highest proportion of men was in the manufacturing industry (high or medium innovation rate at 87% and low or medium innovation rate at 86%, respectively). We examined in more detail any differences between characteristics for men and women; proportions of the two groups and differences between them are not the same as characteristic differences.

The generality was limited by the choice of sub-industries and types of municipality, as well as by several additional division criteria. We continuously worked with a limited number of comparisons that we believe provide increased opportunities, overviews and conclusions. These are divisions into four sub-sectors, distribution of answers in three different types of municipality, turnover of small enterprises divided into three groups, number of employees in three groups of small enterprises, three groups of start-up years, gender (male or female), age of interviewees (divided into three age groups), entrepreneurs divided into domestic or foreign backgrounds and with three options for the effects of the pandemic. All relationships were tested for significance at the 95% level.

7.4 Three Regional Groups

One division basis used was to divide the material into three regional groups based on all of Sweden's municipalities: firstly, large cities and municipalities close to the city; secondly, larger cities and municipalities close to larger cities and, thirdly, smaller cities or urban areas and rural municipalities.

Firstly, there are three divisions for the three regional types where there were no significant differences. This applies when comparisons are made as to what applies to relative proportions between municipality types for men and women, respectively. Of course, it can be difficult to divide all municipalities into three groups, but even if metropolitan areas were to be compared with other municipalities, the same result would be obtained. The results will be exactly the same as each gender's relative share in the survey.

Secondly, women and men have similar opportunities to run companies in different types of regions. This conclusion is reinforced by the fact that age differences for both men and women seem to be unimportant for the possibilities of running companies in these types of regions.

Thirdly, the types of regions in which interviewees operate seem to be irrelevant to how they experienced the effects of the pandemic. This was measured by a question concerning whether entrepreneurs in different regional types assessed the effects of the pandemic as positive, negative or no impact.

However, there were differences regarding industries, sales, number of employees, start-up years and foreign background between the two of the region types. Large cities and municipalities close to metropolitan areas had relatively few companies with a low degree of innovation in the manufacturing industry, as well as many entrepreneurs in the hotel and restaurant industry, which seems reasonable due to a larger population base. Other factors that stand out for this group of municipalities are that many companies had a low turnover and few employees, and there were many relatively young companies.

Finally, with regard to the group of smaller cities or towns and rural municipalities, this group had a relatively large number of companies belonging to manufacturing industries with lower technology and few companies in the hotel and restaurant industry. There were also relatively many companies with high turnover, as well as a high proportion of companies with more than 20 employees and a high proportion of older companies. This group also had relatively few entrepreneurs with a foreign background.

In sum, there were differences between the most densely populated municipalities and the most sparsely populated municipalities, which should be exciting to study in more detail. There were many indications that in sparsely populated environments, companies are older and have higher turnover and more employees, while the proportion of new and young companies is low, which may indicate low dynamics.

7.5 Entrepreneurship in Four Sub-Business Sectors

It appears from the Method and Selection section that the selection took place from the four sub-sectors:

A. Manufacturing—High and medium technology (SNI 20–21, 26–30)
B. Manufacturing—Low and medium technology (SNI 10–19, 22–25, 31–33)
C. Service—Retail (SNI 47)
D. Hotel and restaurant (SNI 55–56)

For each industry, 300 telephone interviews were conducted. It is worth noting that some measurements can be assumed to show the same thing; for example, the probability was high that companies with the most employees would have higher turnover than companies with few employees, and older companies often also have more employees than younger ones.

Manufacturing industry with a high or medium degree of innovation (A) showed no differences for different municipal groups, had a relatively low proportion of companies with low turnover and had a high proportion of companies with high turnover. This also means that this sub-industry had few young companies with few employees and many older companies with relatively many employees. Furthermore, it is evident that this sub-industry had few younger entrepreneurs and rarely had entrepreneurs with a foreign background. Relatively many of the companies in this group stated that the pandemic did not have any effect on development, although few entrepreneurs stated that the pandemic had caused any positive development. Finally, the proportion of men was significantly higher than the proportion of women.

The manufacturing industry with a low or medium degree of innovation (B) shows broadly the same pattern as sub-industry A, except for a low proportion of small companies with high turnover and many employees. However, this sub-industry had an equal proportion of older companies, which indicates a lower growth rate in sub-industry B compared with sub-industry A. It would therefore be of interest to study in more detail the significance of the degree of innovation in small companies in the manufacturing industry for their growth. Sub-industry B also had the highest shares for the region-type smaller cities or urban areas and rural municipalities, and it had the lowest share for the region-type large cities and municipalities close to the city. This is a factor to take into account when analysing different levels of innovation.

For the sub-industry retail companies (C), there were no significant differences in terms of different regional types. However, this sub-industry had relatively few companies with low turnover but relatively many companies with few employees and relatively many companies with start-up years between 1991 and 2010. The relationships between the key figures for these companies thus differed compared with previous sub-sectors. Regarding comparisons between men and women, there were no significant differences, which also applied to age groups for interviewees. There were relatively few entrepreneurs here with a foreign background. A high proportion of entrepreneurs (close to 60%) had positive experiences of the pandemic, while only 16% had negative ones. This is clearly different from the other sub-industries studied. For example, for the sub-sector hotel and restaurant (D), the corresponding proportions are 9% positive and 34% negative. Other results for sub-sector D are a relatively high proportion of entrepreneurs with a foreign background, high proportions of young entrepreneurs, high proportions of women, relatively many young companies, low proportions regarding number of employees and turnover, and most companies in region type A and least in region type C.

7.6 Sales Pattern

Interviewees were asked about the share of sales in the local market (i.e., within ten miles) and the proportions of their sales for export and import. With regard to the local market, there were more women than men who answered "To a very large extent", while the proportion of men who stated that exports were higher than the proportion of women. Note that there were no significant differences for the "Yes to a very large extent" option, either for export or for import.

One explanation for this may be that women are overrepresented in the retail and hotel and restaurant sub-sectors. The companies in these industries have low values; in the hotel and restaurant industry, only 1 in 20 companies export and 1 in 10 companies import, while 9 out of 10 companies have fairly or very large sales in the local market. In addition, men are overrepresented among the elderly, as well as in larger small companies with higher turnover, all of which are indicators of higher export shares, something that also emerged in the responses to the survey. With regard to imports, a similar pattern obtains: the majority of small companies with high export shares also have high import shares.

Six out of ten entrepreneurs had no exports. Companies with exports exist mainly in the manufacturing industry, for companies with higher turnover, with more employees, and those which have been on the market for long. Two out of ten entrepreneurs had fairly or very large exports. Five out of ten companies had no imports, and one out of four companies had fairly or very large imports. This mainly applies to companies in the manufacturing industry with a high or medium degree of innovation. Finally, in terms of sales in the local market (here defined as within a radius of 100 km), nine out of ten companies had some sales in this market. High values were obtained for companies in the retail sub-sector as well as in hotels and restaurants, for municipal groups in large cities and municipalities close to cities, the smallest companies, those with few employees and the youngest companies. Most of these groups had relatively more women, which largely explains the reported differences.

7.7 Impact and Support during the Pandemic

Regarding the overall positive or negative impact of the pandemic, there were no differences between women and men. About six out of ten entrepreneurs experienced negative effects, while four out of ten experienced positive effects or no impact.

Similar results were obtained concerning how profitability has been affected. There were major differences between different industries. Four out of ten small business owners in the retail trade believed that profitability has improved, while more than eight out of ten business owners in hotels and restaurants believed that it has deteriorated. There were no significant differences within different types of municipality. However, companies with the lowest turnover, as well as the youngest companies, believed to a greater extent that profitability has deteriorated. We observed no significant differences between men and women. This also applies to the answers to the question about how sales and order intake have been affected. There were also similar patterns regarding the answers to the question about the development of profitability.

During the coronavirus pandemic, research reports have already shown that younger companies have encountered greater challenges than established companies. This is because young companies in many cases have not had time to fully develop their business, which is also noticeable in financial key figures. The youngest companies included in this current study, those established between 2011 and 2020, have an equity-to-assets ratio of 36%, while the corresponding ratio for the group of companies established before 1991 is 48%. Through the survey, the companies also reported various changes, negative as well as positive, that have arisen in various areas as a result of the pandemic.

Opportunities for companies to obtain external financing are radically affected during crises. In addition, financing in smaller companies is associated with extra risks, a situation which escalates when a global pandemic breaks out. Brown and Rocha (2020) have shown in an international study that financing of new companies has decreased radically during COVID-19 and early sowing financing has almost completely disappeared.

It may be natural that initial phases among newly established companies are extra sensitive, with higher risks where any return is some way into the future, but the relationship can also be transferred to smaller companies in general where "liabilities of newness" affect risk levels and thus opportunities to gain access to external capital. Kuckertz et al.'s (2020) recent studies of small companies in Germany strengthened this picture wherein many start-ups are not "bankable"—that is, they have insufficient opportunities to provide collateral for loans and have unclear development plans, which lead to poorer interest rates—but also that they can be excluded from national support programmes during a crisis.

A Swedish study by Thorgren and Williams (2020) showed the importance of smaller companies having a stable financial situation when a crisis period starts. With the outbreak of COVID-19, most of the demand in many industries disappeared during the first months, while companies were still bound by fixed costs such as salaries, premises and current contracts. There was thus a clear demand for good liquidity during this shocking first period. Companies that were not sufficiently liquid could also find it difficult to apply for short-term loans because they already had a high debt-to-equity ratio. Coupled with this, COVID-19 created increased uncertainty and thus reduced the incentives for companies to take out new loans.

Regarding liquidity, just over four out of ten entrepreneurs stated that it had deteriorated, while just under two out of ten entrepreneurs stated that it had improved. Just over four out of ten stated that liquidity had not been affected. The highest proportion of negative impacts (seven out of ten) was reported by entrepreneurs in hotels and restaurants, while three out of ten entrepreneurs in the retail sub-sector reported an improvement. Here, 50% of the companies in the sub-sectors in the manufacturing industry reported no impact on liquidity. Entrepreneurs with the lowest turnover, few employees and young people (both for the company and for its leaders this year) reported half a negative impact on liquidity. Entrepreneurs with a foreign background also reported a highly negative impact. Finally, it can be mentioned that entrepreneurs who reported a positive impact of the pandemic believed to a large extent (60%) that liquidity had improved. No significant differences between men and women were evident here.

Interviewees were also asked how deliveries to and from small companies had been affected during the pandemic. Just over 50% of the companies had not seen any impact, while just over 40% stated that deliveries had been negatively affected. High values for non-impact were obtained for the manufacturing industry with a low degree of innovation, while deterioration in deliveries was reported to a high degree (just over 50%) by small entrepreneurs in the retail trade. No significant differences were found between small businesses in different types of municipality. No significant differences were shown between women and men, nor between small entrepreneurs in different size classes, or according to their start-up years, turnover or between domestic and foreign small entrepreneurs.

Regarding opportunities to recruit staff, about two out of three entrepreneurs stated that this was not considered during the pandemic case. Just under 10% reported improvements, while few (about 5%) reported deterioration. These relationships were largely repeated for all the different divisions. Consistency between women and men was high, with just under 10% reporting improvements, twice as many reporting no impact, two out of three reporting that recruitment was not relevant, and only just over 5% who stated that opportunities had deteriorated. It was mainly entrepreneurs stating that recruitment was not relevant who reported negative effects of the pandemic.

7.8 Support Programmes—Needs and Use

The public sector has set up various special resources and programmes with the aim of supporting business during the pandemic. The three support resources that companies have used to the greatest extent are reduced employer contributions, compensation for employees' sick pay costs and short-term layoffs. Just under one in five used adjustment support and deferral of VAT and employer contributions. Only 2% of the companies used special financial support.

As previously pointed out, entrepreneurs answered a question concerning the extent to which they felt that different areas had affected their companies during the pandemic; the answers were given on a 5-point scale from "decreased a lot" to "increased a lot". This concerns six different areas: sales, profitability, liquidity, deliveries, recruitment and external financing. To further analyse whether companies' situations during the pandemic had an impact on their use of the various state aid programmes, users and non-users of aid programmes were compared. The support programme for short-term layoffs has been taken as an example, and for each of the six areas, the companies have indicated, on the 5-point scale, the extent to which the pandemic led to deteriorations or improvements. An average value has been calculated that has been compared for those who used or did not use this support programme.

This match shows a clear pattern. The companies that used the support programme for short-term redundancy reported a lower average value for all six areas where effects from the pandemic have been studied—that is, these companies deteriorated in these areas. This difference is also significant for the areas of sales, profitability, liquidity and deliveries. It may seem natural that it is the companies that experienced the biggest negative changes during the pandemic that also had the greatest need for support measures.

Although companies chose to use the support programmes specifically set up during the pandemic, the impact of these efforts may vary. To clarify the surveyed companies' perceptions of the effect of the aid on their activities, a special question was included in the survey where the respondents were asked to give an overall assessment of the importance of the aid in saving the company, on a scale from small to crucial.

We have previously stated that the support in the form of reduced employer contributions is what about 90% of the companies used, but only a small part of these assessed that this form of support became of decisive importance for the business. The adjustment support attracted just under one in five, but as many as 34% of this group stated that this support was absolutely essential for their activities during the pandemic. The forms of support that just over 40% of the users considered to have provided little or no significance were those that provided reduced employer contributions and compensation for employees' sick pay.

Women as leaders of smaller companies had a higher degree of activity with regard to applying for and using the current support programmes. This group corresponds to 19% of all companies included in the study, while between 20% and 26% of the companies that actively used programmes, or announced without support, were women-led companies. Based on answers to the question about the quality of the support programmes, it also appears that the support used by companies having women as operational business leaders was assessed as crucial to the companies' activities during the pandemic to a greater extent than was stated by companies led by men.

The literature suggests that women and men, in their roles as business leaders, can generally have different perspectives for leading and developing their businesses and that these differences are activated when crises and other situations of genuine uncertainty arise. McGrath (2010) argued that women in such situations strive to minimize the risks that arise while men are more focused on uncovering and developing potential business opportunities. Manolova et al. (2020) have applied this to how women-owned companies have so far handled two coronavirus waves, reaching the conclusion that women have a higher presence in certain industries, such as hotels and restaurants, which have been exposed to traumatic shock effects during the pandemic much more than other industries, and this has adversely affected the opportunities to actively influence development. Two surveys of women-owned companies were conducted in the spring and autumn of 2020 within the framework of this study, which indicates that women, through support programmes and networking, have created the conditions for a restart. There are also indications that women have special abilities to develop business models, combining risk minimization with efforts for business development.

The results of our study indicate that women have at least as high an activity level as men with regard to applying for and using available support during the coronavirus pandemic. However, studies including that by Cowling et al. (2019), which concerned bank loans during the financial crisis in 2008, indicate that women apply for loans to a lesser extent than men in such crisis periods, but at the same time that women who apply for loans are more successful, in that their applications are accepted to a greater extent. This is explained in the study by the fact that women apply for smaller amounts and have better-developed applications, which in turn is explained by women being aware that they need to compensate for a negative entry value at the time of application (Malmström and Wincent 2018).

7.9 Support Programmes—Different Background Factors

Eight out of ten entrepreneurs did not believe that it was relevant to obtain external financing. Only 2% of entrepreneurs used bank loans with a government loan guarantee, which may be due to external financing not being relevant during this period. There was also a pattern in the use of various possible forms of state aid from which small businesses were able to benefit. The support that was primarily used was in forms that reduced companies' costs.

Of state forms of support, entrepreneurs mainly benefited from reduced work fees (88%), compensation for sick pay costs (65%) and short-term layoffs (47%). Few entrepreneurs, just under 20%, notified or laid off staff without using the redundancy support. Adjustment support was used by 18% of entrepreneurs, while deferral of paying VAT and employer contributions, which should be seen as support that pushes costs forward in time, was used by 17% of entrepreneurs. The share of adjustment support can possibly be seen as the differences in the companies' turnover being small.

The result shows that in terms of reduced employer contributions, there were few differences for our different division bases, apart from a higher proportion for small companies with the most employees. Here, 93% of entrepreneurs stated that they used this form of support. It is also interesting that, of those who used this support, approximately, as many entrepreneurs had positive experiences as negative ones.

The forms of support offered receive overall positive reviews. Nearly six out of ten small businesses stated that this support had been decisive or very or fairly important. For small business owners in hotels and restaurants, eight out of ten stated that this was the case. There were no differences between different types of municipality or number of employees. However, companies that had been active for fewer years seemed to agree more with this statement.

Four out of ten small businesses had waived or reduced wage withdrawals and benefits during the pandemic. This mainly applies to small business owners in hotels and restaurants, where seven out of ten business owners stated that this was the case. There were no differences between different types of municipalities or between women's and men's entrepreneurship. The age of employees did not seem to matter either, though to a greater extent foreign small entrepreneurs stated that this was the case.

Two out of three small business owners stated that the state had helped small businesses cope with the effects of the pandemic very or fairly well. There were large differences between industries (the hotel and restaurant share was just over 50%, while the manufacturing industry was between

70% and 75%), but not between municipality types, number of employees, companies' start-up years, women and men, or entrepreneurs' age.

Regarding the question of how the motivation of small businesses was affected by the pandemic, almost 20% stated that it had increased, while six out of ten stated that their motivation had not been affected. The highest proportions reporting that motivation was not affected were in the manufacturing industry, where just over seven out of ten stated that this was the case, while the proportion of small entrepreneurs in the retail trade who stated a positive effect was 25%. In the restaurant and hotel industry, half of the entrepreneurs reported a negative impact. Entrepreneurs reporting that motivation was unaffected tended to be within the municipal type smaller city or urban areas and rural municipalities, within companies with relatively high turnover, relatively many employees, companies with many years on the market, male entrepreneurs, older entrepreneurs and entrepreneurs without a foreign background.

Regarding the question about how the pandemic had affected entrepreneurs' fear of failure, almost seven out of ten stated that the pandemic had not affected this fear. Relatively high values were obtained for the sub-sector hotels and restaurants (47%), young companies (40%), women (38%), younger entrepreneurs (39%) and entrepreneurs with a foreign background (43%).

When asked if the pandemic had led companies to discover and want to develop new business opportunities, almost 40% of entrepreneurs stated that this was the case. This mainly applies to entrepreneurs in hotels and restaurants (55%). Regarding the entrepreneurs' need for new skills development, almost eight out of ten small entrepreneurs stated that they had not experienced such a thing. Here, too, there are higher values for hotels and restaurants, as just over 30% stated such a need. Similar values exist for managers with foreign backgrounds and for younger entrepreneurs.

7.10 Pandemic—Future and Employment

Processes to start and run a business are always associated with uncertainty and risk-taking. The ongoing global pandemic has so far had a major impact on companies' opportunities to conduct commercial activities. Both supply and demand have declined for most industries, and companies have been forced to take a long list of measures, such as redundancies, advanced investments, and—during the most intense phases of the pandemic—closures and bankruptcies have also increased significantly. It is therefore natural to assume that business leaders and owners, as people responsible for their respective companies, today feel an increased anxiety about the future. This concern can thus negatively affect the entrepreneur's self-confidence and inhibit the driving forces required for a restart of the business after the pandemic has subsided (Wennberg et al. 2013).

The shockingly rapid onset of the pandemic and the far-reaching negative effects that have followed have made it natural to ask business leaders if this has affected their fear or anxiety about continuing to fail as entrepreneurs. This question could be answered on a 5-point scale from "decreased a lot" to "increased a lot". Almost 30% of the companies reported a large or small increase in such fear, while more than two-thirds were not affected at all, and the group with reduced anxiety was small, at about 4%.

A comparison between the sexes on the 5-point scale shows that business leaders who are women had a higher average value than men in the same role. The difference was significant and thus indicates that women have been affected more by the pandemic, which has led to them being more anxious about failing as entrepreneurs than men are. Previous studies also indicated that women perceive risk aspects as dominant during crisis periods—in other words, that women prioritize decisions and action to reduce risks (Cacciotti et al. 2016; Lee et al. 2020).

Corresponding analysis at the industry level shows that business leaders in the hotel and restaurant industry have a concern about failing as entrepreneurs to a much greater extent than in the other three industries. We have also previously noted that the proportion of women as operational leaders for companies in the hotel and restaurant industry is significantly higher than in the other industries, which is also the main reason why women have a greater presence and thus a higher degree of worry about failure in the future when all companies are included in the analysis.

Similarly, studies have found that financial crises, sharp economic downturns and natural disasters can affect entrepreneurs' motivation to run companies. Our study shows that men in the role of operational business leaders have a higher motivation than female leaders to run their business after the ongoing coronavirus pandemic. It should be noted, however, that the motivation of both men and women has decreased rather than increased, and that the motivation of female business leaders has decreased the most.

As can be seen, the workforce has decreased in companies led by both women and men, by 299 and 657 people, respectively. Employment has increased by almost 300 people in the industry category where companies have a close connection to higher technology. As expected, the reverse is true for companies in the hotel and restaurant industry, which have seen a reduction in employment corresponding to 877 people.

The number of employees in the smallest size class, 5–9 employees, has decreased by 666 individuals and about half that number is among companies with 10–19 employees. The largest companies included in the study have increased marginally in size, measured by the number of employees. The two regional categories, large cities and larger cities and the surrounding area, have both been reduced in staff by up to 500 people each. However, the regional grouping of smaller cities and towns and the surrounding area has virtually maintained the same level of employment over the past nine months. It can also be seen that the group with the oldest companies, established in 1990 or earlier, together has increased its number of employees by 170 people, while the younger companies have decreased by 5–600 employees.

7.11 Conclusions

The purpose of this chapter is to assess how the pandemic has affected Swedish small businesses in four sub-industries. There is specific interest in highlighting differences and similarities between women's and men's entrepreneurship within different classification bases, based on responses from 228 women and 972 men who had the role of operational business leaders and/or owners. The shares regarding men and women depend on how many of each gender is represented in the various sub-sectors, of which there are two in the manufacturing industry and two in the service sector. In the various sub-sectors, women's shares vary between 13% and 28%, with the lowest shares in manufacturing industries and the highest share in the hotel and restaurant sub-sector. This report analyses the similarities and differences between companies run by women and men, how small businesses have taken advantage of possible government measures, the significance of these measures and how these entrepreneurs perceived the future prospects of the pandemic's effects over six to seven months from March to October 2020.

7.11.1 The Total Effects of the Pandemic Varied Greatly between Sub-Sectors, but the Total Effects on Employment Were Limited

The 1200 small businesses interviewed employed a total of about 15,000 people. Compared with 2019, the companies as a whole reduced employment in 2020 by approximately 6% or just over 950 people. The smallest companies lost the most employees, while companies in the largest size class saw a slight increase. On the one hand, there were fewer employees in small companies with women as leaders, which relatively means a greater effect than for men, because women relatively dominate in the smallest small companies. Men in the role of business leaders, on the other hand, dominate in, for example, the sub-industry of manufacturing with high and medium-high technology, an industry that has increased employees during the same period. In terms of sub-sectors, the largest reductions have taken place in hotels and restaurants.

7.11.2 Small Businesses Stated that they Benefited Greatly from State Support Programmes

Ranked by utilization rate, cost-cutting support was the most widely used. Such support mainly comprised reduced employer contributions (88%), compensation for sick pay costs (65%), short-term layoffs (47%)

and adjustment support (18%). There were also deferrals of VAT and employer contributions (17%), a programme that provided opportunities to postpone costs. The lowest utilization rate was found for the financial support with a government loan guarantee. For the latter, one reason for the low rate is that eight out of ten small companies reported that external financing was not relevant during the pandemic.

Proportions of companies stating that support was of great or decisive importance varied between 58% and 87%. There were no differences between women and men in terms of utilization rate, except that women had a higher utilization rate for adjustment support and, to a greater extent than men, believed that the programmes were of decisive importance to the company. It was mainly companies with poorer financial development that requested state aid, which is natural.

7.11.3 In some Areas, there Were Significant Differences between Women and Men

For our selected sub-industries, there were some significant differences between women and men. This was the case in manufacturing, where men in the role of business leaders are dominant; and in the hotel and restaurant sub-industry, where women are overrepresented, men considered to a greater extent that their motivation was unaffected by the pandemic, while women believed that their motivation had decreased. Similarly, women reported to a greater extent than men that their fear of failure as an entrepreneur had increased. There is, of course, a connection between entrepreneurs reporting reduced motivation and increased fear. In addition, women-led companies have lower turnover and fewer employees than companies with men as business leaders. Women are also overrepresented in management roles for younger companies. The proportion of women with a foreign background who are entrepreneurs is lower than the corresponding proportion for men.

7.11.4 For Most Comparisons between Women and Men, there Were no Significant Differences

There were a number of areas where comparisons between women's and men's entrepreneurship showed no significant differences, such as between different regions in the country; in terms of how small businesses perceive that the state has helped them cope with the effects of the pandemic; regarding the need for new skills, where both groups (80%) say that there is no such need; and with regard to new business opportunities, with both genders to the same extent (about 40%) stating that they see such opportunities.

In previous research, there are summaries of similarities and differences between men and women as small businesses, see, for example, Holmquist and Sundin (2015). Our study used four sub-industries, two in the manufacturing industry and two in the service sector. There were more female than male small entrepreneurs in the two studied service industries and more men than women in the manufacturing industry compared with their relative share in the total sample. This was despite the fact that we chose a lower limit of at least five employees when selecting companies for the sample, but like the study above, we saw greater similarities between women and men than differences. Some further examples of this are the following.

There were no differences between women and men regarding the positive or negative effect of the pandemic. The majority of both genders feared a negative impact. The proportion of entrepreneurs who believed that motivation had increased was equally large for both genders. Just over four out of ten women and men had reduced or waived salaries or other remuneration during the pandemic, and in the sub-sector hotels and restaurants, this figure was seven out of ten for entrepreneurs of both genders. There were no differences between regions, number of employees or age of the entrepreneurs.

Additional areas where we did not see differences between men and women were in their perception of the pandemic's effect on liquidity and profitability, the ability to recruit staff and obtain external financing, assessment of the effects of government measures, the effect on sales and order intake and how entrepreneurs viewed future uses of different digitization possibilities.

Our conclusion from this is that there are more similarities than differences and that it is, therefore, exciting in the future to analyse in more detail similarities between effects for women's and men's entrepreneurship.

References

Brown, R., & Rocha, A. (2020). Entrepreneurial uncertainty during the COVID-19 crisis: Mapping the temporal dynamics of entrepreneurial finance. *Journal of Business Venturing Insights, 14*, e00174.

Cacciotti, G., Hayton, J. C., Mitchell, J. R., & Giazitzoglu, A. (2016). A reconceptualization of fear of failure in entrepreneurship. *Journal of Business Venturing, 31*(3), 302–325.

Carstensen, L. L., Shavit, Y. Z., & Barnes, J. T. (2020). Age advantages in emotional experience persist even under threat from the COVID-19 pandemic. *Psychological Science, 31*(11), 1374–1385.

Cowling, M., Marlow, S., & Liu, W. (2019). Gender and bank lending after the global financial crisis: are women entrepreneurs safer bets?. *Small Business Economics*, 1–28.

Davidsson, P. (2020). Guidepost: Look out! See change? Sea change ahead! *Academy of Management Discoveries, 6*(3), 321–324.

Eurostat. (2016). Aggregation of manufacturing based on NACE Rev 2. Aggregations on services based on NACE Rev 2.—https://ec.europa.eu/eurostat/cache/metadata/Annexes/htec_esms_an3.pdf.

Holmquist, C., & Sundin, E. (2015). *25 år med kvinnors företagande: Från osynligt till drivkraft för tillväxt*. Stockholm: Tillväxtverket.

Kuckertz, A., Brändle, L., Gaudig, A., Hinderer, S., Morales Reyes, C. A., Prochotta, A., Steinbrink, K. M., & Berger, E. S. C. (2020). Startups in times of crisis—A rapid response to the COVID-19 pandemic. *Journal of Business Venturing Insights, 1*, e00169.

Lee, C. K., Cottle, G. W., Simmons, S. A., & Wiklund, J. (2020). Fear not, want not: Untangling the effects of social cost of failure on high-growth entrepreneurship. *Small Business Economics*.

Malmström, M., & Wincent, J. (2018). Bank lending and financial discrimination from the formal economy: How women entrepreneurs get forced into involuntary bootstrapping. *Journal of Business Venturing Insights, 10*, 1–8.

Manolova, T. S., Brush, C. G., Edelman, L. F., & Elam, A. (2020). Pivoting to stay the course: How women entrepreneurs take advantage of opportunities created by the COVID-19 pandemic. *International Small Business Journal: Researching Entrepreneurship, 38*(6), 481–491.

McGrath, R. G. (2010). Business models: A discovery driven approach. *Long Range Planning, 43*(2–3), 247–261.

Newman, A., Mole, K. F., Ucbasaran, D., Subramanian, N., & Lockett, A. (2018). Can your network make you happy? Entrepreneurs' business network utilization and subjective well-being. *British Journal of Management, 29*(4), 613–633.

Reymen, M. M. J., Adries, P., Berends, H., Mauer, R., Stephan, U., & Van Burg, E. (2015). Understanding dynamics of strategic decision making in venture creation: A process study of effectuation and causation. *Strategic Entrepreneurship Journal, 9*, 2351–2379.

Sarasvathy, S. D. (2001). Causation and effectuation: Toward a theoretical shift from economic inevitability to entrepreneurial contingency. *Academy of Management Review, 26*(2), 243–263.

Thorgren, S., & Williams, T. A. (2020). Staying alive during an unfolding crisis: How SMEs ward off impending disaster. *Journal of Business Venturing Insights, 14*, e00187.

Wennberg, K., Pathak, S., & Autio, E. (2013). How culture moulds the effects of self-efficacy and fear of failure on entrepreneurship. *Entrepreneurship & Regional Development, 25*(9–10), 756–780.

Wenzel, M., Stanske, S., & Lieberman, M. B. (2020). Strategic responses to crisis. *Strategic Management Journal*, (March), 7–18.

Part III

CSR, Large Companies and COVID-19

8

Corporate Sustainability and COVID-19 Responses in West Africa: The Potential for Sustained Linkages Between Philanthropy and CSR Practices

Adaeze Okoye and Ijeoma Nwagwu

8.1 Introduction

The unprecedented pandemic of 2020 has triggered global responses from companies and various charitable donations to government and development agendas. This chapter examines such donations through the lens of corporate sustainability. Corporate sustainability (CS) and Corporate Social Responsibility (CSR) will be used in this chapter as alternative themes on the same subject matter. The specific focus of the work is to examine whether the recent type of corporate philanthropy within CS bears any linkages to a more sustainable approach relevant for African human development. This chapter is written during the

A. Okoye (✉)
University of Brighton, Brighton, UK
e-mail: a.okoye@brighton.ac.uk

I. Nwagwu
Lagos Business School, Lagos, Nigeria

A. Sörensson et al. (eds.), *Corporate Responsibility and Sustainability during the Coronavirus Crisis*, Palgrave Studies in Governance, Leadership and Responsibility,
https://doi.org/10.1007/978-3-030-73847-1_8

pandemic so it takes an evaluative approach of actions carried out so far, while making potential suggestions for the future.

Corporate sustainability and COVID-19 responses are best examined in context. The context examined in this chapter is West Africa. West Africa is a key region of Sub-Saharan Africa located towards the Western end of the continent covering 8 million square kilometres of diverse ecosystems and roughly ¼ of the African continent. (USGS, EROS 2020) It has a population of over 391 million (UN 2019) within 17 countries (UN STATS 2020) including Benin, Burkina Faso, Cabo Verde, Cote d'Ivoire, Gambia, Ghana, Guinea, Guinea-Bissau, Liberia, Mali, Mauritania, Niger, Nigeria, Saint Helena, Senegal, Sierra Leone and Togo (although the economic union, ECOWAS membership list does not have Mauritania [left in 1999] or the British Overseas Territory of Saint Helena). The World Bank in its overview of Western and Central Africa notes, 'With 12% of its population being under the age of 15, Western and Central Africa has one of the youngest populations in the world' (World Bank 2020).

A majority of these West African countries are resource-rich and rely on the export of commodities and dominant industries in the commodities sector. This fuelled high growth in the mid-2000s before a downturn recently following the fall in commodity prices (World Bank 2020). In spite of this potential, there is a significant underperformance in human development with significant gaps in education, health and skills. The Human Capital Index evidenced that under current conditions, children born in Sub-Saharan Africa today will only reach 40% of their productivity potential in adulthood due to deficits in human capital investment (World Bank 2020).

Since the late 1990s, the conception of the state's role in development has changed, alongside privatization and liberalization policies came the realization that with the changing context came changing responsibilities for both states and businesses (World Bank 1997). This coincides with the rise of CSR as a concept alongside complementary themes such as corporate social performance, corporate citizenship and corporate sustainability. This reflects the expectations that private enterprises would be made to take into account the public interest, because they have gained much more influence over hitherto public spheres, and thus re-evaluate their relationship with society (Lydenberg 2005). It has been stressed that 'in Latin American and Africa, nations dismantled trade barriers and adopted stringent controls on government spending in the hope of making rapid strides to end poverty' (Lydenberg 2005, p. 10). This aspiration did not materialize, instead it has become evident that the multi-stakeholder partnership approach targeted at development goals is necessary. The UN SDG 17 focused on capacity building, and multi-stakeholder partnership for achieving the sustainable development goals acknowledges this new role.

There is evidence that corporate philanthropy is the dominant type of CSR on the African continent (Benon-be-isan Nyuur et al. 2014) (Idemudia 2014). This chapter seeks to re-evaluate the role of such corporate philanthropy in the light of the COVID pandemic and suggest potential ways in which such responses can be embodied in sustained corporate responsibility practices geared towards sustainable human development.

It will examine: CSR types with a focus on corporate philanthropy, COVID private sector coalition platforms set up in two West African countries, specific company philanthropy examples and any emerging linkages with sustainable development agendas. The chapter will indicate the potentials and limitations of existing corporate giving and how evolving post-COVID corporate practices may lead towards better sustainability.

8.2 CSR Typology: Philanthropy to Sustained CSR Strategy

CSR and Corporate Sustainability (CS) are not mutually exclusive, instead they are two themes which refer to complementary aspects of the business and society relationships. Deloitte (2020) points that 'Sustainability is a comprehensive approach to management of organizations which is focused on creating and maximizing long-term economic, social and environmental value. It is a response to the challenges of the modern world facing organizations from the public and private sectors'

ing, assisting individuals, e.g., children, aged or physically challenged who may not ever be able to fend for themselves. Notice that this is the genuine philanthropy that asks nothing back. (p. 17)

This typology characterizes some of the complexity that exists within corporate philanthropy. Transformational philanthropy becomes an ideal type, where there is the potential for targeting underdevelopment and helping innovative change. In the face of the pandemic, many funds have been set up and donations received. However, it is necessary to examine these developments as one would seek to avoid a soothing philanthropy which does not address the root causes of the issues, in this case the health systems deficit, education gap and lack of infrastructure, rather it could be a short term genuine act of support without a transformative potential.

8.3 COVID Responses: Country Level

Nigeria and Ghana have had some significant impact from COVID-19. A UNICEF situational report of June 2020 states: 'As of 15th June 2020, Ghana remained the second most impacted country in the West and Central African region after Nigeria, ranking third in the number of cumulative cases in the WHO Africa region, following South Africa and Nigeria. The number of people confirmed to have contracted the coronavirus in Ghana now stands at 11,964' (UNICEF 2020).

In Nigeria the Private Sector Coalition Against COVID-19 (CACOVID, Nigeria) and in Ghana COVID-19 Private Sector Fund were set up in response to the unprecedented pandemic which affected both countries in 2020. CACOVID Nigeria was formed on 26 March by an initiative led by Aliko Dangote (reputed as Africa's wealthiest man and backed by Access Bank Group, Zenith Bank, Guaranty Trust Bank, and several others, all part of Nigeria's private sector; Africa Business Magazine 2020). CACOVID describes itself as 'The Coalition Against Covid-19 (CACOVID) is a Private Sector task force in partnership with the Federal Government, the Nigeria Centre for Disease Control (NCDC) and the World Health Organisation (WHO) with the sole aim of combating Coronavirus (COVID-19) in Nigeria' (2020 CACOVID website CACOVID (2020b)). The total contribution as of 30 June 2020 stands at roughly USD 79 million (CACOVID list of contributors 30 June 2020). Although donations have come from a diverse range of organizations, the partnership appears driven by the wealthy dominant shareholders of indigenous companies. The report notes that major private players include 'Segun Agbaje (Guaranty Trust Bank), Jim Ovia (Zenith Bank), Herbert Wigwe (Access Bank), Tony Elumelu (United Bank for Africa), Abdulsamad Rabiu of BUA Group, Folorunsho Alakija of Famfa Oil Limited, Oba Otudeko (First Bank), Femi Otedola of Amperion Power, billionaire businessman Mike Adenuga of Globacom and the Nigeria Deposit Insurance Corporation have provided \$2.59m each. The Nigerian National Petroleum Corporation alongside some oil companies has pledged \$30m to the Nigeria Centre for Disease Control to improve patient care, medical supplies and equipment' (Africa Business Magazine 2020).

The mission and focus are on health: 'provide direct support to private and public healthcare's ability to respond to the crisis by providing funds to set up several testing, isolation and treatment centres in all geo-political zones; aggressively increasing general public's awareness, education and buy-in to prevent panic and resulting chaos' (2020 CACOVID website CACOVID (2020b)). The direct focus is on the provision of medical facilities in the six geopolitical zones. These appear to be COVID-specific treatment centres which will 'involve the creation of testing, isolation and treatment centres, and include the provision of Intensive Care Units (ICUs) and molecular testing labs' (CACOVID Press release 3, 2020 CACOVID (2020a)). The website contains pictures of isolation centres built in Yaba, Lagos.

This coordinated and immediate response will provide immediate short-term relief and enhancement of the capacity of the country to deal with COVID-19; however, there is not yet any evidence of how this will fit into a long-term capacity enhancement for Nigeria.

Nigeria with a population close to 200 million has approximately 5% health insurance coverage (Awosusi et al. 2015). Nigeria is a federation of 36 states and a Federal Capital Territory by virtue of the 1999 Constitution, having also 768 local governments and 6 area councils (Omar 2012). Therefore, there are three tiers of health care—federal, state and local authority (Scott-Emuakpor 2010). The WHO observes that there is also a human resources challenge in this area, because, while Nigeria has a large stock of health care professionals, they are densely located in urban areas (2020). Nigeria also recognizes three modes of health care delivery: orthodox, alternative and traditional (WHO 2020). There is also a major health care infrastructure deficit with very low bed per thousand population—0.9 in 2015 (PWC 2016). On the one hand, the potential for public-private partnerships to boost provision of health care infrastructure and provision had already been noted prior to the COVID pandemic; however, there is some doubt that the narrow scope of CACOVID will ameliorate or impact heavily on this agenda.

On the other hand, Ghana is by virtue of its 1992 Constitution, a unitary republic with features of decentralization (Antwi-Boasiako 2010). The country has 16 Administrative regions, with the capital of the country as Accra city (Sarfo and Karuppannan 2020). Ghana has an estimated population of about 30 million with a moderately successful health care system. It has over 50% health insurance coverage (Drislane et al. 2014). Nevertheless, there is also an urban concentration of facilities and provision of health care. The Ghana COVID Private Sector Fund was set up by the business community in response to the anticipated shortfall and missed targets in health by the government of Ghana (GoG). Specifically, the rationale was 'for the private sector to support the GoG effort to win the C-19 War' (Ghana COVID-19 Fund website 2020). Therefore, they aim 'to partly finance GoG's interventions and equip select health service and supply chain facilities and activities in the fight against Covid-19' (Ghana COVID-19 Fund website 2020).

This is similar to the approach taken in Nigeria although it is more explicit on the facilitative role it seeks to play in support of government effort. The scope is still COVID-specific. The fund just completed Ghana's first infectious disease centre in July 2020, located within the Ga East Municipal Hospital Accra and intends to construct similar facilities in other regions such as Kumasi, Tamale and Takoradi (Aug 2020, GhanaCovid19Fund News).

Overall, both country-level coalition responses represent emergency responses to an unprecedented pandemic but they also highlight three potential key developments which could have sustainable future implications. These are, firstly, the large-scale involvement of indigenous small and medium-sized enterprises (SMEs) in the private sector responses; secondly, the creation of a collaborative partnership based platform; and thirdly the presence of long-term and short-term objectives.

8.4 COVID-19 Responses: Institutional Practices

This next section of the chapter explores illustrative cases of large multinational enterprises' (MNEs') response—Lafarge in Nigeria and Unilever in Nigeria and Ghana—in terms of their approach to and practice of corporate social responsibility and sustainability, their response to the COVID-19 crisis in a complex environment marked by deepening poverty and climate change issues. These examples are chosen as indicative of MNEs active in the West African region.

With tens of thousands of employees and businesses that span diverse supply chains across the globe, these companies have inevitably encountered setbacks and occasionally taken deliberate missteps leading to negative impacts on society. However, these large companies have a stated intention of integrating sustainability into their core values, not only from a sense of ethical correctness but also from a recognition that it makes good business sense to do so in a competitive global environment. In the competitive global marketplace, stakeholder value—based on the economic, ecological and social impacts a company has on a range of stakeholders—is increasingly recognized as a way to achieve competitive advantage.

The COVID-19 crisis provides a perfect setting in which to consider the corporate social responsibility tenets and practices of these companies and what that might portend for the future. Moreover, what these giant companies say and do with respect to their corporate social responsibility is highly influential in the business landscape of emerging market economies such as Nigeria, where over 90% of the ecosystem is made up of small and medium enterprises employing less than ten people. Many of the latter companies are also at the early stages of formally institutionalizing corporate social responsibility and sustainability frameworks and to some extent consider companies such as Lafarge and Unilever as exemplars in the field of sustainability. In exploring Lafarge Africa and Unilever as illustrative cases, we offer some initial examination of how the COVID-19 pandemic has influenced CSR and sustainability.

8.4.1 Lafarge Africa Plc.

Lafarge Africa Plc. is a leading building materials company, specializing in building materials across Africa. The company is a member of the LafargeHolcim Group, a global industry leader in the manufacture of cement, aggregates and concrete. The company has been profitable over much of its history, since 1833, with a third of its sales coming from markets outside of Western Europe and North America. Over half of these were in Africa and Asia Pacific countries such as Bangladesh, Morocco, Zambia and China (Laszlo 2008). Lafarge's presence in Nigeria and similar emerging markets presents a unique set of social challenges including land use and pollution issues in relation to poor local populations faced with new cement plants or quarries, avoiding corruption practices and respecting labour standards, and modernizing old cement plants with workforce reduction involving hundreds of employees. To give an example: it was sued in the Federal High Court, Abeokuta Nigeria in 2019 by the Ewekoro community of Ogun state, Nigeria, for alleged pollution by cement dust (Ramon 2019).

Lafarge Africa Plc., sustainability practices are driven by the LafargeHolcim Group's Sustainability Strategy—(The 2030 Plan—Building for Tomorrow) This encapsulates the company's approach to navigating these myriad challenges and making its operations more sustainable in an industry perceived as being both dirty and energy inefficient. The strategy revolves around four areas—Climate, Circular Economy, Environment and Community. The strategy aligns with the majority of the United Nations Sustainable Development Goals and reports using the Global Reporting Initiative's (GRI's) G4 reporting standard. Lafarge in Nigeria participates actively with other businesses through the United Nations Global Compact, as well as the United Nations Private Sector Advisory Group, to drive its sustainability framework on a collective platform. The COVID-19 crisis would cause the company to publicly restate its corporate social responsibility position.

Lafarge Africa would find itself at the centre of the Coronavirus crisis when on 27 February 2020, Nigeria recorded its index case of the virus in the person of an Italian man who had visited a Lafarge factory as a vendor of one of the company's suppliers (Reuters 2020). The company was thrust into the arena of action against coronavirus as its public perception weighed heavily against its corporate image and its share prices fell on the Nigerian Stock Exchange. Lafarge Africa CEO contested assumptions that the company's tumbling share prices had anything to do with the negative press associated with the coronavirus index case. Faced with negative press, the company proceeded to make a targeted and very visible response to the coronavirus pandemic. It leveraged its vast resources to shut down facilities where employees had been exposed to the virus through the index case, a process of shutdown that would prove more painful to smaller companies in the region when the government eventually enforced lockdowns.

Lafarge Africa went further to convert two of its facilities to isolation centres, provided infrastructural support such as ambulances, generators, personal protective equipment for health personnel to states where their facilities are located. They also contributed an N500 million intervention fund to provide medical infrastructure, food and essential medications to its host communities. In the second phase of the intervention, Lafarge distributed food and medical supplies to its host communities targeting 60,000 beneficiaries across 10,000 families.

Lafarge Africa CEO, El Dokani said:

> *"Lafarge's intervention is built on the insight that a combination of interventions is required to contain the spread of COVID-19". He said that these critical interventions include providing personal protection equipment for the medical staff who have to come into close contact with COVID-19 patients, the provision of testing kits which enable the quick identification and isolation of infected people, ambulances to safely transport infected people and the provision of decent isolation centres to accommodate them. He further commented on*

Lafarge's intervention, "The fight against COVID 19 will be won only if this trio is effectively deployed -testing kits, protection equipment and isolation facilities. Lafarge Africa is determined to work with Nigerians and the Nigerian Government in the fight against COVID-19 in Nigeria." (Thomas 2020)

In the wake of the coronavirus, Lafarge Africa was forced to ramp up its social investments and target them for emergency food aid as well as health and safety measures. At least momentarily, the broader focus of its corporate social responsibility in the country would narrow, deprioritizing for the moment the company's long-term commitment to education, public health broadly, affordable housing, environment, climate and circular economy. The temporarily de-prioritized areas remain key parts of Lafarge's corporate social responsibility vision but were not focal points of attention in the Coronavirus crisis. Below is a description of the other areas Lafarge regularly acts within its corporate social responsibility framework.

The strategy for social investments in Lafarge is informed by their sustainability ambitions. Under the Communities' pillar, localization of the plan in Nigeria focuses the commitment to four sub-pillars: Shelter/Infrastructure; Education; Health and Safety; and Economic Empowerment.

In recent years, as concerns about the impact building materials can have on the environment have grown, efforts have been made to make firms in the sector address and reduce their emissions. According to a 2018 report by the think-tank Chatham House, over 4 billion metric tons of cement are produced annually which accounts 'for around 8% of global CO_2 emissions.' Lafarge Africa attempts to reduce the CO_2 emissions associated with its production of cement in Nigeria as well as the impact of that process on the lives of local communities surrounding its plants.[1] Lafarge continues with a focus on thermal substitution rates (use

[1] A chemical reaction occurs when the raw material (limestone—CaO_3) is converted into lime – CaO, used for clinker in the kiln at an extremely high temperature. Lafarge uses the Clinker factor management, which enhances assessments for improvement; partial substitution of clinker in final cement products with alternative mineral components such as fly ash. This reduces the carbon emissions from mining new resources and emissions from the chemical process of calcination. Fossil fuel burning, Burning of fuels required to heat kilns to the high temperatures is needed for the calcination process.

of alternative fuels like biomass) within manufacturing processes. Lafarge Africa has also been exploring alternative 'zero waste' fuel options, injecting agricultural waste (biomass) into their cement kilns as an alternative energy source.

Waste materials are co-processed as alternative energy and raw materials for different aspects of the cement manufacturing process. The purchase of biomass from local suppliers has created new streams of income for local companies and impacted the livelihood of hundreds of Nigerians. Beneficiaries include waste gatherers, collectors and transporters, amongst others. Lafarge Africa Plc. works with local suppliers (SMEs) to ensure that goods supplied—that is, raw materials and waste products—meet international quality standards.[2]

Lafarge adopts a strategic approach to collecting, transporting, processing, recycling and disposing of different types of waste within plants and offices. Lafarge plants have waste management procedures that are in line with national environmental (waste and sanitation) regulations.

Lafarge can demonstrate corporate investments in food aid and health and have expanded dramatically in two states hosting Lafarge facilities, and a comprehensive approach to the pandemic is shown in these areas by the company. However, there is a need to (perhaps in collaboration with other companies through PSAG and UNGC local network) geographically broaden what appears to be a model holistic approach to addressing coronavirus impacts across the country. Furthermore, companies must also not lose sight, in focusing on the pandemic, in supporting routine health services such as maternal and child health services. There is evidence of drop in vaccinations, antenatal services and care for persons suffering endemic diseases such as malaria, tuberculosis and HIV as the focus of public health resources and attention moves to the coronavirus (Hogan et al. 2020). Areas of corporate social responsibility related to the environment and circular economy still need to be front and centre of corporate social responsibility in African countries considering that Africa

[2] Nikoy Nigeria Limited and Al Bari Nigeria Limited are examples of such SMEs. Nikoy is a biomass waste collection Company that generates income through the collection of waste (palm kernel shells used in the Geocycle solution for heat production). Al Bari is a waste collection company that sources various biomass types from communities across the Country and supplies to Lafarge Africa Plc.

is the continent most negatively impacted by climate change and that this is more strategically linked to the company's business objective and expertise. Following the analogy above this may be classed as a soothing philanthropy which is not yet on the threshold of a transformational philanthropy.

8.4.2 Unilever

Unilever is a consumer goods company whose products include household items, beauty, personal care products, pharmaceutical products, food items, and many more. Unilever operates in over 100 countries including Ghana and Nigeria.

Unilever has three big goals under its global **Unilever Sustainable Living Plan** (2010) to achieve social, environmental and economic performance across the value chain, underpinned by nine commitments and targets. They are also focused on those areas that can drive the biggest change and support the UN Sustainable Development Goals (SDGs). The three big goals include the following:

(a) Improving health and well-being for more than 1 billion by 2020
(b) Reducing environmental impact by half by 2030 and
(c) Enhancing livelihoods for millions

Unilever is particularly well placed as its core products include soaps, and this has allowed it to partner with UK Department for International Development for a COVID-19 handwashing campaign (Unilever 2010). This is tailored to specific countries across Africa including Ghana. Unilever confirms: 'the initiative – backed by £50 million [roughly USD 70 million) each from Unilever and UK aid—will support programmes aimed at raising awareness and changing behaviour, to make sure people are washing their hands with soaps regularly and disinfecting surfaces' (Unilever 2010).

With the onset of COVID-19, the company also commenced donation of its food and hygiene products in Nigeria and Ghana (GhanaTimes 2020; Marketscreener 2020). The rationale for Unilever's donations can be found in statements by the Director of Corporate Affairs and Sustainable Business, Ghana and Nigeria. She states that 'as a purpose driven organization, we understand the need for proper hygiene during a crisis of this nature. We are also aware that the restriction of movement has affected the livelihood of many and that is why we are sending food and hygiene products worth 200 million Naira [roughly USD 500,000] to Nigerians who need them' (Marketscreener 2020). The donations were made in collaboration with Ministries of Health in Ogun and Lagos and other states, as well as non-profit organizations with direct access to vulnerable populations.

Operationally, specific protocols were outlined for staff to ensure the utmost safety of staff and the communities. They include the prohibition of travel staying at home if experiencing flu-like symptoms, maintaining hygiene and social distance with customers, office-based staff working from home, using sanitizers and many more. Field sales employees were required to connect with customers virtually wherever possible and minimize the use of public transport, if a customer visit is necessary (Unilever, COVID Disclosure 2020).

8.4.3 Lessons from the Illustrative Cases

Overall, Lafarge and Unilever advance a clearly defined formal sustainability and corporate social responsibility agenda, tackling major challenges facing emerging markets that include health and well-being, climate and energy, environment, communities. These organizations also leverage global frameworks within their CSR scheme, such as the United Nations SDGs, GRI and participate in global networks such as the United Nations Global Compact (UNGC) and PSAG. Unilever focuses on health and well-being, livelihood and environment. Lafarge deals with manufacturing building products while Unilever produces mainly food, personal and household items. However, in the face of COVID responses, it is still an emerging picture which indicates cooperation with some relevant stakeholders in areas of expertise developed pre-COVID.

There is an existing framework of corporate social responsibility incorporated into both companies, and, with the COVID outbreak, there has been a greater wave of philanthropic activities in both companies. They have deployed corporate philanthropy in saving lives and livelihoods through food aid, monetary and product donations, as well as health provision in the current climate. As economic recession takes hold in the region, the question is to what extent these companies can continue to provide these interventions to support the social safety net for the poor and vulnerable whilst advancing other aspects of their corporate social responsibility portfolio, particularly commitments related to the climate. Further, to what extent will the philosophy and forms of corporate sustainability change in response to systemic human capital investment deficits laid bare by the pandemic?

Alongside a health and educational crisis, the COVID-19 crisis has sparked a food security crisis in Africa, as documented by the World Bank, with agricultural production potentially contracting between 2.6% in an optimistic scenario and up to 7% if there are trade blockages. Food imports would decline substantially (as much as 25% or as little as 13%) due to a combination of higher transaction costs and reduced domestic demand (Zeufack et al. 2020). Already Nigeria reports growing food insecurity and economic challenges resulting from food inflation prompted by disruptions in the food value chain owing to COVID-19 lockdowns and import disruptions (PWC Nigeria 2020). These patterns are manifest across the region and in varying forms globally, calling for a deeper corporate commitment to transformational philanthropy within a multisectoral framework.

8.5 Conclusion

There is a rise of soothing philanthropic giving, in the face of the unpredictable circumstances of COVID-19. As Ahen and Amankwah-Amoah (2018) propose, this will gain public relations kudos for the corporations involved and also arises from a genuine response to the situation. However, there is a deeper potential to elevate this to transformational philanthropy, not only by linking with other aspects of CSR—ethical, legal and economic—but also by linking with wider sustainable development goals and seeking truly innovative ways of transforming the lives of communities and consumers beyond palliative responses. There are a number of key observations which indicate prospective potential and further scope for future research.

Firstly, the rise of national platforms of public-private partnerships to tackle the insufficiency of government capacity such as that seen in CACOVID and Ghana COVID-19 private sector fund can act as an emerging template for private sector collective action to tackle issues of public interest. The potential to demonstrate collective goodwill and community interest and also deliver on government target need areas is exemplary. This can also be seen in the dominance of indigenous SMEs in these coalition platforms, and this could become a template for collaborative efforts that draw on local content as well as multinational activity potentially leading to more sustainable Afro-centric practices. Nevertheless, the actual funds derived and the ability—to maintain momentum in acquiring such funds outside of the emergency situation such as COVID—will be ascertained more adequately in future. The CACOVID funding thermometer indicates approximately 35% achievement of the 120 billion naira target, with a list of contributors on the website, as of 30 June 2020.

Secondly, Unilever in its handwashing campaign which brings together home country development aid body (in this case, UK)—an ethical aspect and its strategic product (soap)—allows the company to demonstrate CSR and philanthropy from a basis of its own business capability and expertise.

Thirdly, the CSR strategy of companies will not prevent legal responsibilities which may arise as communities may still bring class actions on cases of alleged pollution even where they are in receipt of corporate giving. This underlies Carroll's typology of CSR which embodies the legal, ethical, economic and philanthropic.

Finally, while the immediate short-term response of delivering palliative care remains important in such a complex environment, with the immediate needs of communities, whose food security have been severely affected by COVID-19 and the preventative policies adopted by their governments. Nevertheless, the long-term sustainability of CSR action in the face of COVID-19 is a key concern as human development on the African continent is essential to global SDGs. The potential underlying themes of poverty, hunger and vulnerability of health systems exposed by COVID in this context are long-term challenges. Therefore, the comprehensive yet targeted platforms, which the responses provide, could be translated into wider post-COVID sustainable responses.

References

Africa Business Magazine. (2020). Nigeria: Group forms coalition to mobilize business sector to provide resources in efforts fight against Covid-19. *Business & Human Rights Resource Centre*. Retrieved September 7, 2020, from https://www.business-humanrights.org.

Ahen, F., & Amankwah-Amoah, J. (2018). Institutional voids and the philanthropization of CSR practices: Insights from developing economies. *Sustainability, 10*(7), 1–27.

Antwi-Boasiako, K. (2010). Administrative decentralization: Should districts and regions elect their own leaders in Ghana? *African Social Science Review, 4*(1). Retrieved from https://digitalcommons.kennesaw.edu/assr/vol4/iss1/3.

Awosusi, A., Folaranmi, T., & Yates, R. (2015). Nigeria's new government and public financing for universal health coverage. *The Lancet Global Health, 3*(9), e514–e515.

Benon-be-isan Nyuur, R., Ofori, D. F., & Debrah, Y. (2014). Corporate social responsibility in Sub-Saharan Africa: Hindering and supporting factors. *African Journal of Economic and Management Studies, 5*(1), 93–113.

Carroll, A. B. (1991). The pyramid of corporate social responsibility: Toward the moral management of organizational stakeholders. *Business Horizons, 34*(4), 39–48.

Chen, J., Patten, D., & Roberts, R. (2008). Corporate charitable contributions: A corporate social performance or legitimacy strategy? *Journal of Business Ethics, 82*(1), 131–144.

Deloitte. (2020). Retrieved September 7, 2020, from https://www2.deloitte.com/ru/en/pages/risk/solutions/sustainability-and-csr.html.

Drislane, F. W., Akpalu, A., & Wegdam, H. H. (2014). The medical system in Ghana. *The Yale Journal of Biology and Medicine, 87*(3), 321–326.

GhanaTimes. (2020). Unilever Ghana supports more institutions on Covid 19. June 22. Retrieved September 7, 2020, from https://www.ghanaiantimes.com.gh/unilever-ghana-supports-more-institutions-on-covid-19/.

Helly, D. (2013). Philanthropy in Africa and the future of EU's development policies: Useful synergies? Retrieved from https://cadmus.eui.eu//handle/1814/28978.

Hogan, A., Jewell, B., Sherrard-Smith, E., et al. (2020). *Potential impact of the COVID-19 pandemic on HIV, Tuberculosis, and Malaria in low-income and middle-income countries: A modelling study*. Lancet Global Health. Published online 13 July 2020. Retrieved September 7, 2020, from https://www.thelancet.com/journals/langlo/article/PIIS2214-109X(20)30288-6/fulltext#seccestitle10.

Idemudia, U. (2014). Corporate social responsibility and development in Africa: Issues and possibilities. *Geography Compass, 8*(7), 421–435.

Laszlo, C. (2008). *Sustainable value: How the world's leading companies are doing well by doing good*. Stanford University Press.

Lydenberg, S. (2005). *Corporations and the public interest: Guiding the invisible hand*. Berrett-Koehler Publishers.

Marketscreener. (2020). Unilever Nigeria: Supports Covid Nigeria fight with food and hygiene. Retrieved September 7, 2020, from https://www.marketscreener.com/quote/stock/UNILEVER-NIGERIA-PLC-8252801/news/Unilever-Nigeria-supports-COVID-19-fight-with-food-hygiene-30582338/.

Montiel, I. (2008). Corporate social responsibility and corporate sustainability: Separate pasts, common futures. *Organization & Environment, 21*(3), 245–269.

Omar, M. (2012). Ensuring free, fair, and credible elections in local governments in Nigeria. *Developing Country Studies, 2*(11/12), 75.

Private Sector Coalition Against Covid-19 (CACOVID). (2020a). Retrieved September 7, 2020, from https://www.cacovid.org/pdf/cacovid_press_release_3.pdf.

Private Sector Coalition Against Covid-19 (CACOVID). (2020b). Retrieved September 7, 2020, from https://www.cacovid.org/#partners.

PWC. (2016). Retrieved September 7, 2020, from https://www.pwc.com/ng/en/assets/pdf/pwc-ppps-the-antidote-to-nigerias-healthcare-infrastructure-deficit.pdf.

PWC Nigeria. (2020). Responding to the impact of Covid-19 on Food Security and Agriculture in Nigeria. Retrieved September 7, 2020, from https://www.pwc.com/ng/en/publications/impact-covid-19-food-security-nigeria.html.

Ramon, O. (2019). Alleged pollution: Ewekoro community files N1trn lawsuit against Lafarge. *Punch Nigeria Newspapers*, January 10. Retrieved September

7, 2020, from https://punchng.com/alleged-pollution-ewekoro-community-files-n1trn-lawsuit-against-lafarge/.
Retrieved September 7, 2020, from https://ghanacovid19fund.com/background/.
Retrieved September 7, 2020, from https://ghanacovid19fund.com/ghana-employers-association-supports-ghana-infectious-disease-centre-with-cash-and-ppes/.
Retrieved September 7, 2020, from https://www.cacovid.org/pdf/list_of_contributors_to_the_cacovid_relief_fund_as_at_30_June_2020.pdf.
Reuters (2020) 'Nigeria Coronavirus patient works as vendor for Lafarge Africa plc- company statement' 28 February 2020 https://www.reuters.com/article/china-health-nigeria-lafarge-idUSL5N2AS8F4
Sarfo, A. K., & Karuppannan, S. (2020). Application of geospatial technologies in the Covid-19 fight of Ghana. *Transactions of the Indian National Academy of Engineering*, 1–12.
Scott-Emuakpor, A. (2010). The evolution of health care systems in Nigeria: Which way forward in the twenty-first century. *Nigerian Medical Journal, 51*(2), 53.
Thomas, E. (2020). Lafarge Nigeria makes donations to support Nigeria in the midst of a Coronavirus pandemic. *WorldCement News*. Retrieved September 7, 2020, from https://www.worldcement.com/africa-middle-east/08042020/lafarge-africa-makes-donations-to-support-nigeria-in-the-midst-of-coronavirus-pandemic/.
UN. (2019). Retrieved September 7, 2020, from https://population.un.org/wpp/Publications/Files/WPP2019_DataBooklet.pdf.
UN STATS. (2020). Retrieved September 7, 2020, from https://unstats.un.org/unsd/methodology/m49/.
UNICEF. (2020). Ghana Situational report June 2020. Retrieved September 7, 2020, from https://reliefweb.int/sites/reliefweb.int/files/resources/UNICEF%20Ghana%20COVID-19%20SitRep5%201-15June2020.pdf.
Unilever. (2010). Sustainable living plan. Retrieved September 4, 2020, from https://www.unilever.com/sustainable-living/.
Unilever. (2020). 'Covid 19 handwashing campaign to target a billion people worldwide.' 2nd April 2020 https://www.unilever.com/news/news-andfeatures/Feature-article/2020/covid-19-handwashing-campaign-to-target-a-billion-people-worldwide.html

Unilever Covid 19 Disclosure, 2020 4th May 2020. Retrieved September 7, 2020, from https://www.unilever-ewa.com/Images/covid%2D%2D19-disclosures%2D%2D-unilever-nigeria-plc._tcm1283-551141_1_en.pdf.

USGS EROS. (2020). Retrieved September 7, 2020, from https://eros.usgs.gov/westafrica/physical-geography.

WHO | Nigeria. (2020). Retrieved September 7, 2020, from https://www.who.int/workforcealliance/countries/nga/en/.

World Bank. (1997). *World development report 1997: The state in a changing world*. New York: Oxford University Press.

World Bank. (2020). The World Bank in West and Central Africa—Overview. Retrieved September 7, 2020, from https://www.worldbank.org/en/region/afr/western-and-central-africa.

Zeufack, A. G., Calderon, C., Kambou, G., Djiofack, C. Z., Kubota, M., Korman, V., & Cantu Canales, C. (2020). *Africa's pulse, no. 21, Spring 2020: An analysis of issues shaping Africa's economic future*. Washington, DC: World Bank. License: CC BY 3.0 IGO. Retrieved from https://openknowledge.worldbank.org/handle/10986/33541.

9

Board Members' Religious Affiliations and Corporate Governance Practice: An Exploratory Study

Rita Goyal, Nada Kakabadse, and Andrew Kakabadse

9.1 Introduction

Globally, the corporate sector is in the midst of an epidemic that shows little signs of slowing down (Laing and Sigal 2020). Several organizations have been forced to lay off or furlough their employees; their growth prospects are significantly stunted; there is a considerable reputational risk. Still, they need to meet shareholders' expectations (Paine 2020). To survive such an existential crisis, companies need to reinvent themselves by resetting their processes (McKinsey 2020). For the UK's corporate sector, which was already ailing in the aftermath of the Brexit outcome, the blow has been crippling (Mahmood 2019). In the post-COVID-19 world, only the companies which evolve with agility will remain

R. Goyal
Coventry University, Coventry, UK

N. Kakabadse (✉) • A. Kakabadse
Henley Business School, Henley-on-Thames, UK
e-mail: n.kakabadse@henley.ac.uk

A. Sörensson et al. (eds.), *Corporate Responsibility and Sustainability during the Coronavirus Crisis*, Palgrave Studies in Governance, Leadership and Responsibility,
https://doi.org/10.1007/978-3-030-73847-1_9

sustainable (McKinsey 2020). Above all, the COVID-19 pandemic is precipitating corporate governance rules to be rewritten (Kucera et al. 2020). Hence, corporate Boards need to evolve into eclectic and well-informed entities in order to lead their companies to sustainability and long-term success (Barker 2020).

The evolution of corporate governance systems is closely aligned with their environment's cultural settings (Volonté 2015). Institutionalized religion is perceived as a subset of culture and a sociocultural construct (Rost 2017; Kim and Daniel 2016). Haluza-DeLay (2014, p. 261) conceptualizes religion as "beliefs, worldviews, practices, and institutions that cross borders, time and scale from the level of individuals all the way to transnational and trans-historical movements." Historically, tenets of institutionalized religion are claimed to have broadly influenced norms of corporate governance. For example, rules that emerged in Catholic orders, such as the distribution of decision-making, responsibilities and rules, conventions for selection, and the election of leaders and the monitoring of their actions, inculcated learnings, innovation, and the ability to survive in uncertain environments in organizations (Rost 2017). Protestantism shaped corporate governance practices through the work ethics of Protestants which led to capitalism, capitalist institutions, and industrialization in Anglo-American, common law regimes (Weber 1930; Volonté 2015). Fama and Jensen (1983) later compared Protestantism with Catholicism and argued in favor of the former for a more positive impact on corporate governance practices. A relationship between religion (e.g. Protestantism), as a sociocultural variable, and the level of agency costs is claimed to lead to more robust corporate governance regimes (Kim and Daniel 2016). The distinctness of Japanese, American, and German managerial practices is also attributed to the cultural attributes of religion followed in those regions (Volonté 2015).

The Upper Echelon (UE) perspective (Hambrick and Mason 1984) recommends that demographic characteristics of corporate elites—such as their religion and its impact on organizational outcomes—ought to be explored by organizational researchers (Oppong 2014). Nevertheless, organizational literature has generally refrained from conducting a focused study of religion (Rost 2017; Melé and Fontrodona 2017). A reluctance to pursue such an exploration can be on account of the perception that corporate objectives may be in conflict with the tenets of religion (Harrison 2006) and that religion is too detached from the travails of corporate governance (Tracey 2012). A small body of recent academic literature identifies similarities and potential links between religion and corporate governance practices and establishes the need to further explore this relationship (Nakpodia et al. 2020). However, the role of religious affiliations of the corporate elites on corporate outcomes has not yet been explored. In the study, we answer the research question: "*How do board members' religious affiliations shape their perspective and organizational outcomes*?" We now explain the sample set data collection and analysis method adopted in the study.

In this qualitative study, we explore the impact of board members' religious affiliations. We collect primary data through face-to-face, one-to-one elite interviews with 42 corporate elites such as board Chairs, Chief Executive Officers (CEOs), Executive Directors (EDs), and Non-executive Directors (NEDs) of large companies in the UK. This chapter discusses the existing knowledge of corporate elite experiences, backgrounds, and corporate outcomes, as argued by the UE perspective. Afterward, we describe the sample set and explain data collection and analysis strategies in the study before reporting the findings. Finally, we discuss the study's contribution to theory, literature, and corporate praxis, and conclude with a brief discussion of the limitations of the study and suggestions for future research.

Our study findings suggest that directors' religious affiliations are one of the experiences/filters used to interpret complex and uncertain situations. Amid high uncertainty posed by the COVID-19 pandemic, the study's findings may be valuable for boards in crafting suitable response plans. The findings suggest that Directors' value-set drawn from their religious background assist boards in preserving organizations' competitive advantage and support the top management teams to lead through the waves of uncertainty. The severity of this crisis's disruption indicates that the path out will be more of reconstruction rather than a recovery. Thus, directors' religious beliefs and clear value-sets can act as motivators, principles, and standards. Effective governance requires setting priorities, which involves value-led choices of two types—what should be done (ends) and how should it be done (means). There is some suggestion in the extant literature that values serve as motivators, and they guide perception, goals, attitudes, and behavior (Schwartz 2004; Roccas and Sagiv 2010). This study's findings further indicate that values of what is ethical, of what is efficient, honest, and fair, of what is the "right" thing to do. The conventional norms of ethics, values, and beliefs are challenged during this pandemic, as organizations' financial viability is threatened. In such a scenario, Directors with clear value-set and strong beliefs can ensure the moral center continues to guide organizations' responses to COVID-19 crises.

9.2 Upper Echelon Perspective and Board Diversity Research

The UE perspective asserts that if we want to understand organizational performance, we need to "consider the biases and dispositions of their most powerful actors—their top executives" (Hambrick 2007, 334). The theory suggests that corporate decision-makers, while implementing corporate governance norms, often face unforeseen and uncertain situations which they construe/interpret through the filters of their experiences, values, and background (Eisenhardt and Bourgeois 1989; Finkelstein and Hambrick 1990; Boal and Hooijberg 2001). The top managers' diverse experiences give them cognitive complexity which regulates their information-processing tendencies and guides them in choosing alternatives (Hambrick and Finkelstein 1987). A diverse top echelon also leads to more creativity, including varied input in decision-making and considering more alternative solutions to problems (Wiersema and Bantel 1992). As a result, heterogeneous top teams may have improved knowledge base, cognitive abilities, and problem-defining/solving skills (Hambrick et al. 1996).

Boards are a crucial component of effective corporate governance (Demb and Neubauer 1992). The UE perspective also marks a milestone in academic thinking on leadership—as it claims that boards not only function as a team, but their contribution is relevant to corporate performance (e.g. Ferrero-Ferrero et al. 2015; Kipkirong Tarus and Aime 2014).

The best performing corporate boards are known to benefit from their members' diverse experiences, such as their geographic familiarity, cultural understanding, functional capabilities, and thinking styles (Magill 1992; Skroupa 2016). Board members' competencies—such as their qualifications, strategic expertise, knowledge of financial markets and industries, and their ability to manage people—influence boards' decision-making and corporate governance (Huse 2005; Adams and Borsellino 2015; Westphal and Milton 2000). The UE perspective supports and strengthens the preliminary rationale of board diversity research (Johnson et al. 2013) and argues that the impact of a range of corporate leaders' experiences needs to be further explored to understand organizations and their actions (Finkelstein et al. 2009; Buyl et al. 2011).

However, existing board diversity research is overwhelmingly focused on board members' gender (e.g. Harrison et al. 1998; Rao and Tilt 2016; Konrad and Kramer 2006; Khanna et al. 2014; Nguyen et al. 2015; Kakabadse et al. 2015) and ethnicity (e.g. Singh 2007; Miller and del Carmen Triana 2009; Shin and Gulati 2010; and Broome et al. 2011). Gender and ethnicity may not be the only experiences that impact board members' perspectives, and hence more substantive constructs of their thinking need to be explored (Milliken and Martins 1996; Priem et al. 1999; Dhir 2009). A small body of board diversity research explores other less well-explored attributes of board diversity such as board members' functional experience, nationality, and culture, and suggests their role in boards' effectiveness and decision-making (Goyal et al. 2019a, b; Kakabadse et al. 2018). Existing academic knowledge, although limited, seeks to redefine board diversity (e.g. Bassett-Jones 2005; Ararat et al. 2015). Building on the UE perspective, Carpenter et al. (2004) challenge researchers to go beyond the observable attributes of top management teams and explore the deeper constructs of their behaviors. Nevertheless, other experiences of board members such as their religious affiliations—which may also have a bearing on their perspective and hence a valid aspect of board diversity (Ararat et al. 2015; Rao and Tilt 2016)—are not adequately explored for their role in board or firm performance. In this chapter, we aim to address this research gap.

9.3 Participants and Data Collection

Hambrick (2007) argues that opening the black box of social processes involved in corporate decision-making is not only a matter of academic curiosity but also a requirement for scholars who wish to help decision-makers in overcoming any potential biases. Listening to board members' experiences and opinions is considered critical to understanding the behavioral aspects of board processes (Huse 2005). Hambrick (2007) suggests that, ideally, such research should be conducted with "intrusive access" to the decision-makers who "are notoriously unwilling to submit themselves to scholarly poking and probing" (2007, 337). Interviews are widely used research tools to glean authentic information from individuals that cannot otherwise be obtained using secondary data or other modes of primary data (Ritchie et al. 2003). This data collection method has been adopted in a few seminal studies on boardrooms (McNulty et al. 2013; Terjesen et al. 2009; Seierstad 2016).

Therefore, in this inductive and exploratory study, we first collect corporate elites' data through elite interviews. We also believe that in order to obtain authentic information on the subject—that is, their views about religion and its potential role in their contribution—elite interviewing is one of the most appropriate approaches for collecting data. This strategy is also adopted to avoid potentially overlooking the context or critical actors in research (Broome and Krawiec 2008; Broome et al. 2011).

Despite its authenticity and richness of the data procured using elite interviews, it is formidably challenging to approach board members (Broome et al. 2011). Consequently, the initial population of participants is selected from the primary researcher's personal network, and then those participants are asked to provide access to other board members in their network. A purposive, non-probability, convenience sampling and snowball approach is adopted in this research (Tansey 2007). Interviews, which lasted 60–90 minutes, are first audio-recorded, with the participants' explicit consent, and then transcribed using InqScribe software by the primary researcher. In order to assure the participants that their views and identities remain confidential, the interviewees are anonymized and given pseudonyms (participant number) in the study data (Erakovic and Goel 2008). The primary researcher gathered information on participants through secondary sources, such as news articles, interviews, and at times materials made available by participants in advance (e.g. annual reports and other company-specific publications that were not available online).

There are four main categories of questions explored in these interviews with board members. The first set of questions is on religious beliefs and affiliations of the participants' parents/grandparents (three participants were brought up by their grandparents). The second set of questions pertains to the participants' association with religious practices during their impressionable years. The third main theme of questions is around participants' current affiliation with religious beliefs and practices. Finally, participants are probed on the role of religious beliefs and practices in performance/contribution at their workplace (i.e. boardrooms). Participants' descriptions of their religious beliefs and practices and their current association with them are presented in Annexure 1, Table 9.1.

9.4 Findings

Analysis of our data presents three main themes: (1) the impact of religious beliefs/practices on forming board members' value-set, (2) the impact of board members' value-set in shaping their actions/contribution, and (3) the role of board members' value-sets in shaping organizations' strategic aspirations. Themes are explained in this section and supported by quotes from participants and relevant extant literature on the subject.

Participants acknowledge the influence of their religious beliefs and practices on their perspective and, in particular, on their value-set. Participants also indicate the role of those value-sets on their contribution in boardrooms. During these interviews, an interesting observation is about the extent of the impact of board members' religious beliefs even when many of them either have reconsidered their religious affiliation or renounced it altogether. Figure 9.1 shows a pictorial representation of the findings describing the theoretical model which emerges from the research data.

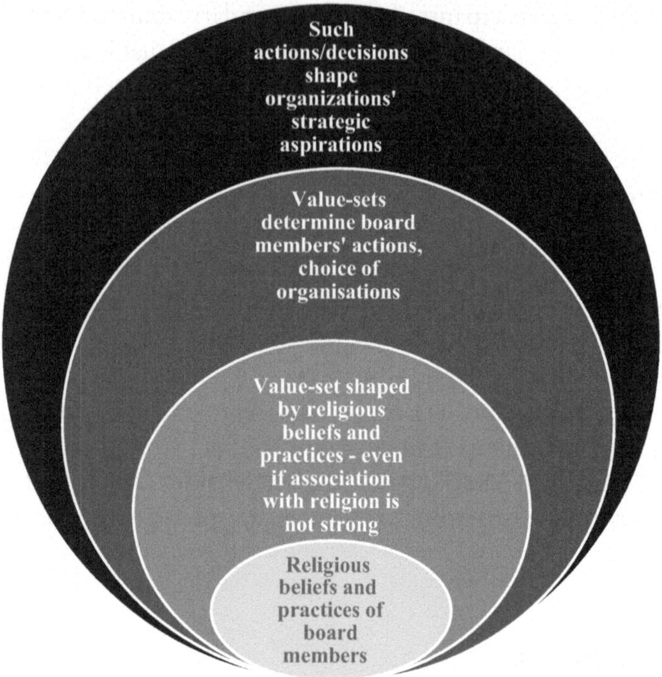

Fig. 9.1 Theoretical model—impact of board members' religious beliefs and practices. (Source: Conceptualized by the authors, based on the study findings)

9.4.1 Religious Beliefs/Practices Shaping Board Members' Values

The data findings indicate that the values instilled during their formative years continue to shape their perspective deeply, even if board members, as adults, renounce their faith or are no longer strongly associated with it. However, quotations in this section are limited to the ones from the participants who claim to have renounced their faith or have become atheists, just to indicate the intensity of the experience on board members' perspective.

Several participants (1) disclosed having had a religious upbringing where institutionalized faith was an integral part of their daily lives or/

and (2) acknowledged the role of their religious upbringing in forming their thinking style. Yet, their association with religion varies: several participants admit that they are "not religious," while few others summed up their association with the church to be limited to "*weddings and funerals*," and a few participants proclaimed themselves to be "lapsed" Catholics. Participants contested the idea of composing boards with an explicit agenda of maintaining religious diversity on boards and considered the idea to be too prescriptive and counterproductive for board effectiveness.

One participant, Respondent 5, who proclaims himself to be an atheist (see Table 9.1 in Annexure 1) explains the role of religion in teaching him humility and a down-to-earth approach to business:

> *Yeah, Religion definitely does have an impact, in the way that you look at life. My [religious] upbringing does teach me to be fair and tolerant. I have picked these up from the Sikh Religion. I measure everything. Am I fair? Is that person fair? There is a lack of ego. Our feet are firmly on the ground, because—and this is where the religious side of me comes out—God can take everything away in a flash.* (Resp. 5)

Another participant, Respondent 8, who proclaims herself to be a lapsed Catholic shares the significance of religious faith which her parents practiced and which she was exposed to in her impressionable years, as follows:

> *Even though I describe myself as a 'lapsed Catholic' now, when I look at my formative years, my former religion was very much a part of that. There is a sense of fairness that I try to bring to the workplace, which is probably, or certainly comes from upbringing. And quite possibly, there is a religious aspect to that. There is the honesty of approach.* (Resp. 8)

However, another participant, Respondent 12, who also claims to be a lapsed Catholic, readily attributes his value-set to his religious upbringing:

> *The Christian values are actually good social values that I adopt, and I follow very dearly. I was brought up with those values. So, I am not a religion fan per se. But I certainly follow Christian practices.* (Resp. 12)

Participant 22 claims that his religious faith makes him reflective and calm as a professional.

> *Religion, for me, is a great stabilizer and a great leveler. It's something which hopefully makes one stop and think about one's behavior. I gather it is the simplicity of faith, having an inner calm to a degree as well.* (Resp. 22)

And finally, a participant who adds another perspective to the argument, who claims that it is not only the religious beliefs and practices of the immediate family but also of the significant external environment, which may shape board members' value-sets. The participant (Respondent 15) shares the impact of their religious school teachings on his thinking style and value-set as follows:

> *I was taught by nuns and monks. And I think the values that you get from that stay with you. So, when you are brought up in strict Catholic or Buddhist values, even if you are not practicing, those values stay with you.* (Resp. 15)

Participants who acknowledge religion's role in forming their value-set have diverse religious backgrounds but acknowledge having been influenced by the religion they were exposed to in their formative years. As per existing knowledge in social psychology, religion is known to have a significant influence on an individual's values (Saroglou et al. 2004; Schwartz and Huismans 1995), which affect attitudes and behavior (Schwartz 1992). Allport and Ross (1967, 434) assert that the "extrinsically motivated person uses his religion whereas the intrinsically motivated person lives his religion." Furthermore, religion influences individuals' belief system by reinforcing some specific values and downplaying others (Rokeach 1969).

Corporate governance literature broadly concedes that religion might be an important medium of expression of individuals' beliefs and values (Volonté 2015). Religion provides society with rules of behavioral relationships and might even affect corporate decisions (La Porta et al. 1999; Hilary and Hui 2009). Thus, religiosity can influence one's intrinsic values or extrinsic values which may result in greater governance stewardship. Yet, in management-related literature and in contemporary institutional scholarship, values are consigned to a marginal position. It is important that focus is brought back to values "in order to understand institutions and their human inhabitants" (Kraatz et al. 2020, 474).

Theorists have also argued that corporate elites' complex decisions are largely a reflection of their behavioral factors (Cyert and March 1963). March and Simon (1958) suggest that decision-makers might bring their own values to an administrative situation. Our study findings suggest that those values may be shaped by those corporate elites' religious experiences, which seem to leave a lasting imprint on their perspective.

9.4.2 Religious Beliefs/Practices and Values Guiding Directors' Actions

In this section, we argue that the impact of religious beliefs and practices that board members were exposed to might not be limited to determining the value-set of board members but may further extend to guiding their actions. Participants in this study narrate their experiences and assert that their value-sets, drawn from their religious faith, influence their actions at their workplace (i.e. boards).

One of the decisions that participants claim is guided by board members' value-sets is their decision to accept/reject a board position in an organization and/or lead an organization. Several participants explain with anecdotes that when their own value-set clashed with the organizations', board members felt obliged to leave board positions in those organizations. One such instance is shared by Respondent 8 who, although now a lapsed Catholic, still finds it challenging to cope with unethical ("sinful") corporate practices (even if those practices are not illegal). She feels the urge to share the information with someone and "confess" her "sin" for working for such an organization. The participant attributes such a desire to the practice of "confessing one's sins" which she was encouraged to adopt as a follower/practitioner of the Catholic faith in her younger days.

> *Doing the right thing is ingrained in the Catholic faith. You actually go through the procedure of saying 'here are my sins.' And throughout my career, one of the things that have stayed with me is about feeling uncomfortable when somebody is doing something that is not ethically or morally right. And needing to fix it or put it right.* (Resp. 10)

She further explains that on one occasion she had to quit her position in an organization when she became aware of irresponsible resourcing of material but could neither stop the practice nor report it to an external agency because of her sense of collective responsibility.

Another participant (Respondent 30) echoes the views of Respondent 8. He argues that he has led organizations which have been a complete contrast to how many companies are often perceived—that is, exploitative, opaque, and unethical—a perception perpetuated by repeated financial wrongdoings, corporate failures, and scandals. He posits that he may have successfully stayed away from working for/leading such unethical organizations because of his value-set, which he derives from religious beliefs and practices as passed on to him from his parents.

> *I instinctively do what most people would consider to be the right thing. You see a lot of the comments on excesses and bad practices in businesses. All the businesses that I have been involved in, they are layers away from that. Now that may be because these are the businesses that I have chosen to work in. Because of the values in me. Because of the values in my upbringing.* (Resp. 30)

This study's findings seem to be aligned with a limited body of extant literature on the influence of board members' value-set on their actions (e.g. Johnson et al. 2013). When religion becomes intrinsic to one's being, it influences one's values, attitudes, and behavior (Huffman 1988; Magill 1992). Marcus et al. (2015) suggest that personal values of loyalty, hard work and a sense of responsibility are desirable and vital to board members' decisions and, consequently, may determine corporate outcomes. Moreover, religion is claimed to be a social norm (Kim and Daniel 2016), and the views expressed by participants in this study also seem to be aligned with the social norm theory (Kohlberg 1967). Kohlberg (1967) argues that social norms shape individuals' behaviors because they want to conform to the norms followed by their peers. Khavari and Harmon (1982) suggest that more religious individuals may have an inverse relationship with the tendency to use illicit substances. UE perspective claims that managers' values determine their strategic choices (Scott and Mitchell 1976; Hambrick and Mason 1984).

Our study substantiates these findings by suggesting a relationship between board members' value-sets (drawn from their association with religious beliefs and practices) and their actions/decisions in organizations (Carpenter et al. 2004). Carpenter et al. (2004) further urge researchers to integrate other determinants of managerial cognition which determine their strategic choices. Not relying on any proxies, in this research we explore and find through first-hand interaction with corporate elites the impact of yet another deeply influential experience, religion, which seems to shape corporate elites' perspective (value-set) and behavior (action). While our study's findings appear to substantiate the argument put forward in existing studies on individuals' need to conform to religious stipulations, we extend the theory to board research.

9.4.3 Directors' Religious Affiliations and Corporate Outcomes

In this section, we focus on the impact on organizations of board members' value-sets, derived from religious beliefs and practices. We suggest that corporate elites who adhere to such value-sets also shape their organizations' vision, mission, and norms, and organizational behavior accordingly. Hence, the impact of religion on board members might not be limited only to their determining their value-set and actions, but transcends to influence shaping organizations' strategic aspirations.

Although a broad range of religions is represented in the sample set (as can be seen in Table 9.1, Annexure 1), a significantly large sample population is from the Christian faith. It is hardly surprising that Christian values and their influence on participants' perspectives are repeatedly referred to during the study. A participant (Respondent 25) acknowledges the role of values derived from his affiliations to religious faiths and practices in setting organizations' strategic aspirations:

> *We have five values that we work towards, that influence our behavior in the organization—treating the people like the way you would like to be treated yourself, with respect, honesty, trustworthiness, and openness. One of the values is caring. A lot of that comes back to those Christian values that I was brought up on.* (Resp. 25)

Another participant, Respondent 29, who has led organizations in the UK, the USA, and Japan, argues that the corporate philosophy in a country is shaped by its corporate elites' practiced religious faith. She substantiates her argument with the example of the long-term corporate vision set by organizations in Japan where, she claims, corporate leaders' religious beliefs reflect in corporate philosophies.

> *In certain cultures, people place a very high value on the heritage of what they have. Their [Japanese] approach to business is always long term. They are not thinking about the next 20 years, [but] the next 100 years. There is a lot of thoughtfulness, mindfulness about their decisions not only worrying about how it will impact them or the next generation but the generation next to that. Preservation of something that is more important for their cultural heritage is often tied around religion.* (Resp. 29)

Another interviewee, Respondent 16—who has led several multinational companies based in the USA and has been a member of boards of a few multinational companies of Indian origin—echoes these thoughts. He states that corporate elites' religious beliefs significantly influence organizations' vision, values, and culture. The participant substantiates his claim with examples of several successful listed companies in India which are family businesses, founded and run by businessmen of the Zoroastrian faith, where the religion of board members shapes the corporate culture.

> *There are corporate cultures and traditions in which certain companies grew and having people from that tradition helped them not only to conform to the tradition but to continue that corporate culture. In some cases, those values are [from] more than a hundred years ago. When people come to the board who still have that tradition, it helps them to conform to who they are and to the values they commit to.* (Resp. 16)

These findings further substantiate the argument of social norm theory (Kohlberg 1967)—individuals seek to conform to their peers' social norms. We suggest that organizations' conforming might be more pronounced if corporate elites in those organizations set those social norms. In the extant literature, Grullon et al. (2009) argue that organizations with more religious employees have more effective monitoring of their managers as compared to organizations with a lesser proportion of religious employees.

Extant literature also informs us that discernible corporate outcomes (such as economic indicators) are more closely associated with values (such as trust) drawn from religious beliefs and practices, rather than religion itself (La Porta et al. 1996). It is argued that several such values, which primarily originated from institutionalized religions (e.g. the Calvinist reformation leading to the creation of multiple churches), might also have shaped best practices of corporate governance such as decentralization of power (Stulz and Williamson 2003). The UE perspective claims that organizational outcomes can be viewed "as reflections of the values of powerful actors in the organization," and such a linkage is no longer merely anecdotal but "can be detected empirically" (Hambrick and Mason 1984, 193).

Our study's findings are aligned with existing literature on the subject but add a revelatory contribution to the theory and literature by indicating a link between board members' religious affiliations and corporate aspirations. Our study findings also suggest a more pronounced impact of religious practices on board members' value-sets, even though formal association with the erstwhile institutionalized religion is loosely held or ceased.

9.5 Discussion and Analysis of Findings

In the aftermath of corporate failure, accounting scandals, and crises of the past few decades, there has been a widespread demand for reforming corporate governance (Volonté 2015). Still, any attempt to associate organizations with religious beliefs and practices has so far drawn inconclusive results. For example, some argue that principles of religiosity may prevent unethical corporate behavior and that companies established in religious environments are less likely to engage in poor corporate governance practices (Grullon et al. 2009; Vitell et al. 2016). Nonetheless, Scandinavian countries are known for their low level of religiosity (Zuckerman 2008) and yet are perceived to be global leaders in best practices of corporate governance, such as corporate social responsibility (Strand et al. 2015). Similarly, a relationship is also projected between preference for certain corporate governance regimes and religious faith of population in those regions. An example of the same is a prevalence of single-tier boards in companies situated in Roman Catholic majority areas of Switzerland and two-tier boards in Protestant-dominant areas (Volonté 2015). Yet, if we broaden the context beyond Switzerland, then we observe that single-tier boards are the norm in the UK and the USA—countries with large Protestant populations. Additionally, two-tier boards are the norm in several countries in continental Europe with large Catholic populations. Additionally, even religious organizations have been mired in unethical practices and scandals (Rost 2017).

It appears that an individuals' religiosity may not always result in an evolved corporate governance system, because religion, as presently understood and practiced by individuals, might be inconsistent with the principles of good corporate governance (Nakpodia et al 2020). Accordingly, the academic inquiry into seeking a relationship between religion and corporate governance is inconclusive and equivocal, and there is no agreement among scholars as to what is an ideal and universally applicable model of a good/bad governance mechanism (Shleifer and Vishney 1997). This chapter provides a potential explanation for the inconclusiveness of these findings and suggests that the relationship may be mediated/tempered through the impact of religion on board members' values, which in turn shape decisions and impact corporate outcomes. We contend that successful and sustainable organizations may be led by board members whose religion-based values are aligned with corporate aspirations and/or who can shape those corporate aspirations according to their value-set.

This chapter does not attempt to pontify or recommend the best corporate governance practices inspired by institutionalized religions. We agree with the contention that corporate governance reforms need to be based on a close and rigorous examination, intellectual analysis, and empirical evaluation, and not be based on articles of faith (Kempf 2008). Prescription of religion-based *best* practices is also difficult because contemporary organizational research lacks the data on which canonical/theological rules may have led to sustainable religious organizations (Rost 2017). Our study findings indicate a gradual process of religious beliefs and practices influencing individuals' value-sets, which in turn guide board members' action and organizations' strategic aspiration.

The global pandemic of COVID-19 has posed new challenges to organizations' social responsibility agenda as their financial viability is under threat. Still, the COVID-19 crisis can be seen as an opportunity to rethink corporate responsibility. Many organizations carry out "cosmetic" or "greenwashing" Corporate Social Responsibility (CSR) initiatives, or perform their social responsibility reluctantly. That approach may not be enough in the current scenario. To cope with the pandemic crisis, increased resources allocation may be required for CSR initiatives, especially for organizations' core business, and critical stakeholders. Organizations need to prioritize and redirect resources in the short and medium term to support vulnerable communities. All these actions require clear values which act as standards for organizational behavior (Schwartz 2004).

Reputation flows from corporate values and tone at the top. Directors with clear value-set and regions beliefs are more likely to be sensitive to community needs as all regions have clear value of charitable giving and caring for others (Ives and Kidwell 2019). The religion, literally means to "reconnect," offers believers self-transcendence. That is uniting a lower, protective self with a more generous, outward-focused, large self. All religions teach "self-transcendence" or pro-social values (Schwartz 2004). Board members with more grounded and clear value-set, which are often derived from their religious affiliation, seem to be facilitating such transcendence toward pro-social values for their organizations.

9.6 Contribution of the Study Findings

Through this study, we make significant revelatory and incremental theoretical contributions (Nicholson et al. 2018). The main contribution of this study is to the UE theory: we argue that board members' (1) religious affiliations are one of the experiences/filters that they use to interpret complex and uncertain situations and (2) value-sets drawn from their religious beliefs and practices may have an intermediary role between their religious affiliations and corporate outcomes. We suggest a process of how the religious beliefs of corporate elites may shape organizational outcome (strategic aspirations) through influencing board members' value-sets and decisions in boardrooms. Additionally, we make an incremental contribution to theory by successfully implementing the theory on individual board members, as the unit of research.

Another novel contribution of this study is regarding the identification of a potential relationship between board members' religious affiliation and their actions/decisions. We attribute the lack of knowledge on the topic in extant literature to well-recorded challenges of accessing boardrooms for academic research (e.g. Hambrick 2007; Leblanc and Schwartz 2007; Zona and Zattoni 2007). Furthermore, while existing literature exploring a relationship between religion and corporate governance is largely focused on a comparison of Protestantism and Catholicism (e.g. Weber 1930; Fama and Jensen 1983; La Porta et al. 1996; Kim and Daniel 2016), our study incorporates perspectives of board members with varied religious affiliations.

In conclusion, in extant literature, the focus is on the macro-constructs of corporate governance such as board structure, the ownership structure of organizations, and centralization of power. We drill down further to cast a light on individual board members' religious affiliations and explore the impact on their perspective, actions, and organizational outcomes.

9.7 Limitation and Guidance for Future Research

The study does not aim to find an all-encompassing definition of religion that can then be prescribed to shape corporate governance. We acknowledge that the definition of religion might vary considerably depending on beliefs and values various religious faiths profess: other significant influences on board members such as geographic locations where such faiths are practiced; the willingness of individual board members to be open to other religious/spiritual influences; and their unique experience of association with religious practices/beliefs. The study does not compare the impact of religion/sects n other faiths and their impact on board members and their actions. Instead, this study presents the journey of 42 board members' relationships with their religious faith, and the impact of these relationships on corporate outcomes. It remains to be seen as to how board members' value-sets shape board processes, board deliberations, and board effectiveness outcomes. Future studies might look into those areas.

Annexures

Table 9.1 Religious affiliation and other attributes of board members in the study

Resp. No.	Gender	Age in 2016	Position(s) held	Religious affiliation (Family)	Religious affiliation (Personal)
1	M	47	ED	Church of England (CoE)	Church of England
2	M	44	CEO	Hindu	Hindu
3	M	52	Chairman	Hindu	Hindu
4	M	55	CEO	Hindu	Hindu
5	M	63	Chairman	Sikh	Atheist
6	M	44	CEO	Hindu	Hindu
7	M	69	Chairman	Sikh	Sikh
8	F	47	ED	CoE	CoE
9	M	76	Chairman	Sikh	Sikh
10	F	59	NED/Partner	CoE	CoE
11	F	51	NED	Catholic	Catholic
12	M	49	ED	Catholic	Lapsed Catholic
13	F	55	CEO	CoE	CoE
14	F	63	Chairperson	CoE	Not religious
15	F	52	ED	Catholic	Lapsed Catholic
16	F	45	ED	Catholic	Catholic
17	M	63	NED/Partner/CEO	Catholic	Not religious
18	M	55	CEO/Board-advisor	Christian	Christian
19	F	54	ED	CoE	CoE
20	F	57	NED/Partner	CoE	Not religious
21	F	47	NED	Christian	Not religious
22	F	54	ED/NED/CEO	CoE	Not religious
23	M	64	NED/CEO	Protestant	Protestant
24	M	68	NED/CEO/CFO/Chair	CoE	CoE
25	M	55	CEO	CoE	CoE
26	M	68	ED	Quaker	Quaker
27	M	70	NED/CEO	CoE	Not religious
28	M	50	ED	CoE	Not religious
29	F	65	NED/Partner/CEO	Buddhist	Buddhist
30	M	65	CEO	CoE	CoE
31	F	48	CEO	CoE	CoE

(*continued*)

Table 9.1 (continued)

Resp. No.	Gender	Age in 2016	Position(s) held	Religious affiliation (Family)	Religious affiliation (Personal)
32	M	69	Chairman/NED	CoE	CoE
33	M	55	CEO	CoE	Not religious
34	F	51	NED/CEO	CoE	Not religious
35	M	50	CEO	CoS	CoS
36	M	67	Chairman/ NED/CEO	CoE	CoE
37	M	69	Chairman	Jewish	Jewish
38	M	60	CEO/Chairman	CoE	CoE
39	F	60	NED	CoE	CoE/Jewish
40	F	57	NED/Chair	CoE	CoE
41	M	68	NED/Chairman	CoE	CoE
42	M	68	Chairman/ CEO/ED	CoE	CoE

Source: Compiled by authors

References

Adams, M. A., & Borsellino, G. (2015). Is there a positive link between corporate governance and board diversity? Lessons from Asia. *Journal of Business Systems, Governance & Ethics, 10*(1), 1–10.

Allport, G. W., & Ross, J. M. (1967). Personal religious orientation and prejudice. *Journal of Personality and Social Psychology, 5*, 432–443.

Ararat, M., Aksu, M., & Tansel Cetin, A. (2015). How board diversity affects firm performance in emerging markets: Evidence on channels in controlled firms. *Corporate Governance: An International Review, 23*(2), 83–103.

Barker, R. (2020). *The corporate governance of coronavirus – What boards should consider*. Policy publications – Corporate Governance Sustainable Business, Institute of Directors, 20 March. Retrieved from https://www.iod.com/news/news/articles/The-corporate-governance-of-coronavirus%2D%2D-what-boards-should-consider.

Bassett-Jones, N. (2005). The paradox of diversity management, creativity and innovation. *Creativity and Innovation Management, 14*(2), 169–175.

Boal, H. B., & Hooijberg, R. (2001). Strategic leadership research: Moving on. *The Leadership Quarterly, 11*(4), 515–549.

Broome, L., & Krawiec, K. D. (2008). Signaling through board diversity: Is anyone listening. *University of Cincinnati Law Review, 77*, 431.

Broome, L. L., Conley, J. M., & Krawiec, K. D. (2011). Dangerous categories: Narratives of corporate board diversity. *North Carolina Law Review, 89*, 759–808.

Buyl, T., Boone, C., & Matthyssens, P. (2011). Upper echelons research and managerial cognition. *Strategic Organization, 9*(3), 240–246.

Carpenter, M. A., Geletkanycz, M. A., & Sanders, W. G. (2004). Upper echelons research revisited: Antecedents, elements, and consequences of top management team composition. *Journal of Management, 30*(6), 749–778.

Cyert, R. M., & March, J. G. (1963). *A behavioral theory of the firm, 2*(4), 169–187.

Demb, A., & Neubauer, F. F. (1992). The corporate board: Confronting the paradoxes. *Long Range Planning, 25*(3), 9–20.

Dhir, A. (2009). Towards a race and gender-conscious conception of the firm: Canadian corporate governance, law and diversity. *Comparative Research in Law & Political Economy*. Research Paper No. 1/2009. Retrieved November 5, 2015, from http://digitalcommons.osgoode.yorku.ca/clpe/116.

Eisenhardt, K. M., & Bourgeois, L. J. (1989). Politics of strategic decision making in high-velocity environments: Toward a midrange theory. *Academy of Management Journal, 31*(4), 737–770.

Erakovic, L., & Goel, S. (2008). Board-management relationships: Resources and internal dynamics. *Management Revue, 19*(1/2), 53–69.

Fama, E. F., & Jensen, M. C. (1983). Separation of ownership and control. *Journal of Law and Economics, 26*, 301–325.

Ferrero-Ferrero, I., Fernández-Izquierdo, M. Á., & Muñoz-Torres, M. J. (2015). Age diversity: An empirical study in the board of directors. *Cybernetics and Systems, 46*(3–4), 249–270.

Finkelstein, S., & Hambrick, D. C. (1990). Top-management-team tenure and organizational outcomes: The moderating role of managerial discretion. *Administrative Science Quarterly, 35*(3), 484–503.

Finkelstein, S., Cannella, S. F. B., Hambrick, D. C., & Cannella, A. A. (2009). *Strategic leadership: Theory and research on executives, top management teams, and boards*. New York: Oxford University Press.

Goyal, R., Kakabadse, N., & Kakabadse, A. (2019a). Improving corporate governance with functional diversity on FTSE 350 boards: Directors' perspective. *Journal of Capital Markets Studies, 3*(2), 113–136. https://doi.org/10.1108/JCMS-09-2019-0044.

Goyal, R., Kakabadse, N., & Kakabadse, A. (2019b). Board effectiveness in FTSE 250 companies: Diversity may hold the key. In A. Levrau & S. Gobert (Eds.), *Governance: The art of aligning interests – Liber amicorum Lutgart Van den Berghe* (pp. 93–108). Cambridge: Intersentia.

Grullon, G., Kanatas, G., & Weston, J. (2009). Religion and corporate (mis) behavior. SSRN 1472118.

Haluza-Delay, R. (2014). Religion and climate change: Varieties in viewpoints and practices. *WIREs Climate Change, 5*, 261–279.

Hambrick, D. C. (2007). Upper echelons theory: An update. *Academy of Management Review, 32*(2), 334–343.

Hambrick, D. C., & Finkelstein, S. (1987). Managerial discretion: A bridge between polar views of organizational outcomes. In L. L. Cummings & B. M. Staw (Eds.), *Research in organizational behavior* (Vol. 9, pp. 369–406). Greenwich, CT: JAI Press.

Hambrick, D. C., & Mason, P. A. (1984). Upper echelons: The organisation as a reflection of its top managers. *Academy of Management Review, 9*(2), 193–206.

Hambrick, D. C., Cho, T. S., & Chen, M. J. (1996). The influence of top management team heterogeneity on firms' competitive moves. *Administrative Science Quarterly, 41*(4), 659–684.

Harrison, V. S. (2006). The pragmatics of defining religion in a multi-cultural world. *International Journal for Philosophy of Religion, 59*(3), 133–152.

Harrison, D. A., Price, K. H., & Bell, M. P. (1998). Beyond relational demography: Time and the effects of surface- and deep-level diversity on work group cohesion. *Academy of Management Journal, 41*(1), 96–107.

Hilary, G., & Hui, K. W. (2009). Does religion matter in corporate decision making in America? *Journal of Financial Economics, 93*(3), 455–473.

Huffman, T. E. 1988. *In the world but not of the world: Religious, alienation, and philosophy of human nature among Bible college and liberal arts college students.* Diss., Iowa State University.

Huse, M. (2005). Accountability and creating accountability: A framework for exploring behavioural perspectives of corporate governance. *British Journal of Management, 16*(1), S65–S79.

Ives, C. D., & Kidwell, J. (2019). Religion and social values for sustainability. *Sustainability Science, 14*, 1355–1362.

Johnson, S. C., Schnatterly, K., & Hill, A. D. (2013). Board composition beyond independence: Social capital, human capital and demographics. *Journal of Management, 39*(1), 232–262.

Kakabadse, N. K., Figueira, C., Nicolopoulou, K., Hong Yang, J., Kakabadse, A. P., & Özbilgin, M. F. (2015). Gender diversity and board performance:

Women's experiences and perspectives. *Human Resource Management, 54*(2), 265–281.

Kakabadse, A., Goyal, R., & Kakabadse, N. (2018). Value-creating boards—Diversity and evolved processes. *Journal of Creating Value, 4*(1), 22–41.

Kempf, D. G. (2008). Corporate governance as religion. *Journal of Regulatory Economics, 33*(1), 117–131.

Khanna, P., Jones, C. D., & Boivie, S. (2014). Director human capital, information processing demands, and board effectiveness. *Journal of Management, 40*(2), 557–585.

Khavari, K. A., & Harmon, T. M. (1982). The relationship between the degree of professed religious belief and use of drugs. *International Journal of the Addictions, 17*(5), 847–857.

Kim, J., & Daniel, S. J. (2016). Religion and corporate governance: Evidence from 32 countries. *Asia-Pacific Journal of Financial Studies, 45*(2), 281–308.

Kipkirong Tarus, D., & Aime, F. (2014). Board demographic diversity, firm performance and strategic change: A test of moderation. *Management Research Review, 37*(12), 1110–1136.

Kohlberg, L. (1967). Moral and religious education and the public schools: A developmental view. In T. Sizer (Ed.), *Religion and public education* (pp. 164–183). Boston: Houghton Mifflin.

Konrad, A. M., & Kramer, V. W. (2006). How many women do boards need? *Harvard Business Review, 84*(12), 1–2.

Kraatz, M., Flores, R., & Chandler, D. (2020). The value of values for institutional analysis. *Academy of Management Annals, 14*(2), 470–485.

Kucera, W., Simala, J., & Noreuil, A. (2020). *COVID-19 and corporate governance: Key issued for public company directors*. Harvard Law School Forum on Corporate Governance, April 29. Retrieved from https://corpgov.law.harvard.edu/2020/04/29/covid-19-and-corporate-governance-key-issues-for-public-company-directors/.

La Porta, R., Lopez-De-Silane, F., Shleifer, A., & Vishny, R. W. (1996). *Trust in large organizations* (No. w5864). National Bureau of Economic Research.

La Porta, R., Lopez-de-Silanes, F., Shleifer, A., & Vishny, R. (1999). The quality of government. *The Journal of Law, Economics, and Organization, 15*(1), 222–279.

Laing, A., & Sigal, L. (2020). Coronavirus pandemic showing no signs of slowing down in Americas – PAHO. *Reuters*, 20 July. Retrieved from https://uk.reuters.com/article/uk-health-coronavirus-who-americas/coronavirus-pandemic-showing-no-signs-of-slowing-down-in-americas-paho-idUKKCN24M2CV.

Leblanc, R., & Schwartz, M. S. (2007). The black box of board Process: Gaining access to a difficult subject. *Corporate Governance: An International Review, 15*(5), 843–851.

Magill, G. (1992). Theology in business ethics: Appealing to the religious imagination. *Journal of Business Ethics, 11*, 129–135.

Mahmood, B. (2019). All the companies that have collapsed or moved abroad since Brexit. *Metro News*. Retrieved from https://metro.co.uk/2019/09/23/companies-collapsed-moved-abroad-since-brexit-10795029/.

March, J. G., & Simon, H. A. (1958). *Organizations*. New York: John Wiley & Sons.

Marcus, J., MacDonald, H. A., & Sulsky, L. M. (2015). Do personal values influence the propensity for sustainability actions? A policy-capturing study. *Journal of Business Ethics, 127*(2), 459–478.

McKinsey. (2020). COVID-19 and the great reseit. Retrieved from https://www.mckinsey.com/business-functions/risk/our-insights/covid-19-implications-for-business.

McNulty, T., Zattoni, A., & Douglas, T. (2013). Developing corporate governance research through qualitative methods: A review of previous studies. *Corporate Governance: An International Review, 21*(2), 183–198.

Melé, D., & Fontrodona, J. (2017). Christian ethics and spirituality in leading business organizations: Editorial introduction. *Journal of Business Ethics, 145*(4), 671–679.

Miller, T., & del Carmen Triana, M. (2009). Demographic diversity in the boardroom: Mediators of the board diversity – Firm performance relationship. *Journal of Management Studies, 46*(5), 755–786.

Milliken, F. J., & Martins, L. L. (1996). Searching for common threads: Understanding the multiple effects of diversity in organizational groups. *Academy of Management Review, 21*(2), 402–433.

Nakpodia, F., Shrives, P. J., & Sorour, M. K. (2020). Examining the link between religion and corporate governance: insights from Nigeria. *Business & Society, 59*(5), 956–994.

Nguyen, D. D. L., Hagendorff, J., & Eshraghi, A. (2015). Which executive characteristics create value in banking? Evidence from appointment announcements. *Corporate Governance: An International Review, 23*(2), 112–128.

Nicholson, J. D., LaPlaca, P., Al-Abdin, A., Breese, R., & Khan, Z. (2018). What do introduction sections tell us about the intent of scholarly work: A contribution on contributions. *Industrial Marketing Management, 73*, 206–219.

Oppong, S. (2014). Upper echelons theory revisited: The need for a change from causal description to casual explanation. *Management: Journal of Contemporary Management Issues, 19*(2), 169–183.

Paine, L. S. (2020). COVID-19 is rewriting the rules of corporate governance. *Harvard Business Review*, 6 October. Retrieved from https://hbr.org/2020/10/covid-19-is-rewriting-the-rules-of-corporate-governance.

Priem, R. L., Lyon, D. W., & Dess, G. G. (1999). Inherent limitations of demographic proxies in top management team heterogeneity research. *Journal of Management, 25*(6), 935–953.

Rao, K., & Tilt, C. (2016). Board composition and corporate social responsibility: The role of diversity, gender, strategy and decision making. *Journal of Business Ethics, 138*(2), 327–347.

Ritchie, J., Lewis, J., & Gillian, E. (2003). Designing and selecting samples. In J. Ritchie & J. Lewis (Eds.), *Qualitative research practice: A guide for social science students and researchers* (pp. 77–108). London: Sage Publications.

Roccas, S., & Sagiv, L. (2010). Personal values and behavior: Taking the cultural context into account. *Social and Personality Psychology Compass, 4*, 30–41.

Rokeach, M. (1969). Value systems and religion. *Review of Religious Research, 11*, 2–23.

Rost, K. (2017). Introduction to the corporate governance of religion. In R. A. Scott & M. Buchmann (Eds.), *Emerging trends in the social and behavioral sciences: An interdisciplinary, searchable, and linkable resource* (pp. 1–10). Hoboken: Wiley-VCH.

Saroglou, V., Delpierre, V., & Dernelle, R. (2004). Values and religiosity: A meta-analysis of studies using Schwartz's model. *Personality and Individual Differences, 37*, 721–734.

Schwartz, S. H. (1992). Universals in the content and structure of values: Theoretical advances and empirical tests in 20 countries. In M. P. Zanna (Ed.), *Advances in experimental social psychology* (pp. 1–65). San Diego: Academic Press.

Schwartz, S. H. (2004). *Mapping and interpreting cultural differences around the world.* In H. Vinken, J. Soeters, & P. Ester (Eds.), *Comparing cultures, dimensions of culture in a comparative perspective* (pp. 43–73). Brill: Leiden, The Netherlands.

Schwartz, S. H., & Huismans, S. (1995). Value priorities and religiosity in four Western religions. *Social Psychology Quarterly, 58*, 88–107.

Scott, W., & Mitchell, T. (1976). *Organizational theory: A structural and behavioral analysis.* Homewood, Illinois: Richard D. Irwin.

Seierstad, C. (2016). Beyond the business case: The need for both utility and justice rationales for increasing the share of women on boards. *Corporate Governance: An International Review, 24*(4), 390–405.

Shin, P. S., & Gulati, M. (2010). Showcasing diversity. *North Carolina Law Review, 89*, 1017.

Shleifer, A., & Vishney, R. W. (1997). A survey of corporate governance. *The Journal of Finance, 52*(2), 737–783.

Singh, V. (2007). Ethnic diversity on top corporate boards: A resource dependency perspective. *The International Journal of Human Resource Management, 18*(12), 2128–2146.

Skroupa, C. P. (2016). Gender diversity on boards: A driver of value. *Forbes*, July 16.

Strand, R., Freeman, R. E., & Hockerts, K. (2015). Corporate social responsibility and sustainability in Scandinavia: An overview. *Journal of Business Ethics, 127*(1), 1–15.

Stulz, R. M., & Williamson, R. (2003). Culture, openness, and finance. *Journal of Financial Economics, 70*(3), 313–349.

Tansey, O. (2007). Process tracing and elite interviewing: A case for non-probability sampling. *PS: Political Science & Politics, 40*(4), 765–772.

Terjesen, S., Sealy, R., & Singh, V. (2009). Women directors on corporate boards: A review and research agenda. *Corporate Governance: An International Review, 17*(3), 320–337.

Tracey, P. (2012). Religion and organization: A critical review of current trends and future directions. *Academy of Management Annals, 6*(1), 87–134.

Vitell, S. J., King, R. A., Howie, K., Toti, J. F., Albert, L., Hidalgo, E. R., & Yacout, O. (2016). Spirituality, moral identity, and consumer ethics: A multicultural study. *Journal of Business Ethics, 139*(1), 147–160.

Volonté, C. (2015). Culture and corporate governance: The influence of language and religion in Switzerland. *Management International Review, 55*(1), 77–118.

Weber, M. (1930). *The protestant ethic and the spirit of capitalism.* New York: Scribner.

Westphal, J. D., & Milton, L. P. (2000). How experience and network ties affect the influence of demographic minorities on corporate boards. *Administrative Science Quarterly, 45*(2), 366–398.

Wiersema, M. F., & Bantel, K. A. (1992). Top management team demography and corporate strategic change. *Academy of Management Journal, 35*(1), 91–21.

Zona, F., & Zattoni, A. (2007). Beyond the black box of demography: Board processes and task effectiveness within Italian firms. *Corporate Governance: An International Review, 15*(5), 852–864.

Zuckerman, P. (2008). An introduction to the sociology of religion. *Sociology of Religion, 69*(2), 234–236.

10

Corporate Social Responsibility and Corporate Reputation During the COVID-19 Pandemic: The Case of Kuwait's Oil Sector

Fajer Al-Husaini

10.1 Introduction

The COVID-19 pandemic took the world by surprise and spread at an alarming level. Unlike recent viruses, COVID-19 was found to be very hard to manage. As a result, and due to the severity of COVID-19, global concern put pressure on governments, corporations, and businesses across the world to respond accordingly. Many of the areas concerning governments' response included health, safety, security, and travel and coordination, and the State of Kuwait was amongst the first to start closing up entry and exit points into the country, with daily meetings being scheduled by the Council of Ministers to discuss and implement crisis response measures that would include the shutdown of businesses, shopping malls, and even medical clinics. Discussions about the responsibilities of what

F. Al-Husaini (✉)
Henley Business School, Henley-on-Thames, UK
e-mail: fajer.alhusaini@pgr.reading.ac.uk

A. Sörensson et al. (eds.), *Corporate Responsibility and Sustainability during the Coronavirus Crisis*, Palgrave Studies in Governance, Leadership and Responsibility,
https://doi.org/10.1007/978-3-030-73847-1_10

each governmental authority needed to do to better combat the spread of this disease were also taking place. Because of its vast organizational and operational capabilities, Kuwait's Oil Sector in particular was summoned by the government to attend the Council of Ministers' COVID-19 meetings. As the country's primary economic driver and most organized sector in Kuwait in terms of crisis management, the Oil Sector was invited to aid the government. No country was prepared for a health crisis of this magnitude, and the Kuwaiti government in particular, although resourceful, realized desirability of support from industry. This was where the Oil Sector's expertise and flexibility of procedures came into play.

The purpose of this chapter is to highlight how CSR during global crises can be implemented to offer significant support on a country-wide level whilst positively impacting corporate reputation. The chapter will indicate how the oil sector was able to identify and implement CSR projects of high visibility and impact on its reputation, highlight the multiple and complex ways in which material support was given, and reputation enhanced.

The rest of the chapter is organized as follows. Firstly, a brief overview of the early responses to the pandemic in Kuwait are presented, then an overview of the oil sector, then the three pillars of CSR in a global crisis are presented, with an emphasis on the media work to connect the Kuwait Oil Sector to the positive response to the pandemic, and finally, the chapter discusses CSR best practice in a global crisis based on the three pillars seen in the work of Kuwait's Oil Sector during COVID-19.

10.1.1 How Kuwait Responded to the Pandemic in the Early Months

The official response from the Kuwaiti Government regarding the COVID-19 pandemic started on 24 February 2020, when all National Celebrations and gatherings were cancelled (TIMES 2020). The State of Kuwait commemorates its National and Liberation Days celebrations annually on 25 and 26 February. These celebrations are regarded as Kuwait's main and most prominent festivities throughout the year, which have been carried out regularly since the 1960s (KUNA 2018). Events normally take place across the country, where companies compete to provide the most elaborate and entertaining festivals as part of their CSR contribution to the inhabitants of the country (Cinemagics 2019). These dates resonate with the people of Kuwait as they recognize Kuwait's independence in 1960, as well as Kuwait's liberation from the Iraqi invasion in 1991 (KUNA 2018)—an event that will forever be engraved in the heart of the Kuwaiti people. Hence contributing showcases corporate citizenship as part of the Kuwaiti society. Families and children wait with great anticipation for these celebrations, and their cancellation for the first time in Kuwait's history left children, in particular, very disappointed (AlQabas 2020b). Suddenly, there was an understanding that the COVID-19 pandemic was a serious social health crisis, which had the power to effectively shut down the country (TIMES 2020). As an unprecedented phenomenon, the impact of the virus on commercial activity was almost completely unheard of. Different business sectors had to deal with a virus that was unpredictable and required a wide range of business decisions to make within the course of a week. These decisions included what needed to be shut down, what will happen to sales, the shift to online business during a forced shutdown, the safety of workers, customers, and so forth. This has led to a call to document the significant shifts in business activity.

The Coronavirus pandemic has created a sense of interconnectivity that has not been experienced during this time and age (Bapuji et al. 2020). Businesses in Kuwait realized that they are part of the societies they operate in, and in turn, societies have also begun to grasp the fact that businesses are an integral part of their everyday lives and a resource that must be called on in a global crisis. In Kuwait, this also means the largest business sector: oil.

10.1.2 The Oil Sector in Kuwait

The Kuwait Oil Sector's mission is to "optimize the value of Kuwait's hydrocarbon resources through exploration, development and production to ensure sustainability" (Kuwait Oil Company 2020f). Whilst the focus is on hydrocarbon resources, the scale and scope of the industry in

Kuwait means that the sector conducts significant CSR activities such as public participation in health events, for example, breast cancer awareness and participation in national day celebrations (Kuwait Oil Company 2020g). These CSR activities are used as part of the sector's strategy to be involved with the community it operates in and effectively maintain a positive reputation for the sector. The Kuwait Oil Sector, in particular, has changed its interaction with society since the outburst of COVID-19. This was evident in its communication efforts which focused on extensive media coverage, social media interaction, and CSR activities and projects that became integral to the Sector's communication. The Oil Sector took a proactive approach to communicate about the safety and precaution measures taken across all of its Companies. A major part of communication was also the development of informative safety awareness campaigns geared towards the general public (Kuwait Oil Company Instagram 2020d), which were launched immediately after the announcement of the COVID-19 pandemic reaching Kuwait in an alarming manner (Kuwait Oil Company Instagram 2020d). The sector also took a proactive approach to ensure the correct information was being shared with the public, thus eliminating chances for the spread of rumours (Kuwait Oil Company Instagram 2020d). These messages included all precautionary measures done in the field, all COVID-19 preventative measures being implemented across the Company, as well as a showcase via videos and photos, about how employees are working under very safe conditions.

Oil sectors around the world are easy targets for negative media attention. They are perceived as money-making giants who are damaging the planet (Theodori and Jackson-Smith 2010), despite the fact that this vital sector plays a critical role in sustaining life as we know it. Oil provides the energy that companies and households operate on, fuel for transport, and for essential production of the food we eat, and almost all of our daily necessities, including medicine (EIA 2020). Yet the public and media, in general, find joy in pointing out the negatives of the sector and thus create a difficult task for oil companies to maintain any positive image.

Kuwait's oil sector consists of the mother company, Kuwait Petroleum Corporation (KPC), which was established in 1980 (KPC 2020). Under

KPC's umbrella are eight different subsidiaries that are concerned with upstream, midstream, and downstream operations. These operations are valued at billions of US dollars and are major contributors to Kuwait's economy. The Kuwait Oil Sector is responsible for securing Kuwait's energy demand, as well as the production and export of oil to international customers—making the State of Kuwait a "reliable supplier of energy to the world" (Kuwait Oil Company 2020i). The sector is not only concerned with the business of oil production, but also responsible for the environment it operates in. The oil sector adheres to international standards for air pollution and has contributed to the environment by developing several natural preserves and oases. Kuwait Oil Company in particular is taking the lead in the Kuwait Environment Remediation Programme, which is the largest and most extensive remediation programme in the world valued at 3 billion US dollars by the United Nations Compensation Commission (UNCC) (Kuwait Oil Company 2020h).

The sector also realizes its corporate citizenship by participating in CSR projects that range from the construction and operation of the Ahmadi Hospital to serve residents of the Ahmadi Governorate, to the implementation of several national-level campaigns such as blood donation campaigns, energy conservation, beach cleans, recycling, and so on (Kuwait Oil Company 2020g). All of the above-mentioned contributions were initiated to generate a positive relationship between the sectors with its various stakeholders. These CSR contributions were carried forward during normal times, whilst, during the COVID-19 pandemic, CSR contribution took new directions due to increased restrictions and the urgent needs of the various stakeholders of the sector.

During the pandemic, the decrease in demand for oil hit the sector hard in terms of the spiked reduction of the price of oil, which reached a staggering percentage drop of 49.29% in March 2020 (Mubasher 2020). This led to an alarming level of reduction in the production of oil, which in turn led to more scrutiny from the public regarding what the sector was going to do in terms of impact on the Kuwaiti economy. Despite these challenges, the Kuwaiti Oil Sector aided the Kuwaiti government during their critical time of need, despite short notice and heavy economic impact on operations (Ktv 2020).

10.2 Kuwait Oil Sector CSR in Response to Government Concerns

The Kuwaiti Government Ministry of Health (MOH) was the governmental body at the forefront of combating the disease. With the number of cases rising substantially, the MOH found itself in the dilemma of ensuring cases were diagnosed quickly, confirmed cases were isolated, and availability of medical supplies were not relinquished (AlJarida 2020). Based on analysis of the response to COVID-19 in Kuwait, three main pillars emerged that required the attention and support from other sectors within the country to help organize a crisis response plan that addressed COVID-19 concerns. These pillars included the following:

(a) Major CSR initiatives
(b) Medium-level CSR initiatives
(c) Media coverage

The Kuwait Oil Sector was involved in all three pillars. Given the sector's flexibility of procedures in crisis response (Oil News Agency 2020), the Kuwaiti government chose to assign the oil sector with urgent procurement of medical devices and requirements (Oil News Agency 2020). The entire state of Kuwait follows the Kuwait Chapter-19 procedure for crisis response, which provides more flexibility for the urgent procurement of needs with less monetary restrictions from auditing. The problem with the Kuwait Chapter-19 is that the auditing system occurs prior and post procurement, which hinders the urgent procurement procedure. This section of Chapter-19 is less rigid for the Oil Sector where the sector has more flexibility from auditing prior to procurement. The sector is rather only audited after procurement, making it faster for the MOH to obtain its required resources through the oil sector. This flexibility in crisis response allowed the oil sector to participate heavily in assisting the Kuwaiti government through the launch of several urgent CSR initiatives to help aid the MOH in the best and fastest ways possible. Major CSR projects that were launched included the following:

10.2.1 Pillar 1: Major CSR Initiatives

Quarantine Facilities: Provision of isolated quarantine facilities with the capacity of accommodating 7000 people (MOH 2020; AlQabas 2020a). This included provision of several secluded locations across the sector's locations such as North Kuwait Ritga Field. The facility, which was constructed in a record time of two weeks, contains all of the health amenities and living requirements necessary for returning citizens during their mandatory quarantine period.

Urgent Procurement of Medical Equipment for the Ministry of Health: Kuwait Oil Company's procurement department was put in charge of purchasing medical equipment urgently for Kuwait's Ministry of Health. These included ventilators, hospital beds, personal protective equipment, and so on. The purchasing department was able to secure all needs in a record time of one week, which led to a major positive impact on the sector's reputation with the Ministry of Health. Acting quickly and responsibly led to the establishment of further trust in the Kuwait Oil Sector, which essentially led to commissioning the construction of the Kuwait Field Hospital by the Kuwait Council of Ministers in decision no (522) (AlAnba 2020b) as explained further below.

Construction of the Kuwait Filed Hospital: The Kuwait Field Hospital was constructed by Kuwait Oil Company (KOC) in collaboration with Kuwait Integrated Petroleum Industries Company (KIPIC) in order to reinforce Kuwait's hospitals with additional facilities to house the rising number of positive coronavirus cases. The building includes wards with a capacity for 200 beds, as well as 40 Intensive Care Unit beds and 19 emergency beds (AlAnba 2020a; Kuwait Oil Company Instagram 2020a). The Kuwait Field Hospital's main objective is to free hospitals for general patients being treated for different diseases who stopped going in for treatment due to fear of exposing themselves to the virus. These included regular patients who are sick from a general flu, to patients who are diagnosed with cancer. The hospitals' bed capacities were quickly diminishing as they were being completely occupied with COVID-19 patients, making health staff very scarce as well. Therefore, moving COVID-19 patients to a controlled setting was critical to stop the spread and free hospital capacities to accommodate other patients.

10.2.2 Pillar 2: Medium-Level CSR Projects

Being a proactive participant in the fight against COVID-19 in the State of Kuwait, the Oil Sector helped the Council of Ministers in providing existing resources that could address logistical needs. Participating with existing resources by identifying capabilities provided grounds for immediate response and relief (AlAnba 2020b) and generated quick-wins in terms of positive perception and reputation amongst stakeholders. This is therefore considered one of the most important elements for successful CSR during pandemics by Kuwait Oil Company's higher management. Kuwait Oil Company was able to extend their immediate help by providing the following:

(a) Providing Kuwait Oil Company's ambulances fleet for the escort of Kuwaiti Nationals returning to the country from Kuwait International Airport to designated quarantine facilities (Kuwait Oil Company Instagram 2020c).
(b) Provision of Kuwait Oil Company's Southwell Hospital to house critical cases from the MOH's Al-Adan Hospital that was already fully occupied (AlAnba 2020c).
(c) Providing Medical Staff from Kuwait Oil Company's Ahmadi Hospital to assist in MOH's hospital Emergency Rooms across the country where hospitals were experiencing shortages in medical staff (AlAnba 2020b).
(d) KOC's Medical Group developed an emergency plan for Ahmadi Hospital, which is home to highly qualified and experienced medical and nursing staff and utilizes the world's latest, state-of-the-art medical equipment. Ahmadi Hospital allocated a complete ward with 31 beds to accommodate any additional patients in the event that Jaber Hospital exceeds its capacity (Kuwait News Agency 2020).

10.2.3 Pillar 3: Media Coverage and Immediate Positive Impact on Reputation

Media content analysis involves the "context of text is analyzed and content refers to words, meanings, pictures, symbols, ideas, themes, or any message that can be communicated" (Neuman 1997: cited in Macnamara 2005). Content from the Kuwait media during the pandemic was analysed qualitatively using the researcher's interpretation of texts (Macnamara 2005). A total of 40 news articles were examined, of which 16 are included. In addition, TV, news, and social media accounts were examined to analyse the impact of oil sector CSR activities on reputation. More than 50 posts were analysed, and a total of 13 were included in here. The articles and social media posts were examined for a period of six months (from February 2020 to September 2020), which was during the period of critical decision-making within the State of Kuwait and its period of consistent lockdowns.

In order to maximize its CSR impact on reputation, Kuwait Oil Company developed targeted media campaigns that would encourage community involvement on a national level. The increased amount of social media use (Suzin Wold et al. 2020) was sought as an opportunity to develop campaigns targeted towards the general public to help encourage a sense of patriotism and establish empathy. Whilst analysing content, the relationship between the media narrative and *Individual Social Responsibility* theory (ISR) emerged as significant. ISR highlights how individuals can have an impact on any social responsibility campaign and suggests that individuals may be drivers of CSR, in which their contribution to social matters adds richness to the CSR initiative being launched (Ebrahim and Buheji 2020). Something as simple as a positive comment directed towards doctors and nurses to encourage and thank them for their efforts may be categorized as ISR, which is what the oil sector has achieved within the campaigns launched throughout the COVID-19 lockdown period.

Several initiatives took place, which could be split into two prominent categories: the first being national communication campaigns (Ktv 2020), and the second, construction projects for needed medical health facilities (AlAnba 2020b). With both categories being highly visible, the amount of media coverage received for the two projects was evident in all local newspapers and on TV channels and social media. The use of social media, in particular, has allowed initial inferences to be derived in regard to the general public's feedback about these CSR projects from the instantaneous option to view comments. Comments on Instagram and Twitter allow us to have a sense of what people think about these projects and hence develop an initial feel of whether these projects have a positive or negative impact on reputation.

The focus on social media during the pandemic showed great promise for the development of national-level social media campaigns to influence the public's perception about the Oil Sector. As people dedicated more of their time on social media (Suzin Wold et al. 2020), a focus on developing messages for this audience was believed to be critical. Kuwait Oil Company's Information Team, therefore, took on the responsibility to develop campaigns with key messages to influence a positive reputation for the oil sector that would build positive momentum towards media coverage of CSR projects at a later stage.

10.2.4 Stay at Home for Kuwait Campaign

The first campaign launched on 18 March 2020 was the "Stay at Home for Kuwait" Campaign (Kuwait Oil Company Instagram 2020e). This campaign was a message that highlighted staying at home as a patriotic act to help prevent the spread of the virus. The campaign showed great success as it caught on nationally, very quickly. All news outlets posted the same message, including influencers on social media as well as participation from the public, allowing the message to go viral. For the entire month of March, this hashtag was a major trend and constituted the launch of several national campaigns as indicated below.

10.2.5 Together United Campaign

This video campaign was developed with the message of unity and patriotism. The video showcased Kuwait's unity during times of crisis, referencing how people from different backgrounds came together as one to do what they can, in order to get through the pandemic. This video also focused on the importance of volunteering, which was very much needed during the first couple of weeks when the pandemic started. People started volunteering their time and effort to manage quarantine facilities, grocery shopping management in consumer cooperatives, distribution of food and amenities to people living in completely locked down areas, and so on.

10.2.6 "May God Protect the White Army" Campaign

National campaigns by the Oil Sector in Kuwait were mainly focused on 'frontliners'—a term that emerged for people working at the forefront of fighting the COVID-19 pandemic. Kuwait Oil Company initiated a national campaign named "May God Protect the White Army" (white being the uniforms worn by frontliners) on 26 April 2020 (Kuwait Oil Company Instagram 2020b). The 'White Army' was a campaign term developed to refer to all medical personnel at the forefront of providing medical care and attention to COVID-19 patients. The campaign included a video that showed how the virus was first reported on in Kuwait, what major impacts it had on our everyday lives, and, in particular, how the virus has impacted the lives of doctors and nurses. The objective of the video was to highlight the fact that although everyone stayed at home to refrain from the dangers of the virus, medical staff were forced to be on duty—forced to face the virus on a daily basis to help people in need. The video showed photos and footage of doctors who were exhausted, working throughout the night and early hours of the morning to secure the safety of Kuwait's inhabitants. The choice of words for this campaign was critical. The word 'Army' was used to make people think of the virus as an enemy of war, in which doctors are 'fighting' against to protect us; therefore, creating an element of seriousness accompanied by emotions of empathy and responsibility. The video therefore paid tribute to these soldiers who sacrificed their own safety to help save our lives. The utilization of promotion on social media was found to be a powerful tool to spread messages to the general public and the Kuwait Oil Company used promoted ads, particularly on Instagram, Twitter, social media news accounts, and influencers. This ensured maximum reach of the required message through social media where the number of reposts and comments exceeded expectations.

In order to fully understand the impact of the national campaigns launched during the COVID-19 pandemic, it is important to explain the general negative feedback that the oil sector has previously received, such as issues pertaining to employment, and concerns related to environmental pollution. Even when launching national campaigns, the KOC has always received at least one negative comment pertaining to the above issues such as:

When are you going to hire us?
KOC burns flares in their facilities, causing air pollution
KOC spills oil into Kuwait Bay.

No matter what CSR, the oil sector posted these perceptions surface on social media. The result is that CSR communication of any sort created the same negative posts taking attention away from any positive messages. In reference to the White Army Campaign, however, the Company came to a realization, which marked an important turning point. Once the Campaign was launched, comments posted on the released video were positive and completely related to the campaign. There was no evidence of negative feedback. This gave an indication that a campaign during a national pandemic in fact unifies opinions and perception of the general public. In a global crisis, the focus becomes dealing with that crisis, with positive response to those that are seen to contribute, and in this case the Oil industry. The campaign was launched in March 2020 and received 4462 views and comments. Below are some samples of the comments received:

May God protect them
May God give them strength and protect them
May God give them strength, our heroes. (Source: Kuwait Oil Company Instagram 2020b)

Negativity towards the company posting content was 'temporarily silenced' as the focus was on portraying Kuwait's doctors and nurses as heroes. Triggering empathy in an audience steered comments away from a negative conversation allowing the company to present itself as a positive, active member of society. Although positive comments were addressed to the doctors and nurses, the usual unrelated negative comments were completely gone, making audiences forget about their negative perceptions momentarily by engaging the public in Individual Social Responsibility (ISR) as described by (Ebrahim and Buheji 2020). ISR means "citizens' decisions, choices and acts to be supportive for social, economic, social and environmental wellbeing." This means that citizens themselves make a decision to participate in CSR activities as evident from the comments addressed to doctors and nurses in the campaign above. In short, where an industry that usually attracts negative comments supports communities in a global crisis, individuals focus on that support and do not post the usual negative messages.

10.2.7 Thank You Kuwait Campaign

The humanitarian job of healthcare professionals went beyond their daily responsibilities, with their resources and ability to treat the ever-increasing amount of people diagnosed with COVID-19 being put to the test as expressed by the late HH the Amir of Kuwait Sheikh Sabah Al-Ahmad Al-Jaber Al-Sabah in his speech to the Kuwaiti people during the COVID-19 Pandemic (Kuwait News Agency 2020).

Learning from the first experience, the sector launched a follow-up campaign to thank medical staff. This voluntary campaign differed from the first campaign as it was conducted without cost, where the campaign required Kuwaiti citizens and residents to develop a message from the heart. The message was in the form of a writing or video to be delivered to medical staff in order to increase health professionals' morale, highlight their efforts, and reassure them that the Kuwaiti people are forever grateful for their selflessness. The doctors were again praised for their work, and beyond that, they became 'heroes.' Whilst contacting employees, celebrities, and even the general public, comments received were

"You are doing something really good and patriotic; this is what we want to see in Kuwait and you are making us proud." "It would be my honor to participate with you and I hope more and more people appreciate the work you are doing for our beloved Kuwait," These were some comments received by Kuwait Oil Company employees who were working tirelessly to spread the campaign. During pandemics, when people feel a sense of patriotism, even a company that is usually consistently criticized can facilitate a national conversation of gratitude and support, associating itself with that support and so disarming criticism.

A website 'ThankyouKuwait.com' and Instagram account 'ThankuKuwait' were created to upload and share all content received from individuals. Content included text messages, photos, and videos from the general public, including Kuwaiti celebrities who expressed their gratitude and support for Kuwait's medical staff.

The 'Thankyoukuwait' website platform hosted thank you messages consisting of posts and videos from the general public that were directed towards Kuwait's healthcare professionals. The website served as a hub that collects content from social media that included the following hashtags:

#Message_from_the_Heart
#Thankukuwait

In a matter of one week, 310 Instagram posts and 609 posts on the website were uploaded and received. Examples of posts from the Thankyoukuwait.com website and the @thankukuwait Instagram Account are introduced below:

"My sincere and heartfelt thanks to all doctors, nurses, para medical staffs and housekeeping & cleaning workers in all the medical facilities in Kuwait."
"Thank you from the heart, a word of gratitude does little for our heroes."
"Thank you for doctors' efforts and fatigue, thank you Kuwait from our hearts, thank you for staying at home. We will win together."
"Thank you very much for your hard work for Kuwait and the people."

A video was developed by Dawood Hussain a famous Kuwaiti Actor and was posted on the Thankukuwait Instagram account.

A video was developed by Bashaar Abdullah, a famous Kuwaiti football player, former captain of Kuwait's national football team, and was posted on the Thankukuwait Instagram account.

Response from medical professionals was outstanding. Some doctors cried when they saw the posts, while others contributed to the campaign by thanking their fellow doctors and nurses for all of their collaborative efforts. The campaign provided doctors and nurses with a sense of community, where they became a unique family that was appreciated by all. The posts below are examples that portray the doctors' reactions to the campaign:

> *"Happy doctors' day. This portrait is made with the pics of doctors and nurses who passed away in this pandemic. Thanks to all."*
> *"Fatigue and sleepiness hit our emergency response heroes after a long day under the sun and during the first day of the holy month of Ramadan while fasting and working for a continuous 18 hours. A thank you message from your colleague...."*

National campaigns during a pandemic which focused on the efforts of others generated a positive impact on reputation by (at least temporarily) silencing negative perceptions and related comments that were visible in most of Kuwait Oil Company's previous posts. By focusing on the creation of empathy towards doctors and nurses and portraying them as heroes, the campaigns launched by Kuwait Oil Company were able to hinder negative comments that were lashed out onto the sector and position themselves as a positive contributor to society, aligned with public interest in dealing with the pandemic and supporting healthcare workers. This was a very different position from the usual attempts to gain support that resulted in the repetition of negative comments. Of course, this in itself does not suggest that negativity towards KOC has permanently receded, only that the organization has managed to align itself with a national sentiment. The correct choice of words for the national media campaigns and the selection of the right causes to support do, however, show how even an organization with reputational problems can bring people together in a crisis. This was evident throughout the entire lockdown period where comments on posts were directly related to the information being posted and there was a clear decrease in the amount of negative feedback on Kuwait Oil Company's Instagram and Twitter accounts. Significant is the move from being seen as doing good to supporting others that are easily recognized as doing good.

Ensuring coverage of activities was also implemented using a proactive approach and is the link between the deployment of corporate resources and the work to develop corporate reputation. The Oil Sector media departments united to control what was said in the media by providing the media with exclusive access to corporate media platforms, so utilizing social media platforms to post consistent progress of CSR activities as well as developing press releases and distributing them to the media as soon as information was gathered and available. Instead of waiting for the press to express interest in covering the sector's stories, the oil sector turned into a media news provider and was rather 'creating' the news said about the sector, therefore initiating and controlling the news being communicated in Kuwait's local media outlets. Such activity sparked interest from the media to cover positive rather than negative stories. Providing the news actually helped the Oil Sector control the narrative being told during the pandemic by showcasing the reality of its quick actions to help the MOH when in need, which diverted the conversation from negative stories associated with production. Below are some sample excerpts from the Kuwaiti media highlighting the Sector's CSR efforts during the pandemic.

(a) Al-Anba Local Newspaper—Twitter Account: "Kuwait Oil Company Announces its willingness and readiness to contribute against the spread of the Coronavirus" (AlAnba 2020b).
(b) Al-Rai Local Newspaper: "Kuwait Oil Company Allocated Entire Wing in its Hospital for the Use of the MOH" (AlRai 2020)
(c) Kuwait News Agency (KUNA) Press Release: "Kuwait Oil Company Allocated Entire Wing in its Hospital for the Use of the MOH" (Kuwait News Agency 2020).
(d) Al-Anba Local Newspaper: "Kuwait Oil Company Provides MOH with its Southwell hospital as a specialized hospital for COVID-19 cases" (AlAnba 2020c).

(e) Kuwait's Ministry of Information—Instagram Account: "Kuwait Oil Company Prepares to Provide MOH with Quarantine Facilities in Ritga Field, North Kuwait Area" (MOInformation 2020).
(f) SNAA NEWS—Local Instagram News Account: "KOC in Collaboration with KIPIC Complete the Construction of the Housing Facilities in the Kuwait Field Hospital in Mishrif Area" (SNAANEWS 2020).
(g) Al-Qabas Local Newspaper YouTube Channel: "KOC & KIPIC Provide Latest Facilities in Kuwait Field Hospital" (Alqabastube 2020).

The above excerpts show that although the sector received extensive media coverage across traditional and social media, the Oil Sector was the actual supplier of news. Using the proactive approach to media coverage, the sector was able to shift media focus into its positive contributions to society.

10.3 CSR Implementation During Pandemics

There are numerous lessons learned from the COVID-19 experience in terms of CSR implementation and its impact on reputation. CSR implementation is now viewed very differently and the realization of its importance to create or maintain a positive reputation is of great significance. Especially within a sector that is frequently the subject of criticism, creating a positive image during a pandemic can be achieved. Strategies for CSR implementation that focus on improving the reputation by implementing CSR initiatives can be segmented into three pillars that directly focused on stakeholder needs as explained below (Fig. 10.1):

Weekly meetings with stakeholders during the pandemic proved to be beneficial for the successful identification and implementation of CSR projects. While attending meetings with stakeholders, oil sector officials were able to identify three major pillars for CSR initiatives. Major CSR involves a high budget, while medium-level CSR involves using existing resources with the least impact on budget, with the third pillar relating to work with the media, including that related to corporate reputation. Working on CSR projects during a pandemic brought a new

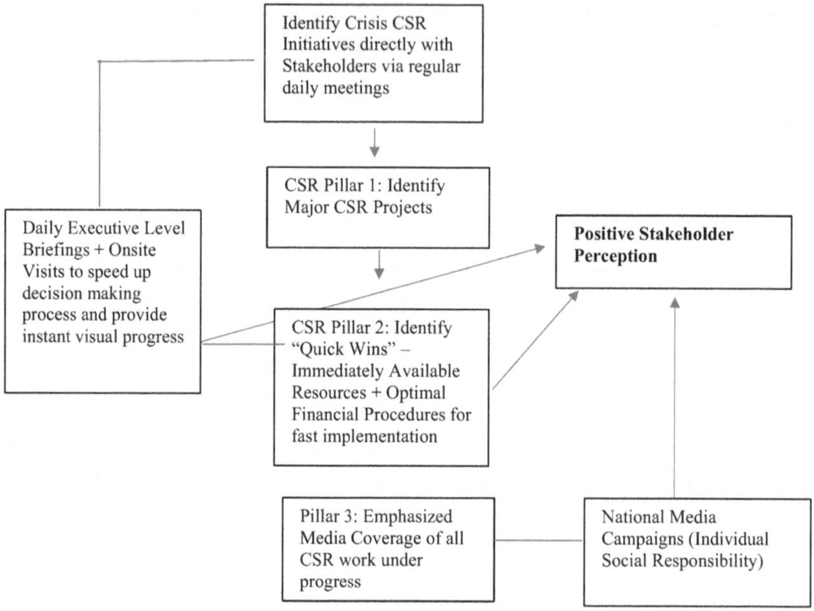

Fig. 10.1 CSR pillars and reputation impact. (Source: Author's own work)

understanding of the term, especially to the Kuwaiti Oil Sector. Companies can now develop stronger CSR programmes by identifying CSR levels as opposed to focusing on a single, highly visual project that would take years to implement and in turn take years to yield or actually see returns on investment in terms of reputation.

Within the overall media strategy 'quick wins'—which are short-term CSR projects that can be done at a low budget and with existing resources. These 'quick wins' allow for immediate returns on investment in terms of reputation and can help start the CSR momentum at the Company. Media coverage and engagement with stakeholders also proved critical to capture the efforts of the work being implemented and obtain a positive influence on reputation. Oil Sector officials did not only attend weekly meetings with the MOH, but rather MOH officials were also invited to the construction site to see first-hand how the construction was progressing. This also allowed for on-the-spot feedback from the CSR receivers, which helped mitigate construction requirements and ensure implementation is directly according to pressing needs. Given that needs were immediately addressed, this gave a positive influence on reputation as the oil sector is now seen as a hero that came to immediate aid and was heavily committed.

Creating CSR projects and programmes can be very expensive, with the potential to quickly consume a large portion of a Company's budget. Implementing CSR projects during the pandemic allowed for the realization that not all CSR projects need immediate cash contributions. The Kuwaiti Oil Sector has an abundance of existing resources that allowed it to act quickly by providing the MOH with immediate needs using available resources that were only reallocated. These available resources included recently abandoned labour homes/chalets that were remodelled to create quarantine facilities. Also available were running construction contracts that helped the oil sector respond immediately to the MOH's need to build the Kuwait Field Hospital. Kuwait Oil Company's Ahmadi Hospital provided new ventilators to hospitals, in addition to lending the services of doctors and nurses. Moreover, an entire wing was dedicated to the purpose of supporting the MOH during the pandemic (AlAnba 2020c). Time is of the essence during a pandemic. Time for CSR implementation was seen as a critical factor for the success or failure of CSR efforts. Through consistent meetings, swift allocation of resources, practical financial procedures in place and constant monitoring of progress, the Oil Sector was able to successfully complete all required CSR projects on such short notice. Therefore, through identifying existing resources, companies can achieve quick-wins to help gain positive reputation.

The success of CSR projects goes hand in hand with media coverage (Balog-Way and McComas 2020). Without coverage from the media, CSR efforts go to waste. The most important element of CSR implementation, which is missed by many, is extensive media coverage. Media coverage allows for companies to show the severity and intensity of the CSR project at hand. Media can help showcase to the public the different layers of work put in by companies to achieve the end result. It shows regular meetings, time, and effort of different members of staff across organizations, highlights collaborations, and can show the endless days and nights where people are working around the clock to help achieve a project that serves the public. The Kuwaiti Oil Sector was able to achieve a positive image literally in a matter of two weeks because of continuously publishing the progress of its CSR projects during the pandemic and becoming a media content provider, rather than wait for the media to cover its stories.

10.3.1 CSR After the Pandemic?

The pandemic showed that regular stakeholder meetings allow for companies to understand their stakeholder's most pressing needs. Stakeholders in return have a deeper understanding of the importance of CSR projects and how companies can put everything in their power to come to their aid. During regular progress meetings with the Council of Ministers, the idea was brought to the table to include the Kuwaiti Oil Sector in the implementation of other major governmental projects. The Kuwaiti Government does not perceive the Oil Sector as a source for money but is now more interested in the experience of its qualified personnel. The future aim is to benefit from the experience and knowledge of Oil Sector personnel in project management, especially in terms of the timely execution of state projects of the highest quality and calibre, in which the Oil Sector showcased its best managerial skills. This in itself is a major positive implication on reputation.

Inviting stakeholders to the site during the construction phase proved to be one of the most efficient means to deliver projects based on expectations and actual needs. On-site visits create a sense of reassurance, show how tiresome and engaged management officials are in the project, and provide instant feedback from the CSR receiver in terms of addressing needs or requirements to change aspects of the project as it is being implemented. On-the-spot feedback provided more satisfaction, as well as eliminated needs for changing certain elements of the project, which saves costs as opposed to the need to change things once construction is completed. The greater benefit was a positive impact on reputation where the stakeholder becomes involved in the project and now understands the work and effort that is exerted to address their most pressing needs through immediate action.

10.4 Conclusion

During times of crisis, it is critical to devise a unified action plan of a collaborative nature. In addition to National Communication Campaigns, the focus on three main pillars of CSR can be a useful tool for positive influence on reputation, which are as follows:

(a) Identify major CSR initiatives to serve massive needs that target a large stakeholder group.
(b) Identify existing resources that can be utilized for immediate action to generate quick wins to generate positive perception with stakeholders.
(c) Utilize media coverage extensively to create a positive reputation.

Understanding the immediate needs of stakeholders can only be achieved by actually meeting with them face-to-face, where consistent meetings have been found to be more beneficial to uplifting the Oil Sector's reputation through showing immediate engagement. The key to achieving a positive reputation from CSR implementation during a pandemic is to quickly identify existing resources that can immediately serve CSR purposes. Translating existing resources into quick action leads to a positive perception where stakeholders believe that their needs are being attended to immediate 'quick wins.' It is also important to identify longer-term needs and establish a mechanism to address these needs, such as more lenient financial procedures that can assist in the implementation of CSR initiatives during crises. A sense of unity is essential to establish a strong relationship with stakeholders, leading by example of patriotism and caring about the state as a whole, which established a very positive relationship amongst stakeholders. As a final remark, the amount of CSR projects being implemented during crises, no matter how extensive, will not be of any use to a sector/company without media coverage and promotion. Using media to make people aware of all the hard work and efforts put forth in CSR is what makes a CSR project successful—allowing it to reach its optimal positive impact on reputation. The ultimate takeaway is: there is no point of CSR without exposure.

References

Agency, O. (2020, March 22). سلطان : نفط الكويت وضعت خطط الطوارئ اللازمة لتجاوز هذه المرحلة الدقيقة https://t.co/oLKeGIzjAF pic.twitter.com/HSF7vcqJl1. Retrieved September 03, 2020, from https://www.oilnewsagency.com/سلطان-نفط-الكويت-وضعت-خطط-الطوارئ-اللا/.

AlAnba, N. (2020a, April 26). بالفيديو النفط يثبت جدارته في إنشاء مستشفى الكويت الميداني خلال أسبوعين. Retrieved September 03, 2020, from https://www.alanba.com.kw/ar/kuwait-news/964237/27-04-2020-بالفيديو-النفط-يثبت-جدارته-إنشاء-مستشفى-الكويت-الميداني-خلال-أسبوعين/.

AlAnba, N. (2020b, March 14). نفط الكويت تعرب عن استعدادها للمساهمة بجهود مواجهة تفشي "فيروس" "كورونا" https://t.co/nz1FKrsRg6 pic.twitter.com/tD8aRm-WetG. Retrieved September 03, 2020, from https://twitter.com/alanba_news_kw/status/1238935863616327681?s=12.

AlAnba, N. (2020c, March 25). صحيفة الأنباء / عاجل: العامر ل "الأنباء": "نفط الكويت" تُسلّم مستشفى الأحمدي القديم ل "الصحة" الأسبوع المقبل كمستشفى عزل لحالات "كورونا" (الكويت) (نفط_كورونا) (مستشفى_الأحمدي) (الكويت). Retrieved September 03, 2020, from http://nabdapp.com/t/70524214.

AlJarida, N. (2020, April 10). "زيادة الإصابات وعودة المواطنين أبرز تحديات "الصحة". Retrieved September 04, 2020, from https://www.aljarida.com/articles/1586448290115300200/.

AlQabas, N. (2020a, April 04). نفط الكويت" وفّرت 7600 محجر للعمالة". Retrieved September 03, 2020, from https://alqabas.com/article/5765548-نفط-الكويت-توفر--7600محجر-للعمالة-الوافدة-خلال--72ساعة-فقط.

AlQabas, N. (2020b, February 24). "إلغاء فعاليات الأعياد.. خوفاً من "كورونا". Retrieved September 03, 2020, from https://alqabas.com/article/5754596-مجلس-الوزراء-يوقف-الاحتفال-بالأعياد-الوطنية-بسبب-كورونا.

Alqabastube. (2020, April 26). إنشاء أحدث مستشفى ميداني.. في أرض المعارض. Retrieved September 03, 2020, from https://www.youtube.com/watch?v=lQ3ZIcLIfbE.

AlRai, D. (2020, March 14). نفط الكويت»: تخصيص جناح عزل كامل في مستشفى الشركة تحت تصرف «الصحة»». Retrieved September 03, 2020, from https://www.alraimedia.com/Home/Details?id=65fb3812-555b-4fa5-9d85-d6a675d43617.

Balog-Way, D. H., & McComas, K. A. (2020). COVID-19: Reflections on trust, tradeoffs, and preparedness. Journal of Risk Research, 23(7-8), 838–848.

Bapuji, H., de Bakker, F. G., Brown, J. A., Higgins, C., Rehbein, K., & Spicer, A. (2020). Business and society research in times of the corona crisis.

Cinemagics, C. (2019, February 24). Kuwait celebrates National and Liberation Day. Retrieved December 05, 2020, from https://www.cinemagics.com/post/kuwait-celebrates-national-and-liberation-day.

Ebrahim, A. H., & Buheji, M. (2020). A Pursuit for A 'Holistic Social Responsibility Strategic Framework' Addressing COVID-19 Pandemic Needs. American Journal of Economic, 10(5), 293–304.

EIA. (2020). U.S. Energy Information Administration – EIA: Independent statistics and analysis. Retrieved December 05, 2020, from https://www.eia.gov/energyexplained/oil-and-petroleum-products/use-of-oil.php.

KPC. (2020). Kuwait Petroleum Corporation KPC at a glance. Retrieved September 03, 2020, from https://www.kpc.com.kw/about/kpc-at-a-glance.

Ktv. (2020, March 20). كوادر #شركة_نفط_الكويت .. جنود مجهولون يعملون على مدار الساعة لتوفير متطلبات السوق من #النفط#الكويت الكويت_تتصدى_لكورونا#COVID19# #قطاع_الأخبار_والبرامج_السياسية pic.twitter.com/q6hChmW3Qh. Retrieved September 03, 2020, from https://twitter.com/newsktv/status/1241023595884748800.

KUNA. (2018, February 24). Kuwait celebrates 57th Nat'l Day, 40th anniversary of nat'l anthem Sun. Retrieved December 05, 2020, from https://www.kuna.net.kw/ArticleDetails.aspx?id=2697122.

Kuwait News Agency. (2020, March 30). في اليوم العالمي للطبيب يجسدون رسالتهم السامية ويتصدرون الصفوف لمواجهة كورونا. Retrieved September 03, 2020, from https://www.kuna.net.kw/ArticleDetails.aspx?id=2882223&Language=ar#.

Kuwait Oil Company. (2020a, April 25). Kuwait field hospital. Retrieved September 04, 2020, from https://www.instagram.com/tv/B_aT5E6jmVg/?igshid=1g28y8qq7c7wm.

Kuwait Oil Company. (2020b, April 26). Retrieved September 04, 2020, from https://www.instagram.com/p/B_cs6RwDb8s/?igshid=1jgd6j87n1la0.

Kuwait Oil Company. (2020c, August 29). Providing ambulances to Kuwait International Airport. Retrieved September 04, 2020, from https://www.instagram.com/p/CEdl6olDped/?igshid=1o2cucjl0429x.

Kuwait Oil Company. (2020d, February 26). COVID-19 awareness. Retrieved September 04, 2020, from https://www.instagram.com/p/B9CJ9Xphee4/?igshid=il8mc7q541k2.

Kuwait Oil Company. (2020e, March 18). Stay at home. Retrieved September 04, 2020, from https://www.instagram.com/tv/B94UTqRj4GQ/?igshid=1pq3vdjll0885.

Kuwait Oil Company. (2020f). 2040 strategy. Retrieved December 05, 2020, from https://www.kockw.com/sites/EN/Pages/Profile/Strategy.aspx.

Kuwait Oil Company. (2020g). Society. Retrieved December 05, 2020, from https://www.kockw.com/sites/EN/Pages/We Care/Social Responsibility/Society.aspx.

Kuwait Oil Company. (2020h). KERP – Kuwait Environmental Remediation Program. Retrieved September 03, 2020, from https://www.kockw.com/sites/EN/Pages/We Care/Soil-Remediation.aspx.

Kuwait Oil Company. (2020i). Our operations. Retrieved September 03, 2020, from https://www.kockw.com/sites/EN/Pages/Profile/Operations/Operations.aspx.

Macnamara, J. R. (2005). Media content analysis: Its uses, benefits and best practice methodology. Asia Pacific public relations journal, 6(1), 1–34.

MOH. (2020, April 2). Retrieved September 03, 2020, from https://www.instagram.com/p/B-fLKOqhYyt/?igshid=fg2d1zcqmhik.

MOInformation. (2020, April 2). Kuwait Oil Company Ritqa quarantine facility. Retrieved April, from https://www.instagram.com/p/B-eVBxlDDLO/?igshid=va7winw1153y.

Mubasher, N. (2020, April 1). تحليل.. سعر برميل النفط الكويتي يهوي 62.4% خلال الربع الأول 2020. Retrieved September 03, 2020, from https://www.mubasher.info/news/3611808/4-62--تحليل-سعر-برميل-النفط-الكويتي-يهوي-خلال-الربع-الأول-2020/.

SNAANEWS. (2020, June 13). قامت شركة نفط الكويت وبالتعاون مع مؤسسة البترول الكويتية والشركة الكويتية للصناعات البترولية المتكاملة "كيبيك" بالانتهاء من تجهيز المبنى المخصص لسكن أفراد الطاقمين الطبي والتمريضي. Retrieved September 03, 2020, from https://www.instagram.com/p/CBYu7hrg9br/?igshid=12ybcsmawa5sd.

Suzin Wold | Sep 16, 2., Tabitha Cassidy | Sep 4, 2., Tabitha Cassidy | Jun 1, 2., Zak Stambor | Apr 17, 2., & Stephanie Crets | May 1, 2. (2020, September 17). COVID-19 is changing how, why and how much we're using social media. Retrieved December 05, 2020, from https://www.digitalcommerce360.com/2020/09/16/covid-19-is-changing-how-why-and-how-much-were-using-social-media/.

Theodori, G. L., & Jackson-Smith, D. (2010). Public perception of the oil and gas industry: The good, the bad, and the ugly. https://doi.org/10.2118/134253-ms.

TIMES. (2020, February 19). Coronavirus affects celebrations marking national holidays. Retrieved December 05, 2020, from https://www.timeskuwait.com/news/coronavirus-affects-celebrations-marking-national-holidays/.

Index[1]

[1] Note: Page numbers followed by 'n' refer to notes.

A. Sörensson et al. (eds.), *Corporate Responsibility and Sustainability during the Coronavirus Crisis*, Palgrave Studies in Governance, Leadership and Responsibility, https://doi.org/10.1007/978-3-030-73847-1

The manufacturer's authorised representative in the EU is Springer Nature Customer Service Centre GmbH, Europaplatz 3, 69115 Heidelberg, Germany. If you have any concerns regarding our products, please contact ProductSafety@springernature.com

Printed and bound by CPI Group (UK) Ltd, Croydon, CR0 4YY
22/09/2026
02221054-0006